"The gifts of this book lie not only
longer with us but also in its remin ... .use in our lives who
are still teaching, still sharing, and still shaping who we are. I am reminded that
tomorrow is never promised for anyone, and to take full advantage of these
great gifts of our heroes with a greater sense of urgency."

Kevin Cox, *President, LKC Advisory and former CHRO,*
General Electric and American Express

"*Lives Lost and Leadership Found: Lessons from Special Somebodies* is a poignant
reminder that we learn leadership not from a book or a class but from a lifetime
of relationships with family, mentors, and colleagues. It is a wonderful reminder
that we should continue to engage fully with people we are close to and understand the very positive impact they have on our lives."

Chris Kastner, *President and CEO, HII*

"Having read many books on leadership, this book has made a unique impact
unlike all those before it. By sharing their most intimate leadership stories,
these authors have successfully given us relatable leadership lessons crafted in
accessible and interesting personal stories. Like me, you may find yourself passing on some of these valuable lessons to others."

Daniel Marsili, *President, The National Academy of Human Resources,*
former CHRO, Colgate-Palmolive Company

"In a poignant testament to loved ones lost, Ian Ziskin and his contributing
authors have captured how losing a special somebody molds our character and
elevates our leadership. This anthology of personal insights has better informed
my emotional journey of dealing with loss, inspiring me with valuable leadership
lessons gleaned from the experiences of others who have lost special somebodies."

Alan May, *retired CHRO, Hewlett Packard Enterprise*

"*Lives Lost and Leadership Found* offers a truly unique perspective on valuable
lessons about life and leadership. Not only do these powerful learnings come
from lost loved ones and the people who experienced the loss, but their stories
represent highly practical insights from many people who might not traditionally be thought of as leaders."

Dr. Ronald D. Sugar, *Chairman Emeritus, Northrop*
Grumman Corporation, and past and current Board Director,
Amgen, Apple, Chevron, and Uber

"Many books provide ideas, tools, and actions to improve leadership. This
remarkable book also touches the heart by sharing how very personal experiences with loss shape identity and leadership. It leads to reflection as much as
instruction. It helped me, thanks."

Dave Ulrich, *Rensis Likert Professor, Ross School of Business (retired),*
Partner, The RBL Group

Lives Lost and Leadership Found

Lives Lost and Leadership Found: Lessons from Special Somebodies explores leadership and transformational change through the lens of personal stories. This unique book gathers insights from dozens of contributing authors who reflect on the profound impact of losing "special somebodies" who helped shape their lives and careers. While emotional, the focus is on growth, leadership, and learning through love and loss rather than grief.

Featuring heartfelt narratives, survey input from 150 leaders, and an exploration of the neuroscience of grieving, this book offers valuable perspectives on resilience, growth, and leadership.

Lives Lost and Leadership Found is a must-read for leaders who seek inspiration and insight from life's most challenging moments, offering valuable lessons on how personal experiences of loss can unlock transformative leadership growth.

Ian Ziskin, President of EXec EXcel Group LLC, has more than 43 years of experience as a business leader, board advisor and member, coach, consultant, CHRO, entrepreneur, teacher, speaker, and author. His client base and corporate work span more than 25 industries and includes Fortune 1000, entrepreneurial, publicly traded, and privately held businesses.

Lives Lost and Leadership Found

Lessons from Special Somebodies

Ian Ziskin
and
The Consortium for Change (C4C)

Foreword By
Dr. John W. Boudreau

Routledge
Taylor & Francis Group

NEW YORK AND LONDON

Designed cover image: © Ian Ziskin

First published 2026
by Routledge
605 Third Avenue, New York, NY 10158

and by Routledge
4 Park Square, Milton Park, Abingdon, Oxon, OX14 4RN

Routledge is an imprint of the Taylor & Francis Group, an informa business

© 2026 Ian Ziskin

ISBN: 9781032955933 (hbk)
ISBN: 9781032949857 (pbk)
ISBN: 9781003585633 (ebk)

DOI: 10.4324/9781003585633

Typeset in Caslon
by KnowledgeWorks Global Ltd.

Dedication

For Ted, Marilyn, and Adam Ziskin, and the special somebodies we all have loved, lost, and learned from as leaders.

And for Dale "Pops" Edwards, my father-in-law, who showed our family the joy of "hearing footprints" (a family inside joke).

Contents

Foreword

Connect in the Moment

by Dr. John W. Boudreau, Professor Emeritus of Management and Organization and a Senior Research Scientist with the Center for Effective Organizations at the Marshall School of Business, University of Southern California

I envy the journey you are about to take! After reading this book, I hope you will be as moved, enlightened, surprised, and inspired as I am.

There are many books, podcasts, courses, retreats, and instruction manuals about the universal human condition of loss, grief, and resilience. This one is different. Ian Ziskin has a long history of masterfully bringing together communities of smart and dedicated professionals committed to improving the workplace and the wider world through their professional work and personal lives. I have been a member and beneficiary of many of those communities over the three decades (or more!) that I've been privileged to be among Ian's "friends for life," as he eloquently puts it. I am honored to get to write this foreword and to play a humble role in getting this work out into the world.

In *Lives Lost and Leadership Found: Lessons from Special Somebodies*, Ian's community ponders personal and universal themes, examining what they have learned about life and leadership through the loss of loved ones, colleagues, and even pets. And each goes a step further to distill lessons about life and leadership from those experiences. Ian has skillfully woven dozens of essays written by this community into relevant themes, and has added his own personal introduction, research, and conclusions, including his moving experience of losing two dear loved ones in close succession. He even includes the song he wrote to help him work through the experience! The generosity and vulnerability of each contributor to this book helps readers feel the universality of the human experience of loss, to feel less alone.

The result is a unique compendium of important lessons, not only about leadership, but about the myriad paths through which we find resilience, acceptance, and peace through the universal experience of loss that we all ultimately face.

I hope your experience of this book is like mine—that it will uplift you, inspire you, bring you to tears, and undoubtedly cause you to get more in touch with your own experiences of loss, grief, and eventual resilience. I hope it will get you thinking about those who are still with you today, and those who may experience the loss of *your* companionship someday. I hope it will offer you lessons that you can apply to your own leadership, and to the future leaders for whom you will be a mentor and role model, whether they be your employees, colleagues, children, family, or community members.

Universal Themes

As so many of the essay authors observe, virtually everyone is, has been, or will be grieving some sort of loss. The authors often remind us to give others the benefit of the doubt, to try to see the behavior of others through their perspectives, to understand that everyone you meet is probably "going through something challenging," and to lead from a presumption of the good in others, even when their situation may make it difficult for them to express "the good" in the best way.

Because loss and grief are so universal, the essay contributors offer a valuable base from which to practice empathy and compassion. Yet, the lessons go beyond empathy and compassion. You will also encounter moving stories that illustrate the importance of having values that provide a North Star (guiding principles) and sticking to those values, even when they are controversial or when others disagree—not shying away from conflict when it is in the service of a larger and important goal.

This book offers a striking testament to our common human desire to share our most powerful and vulnerable experiences of loss, even when the norms of society tell us to hide or repress those feelings. The essay authors are very public figures in their organizations and with their clients, so it is truly inspiring and quite moving to see their willingness to share such intimate and personal experiences. This upwelling of communal sharing is right there below the surface, even for those of us that may seem to have it "all together." I have seen it in yoga retreats, in my graduate and undergraduate classes, and in chance encounters with strangers in restaurants, on plane trips, and virtually anywhere that people come together and choose to communicate.

The Generosity of Sharing Experiences

I resonated with the idea of how important it is to share our experiences of loss with others, as I too have often been surprised by how helpful it has been for me to lean into this vulnerability during difficult times.

For example, my father died after years of struggle with Alzheimer's disease. My mother unselfishly cared for him at home for many of those years. She shared with me this lesson: "You can't change what your father remembers, whether he recognizes you, and how he behaves. What you can do is to go where he is and find a connection to the person he is in the moment."

The last time I saw him, he didn't recognize me. He thought I was a co-worker arriving at his home for a visit. Rather than correcting him, I played the part. My father took me on a tour of the house, showing me pictures of our family from my childhood, proudly pointing out some framed awards, articles, diplomas, book covers, etc., that marked various achievements of my two sisters and me. He turned to me and said, "My son is a fine man, and I love and admire him very much."

Sharing openly with my family as we were grappling with my father's passing was a big reason we got through those times. In the years following, I found that sharing these moments with friends and colleagues navigating a similar form of parental loss has been surprisingly helpful for all involved.

Whether with family, close friends, colleagues, students, or complete strangers, sharing this experience tends to reveal surprising and valuable insights and personal lessons for me. I often write to someone, even years later, to thank them for their generosity and insight, and I have been fortunate enough to receive such correspondence myself.

It's easy to forget how much this universal experience of grief and loss connects us all. This book will remind you.

Addressing the Hard Stuff

Some of the best advice I ever received was from my coach/therapist, Beth Roy (more about her later). I communicated to her a concern I thought was unique at the time, but that I now know is very common to those of us of a "certain age." I shared with her my dilemma about how to process the losses that seem so much more frequent as we age, and ultimately realized the core of this dilemma was the fear of my eventual decline and death. I was particularly concerned about how my decline and passing might sadden my only child, my daughter, and how much I wished to protect her from that sadness.

Beth asked me if I had ever honestly shared this concern with my daughter. I was surprised and astounded when she suggested the radical idea of discussing my decline and death with my "little girl." Beth astutely pointed out that my little girl was now a 40-year-old professional—a child and family therapist with an emerging global reputation as an expert on fear and its effects on schools and other organizations. Beth shared that some of her richest and most rewarding conversations with her father were prompted by a discussion of his mortality. Thus, my "homework" was to set up regular appointments for conversations with my daughter about the "hard stuff," starting with me sharing my fears about my decline and death. Not surprisingly, my daughter was not shocked by the conversation topic. Quite the contrary. The possibility of Alzheimer's disease and the certainty of my passing were things she had been thinking about too. Just as Beth had discovered with her father, my daughter and I discovered that the topic of loss, decline, and death led to some of our richest and most rewarding conversations. It also made so many other "hard things" more discussable.

Perhaps this experience might inspire you to do the hard thing—to have conversations about the things that scare you most so that you can experience support and encouragement from your family, friends, colleagues, and others.

Do It Yourself

As I read this book, an idea occurred to me: we readers could consider the essay we might write *after* losing someone important to us. Whether intentional or not, as I read the essays, each author seemed to be suggesting that we write and share similar essays with our special somebodies *before* they are no longer with us! Many of the writers implied, or actually stated, sentiments such as, "I only wish the wake had been a retirement party, so my loved one would have felt all the admiration and love we had to express."

Just as I was thinking what a profound and original insight I had, sure enough, Ian was one step ahead. His appendix to the book not only makes that suggestion, but he provides a template to guide the essays of would-be authors. I encourage all readers to take Ian's suggestion and guidance to heart. Use his template yourself! Imagine writing your heartfelt observations about the life lessons you have learned from someone and then sharing them with that person now.

Pondering Your Legacy

Of course, this idea works both ways. What lessons would you like to leave with those who are important to you today and who will inevitably experience your passing?

I was talking with an 80-year-old friend in Santa Fe, New Mexico, about how we face our own inevitable deaths. He said, "I know just what you mean. I recently asked each of my children, 'What is the most important lesson that you will have learned from me?'" I must admit my first reaction was that this seemed awfully self-centered. Yet, as I reflected on it, I realized that this question would offer significant insights about the essays that will be written (or remain unwritten) when each of us is gone.

This book will remind you to consider your own legacy. The essay authors repeatedly observe that legacies are seldom found in the wealth, possessions, or even formal achievements and positions of those they lost. Rather, legacy emerges from the personal relationships, interactions, memories, impressions, and lessons that you will leave. Perhaps it's not so self-centered, after all, to ask others what they have learned from you, and incorporate that into your life and leadership.

Reading this book prompted me to seek out some other perspectives about grief, loss, and resilience. Many folks recommended the excellent podcast by Anderson Cooper, *All There Is*. Here are a few impressions that I took away from that podcast as I considered the essays in this book.

From Tyler Perry, "Letting Go":[1]

- "After you lose someone, grief is a fellow-traveler. It is there, even if you try to avoid it. You can try to make yourself so busy that you can avoid facing it, but it is happy to just wait for you to finish whatever you're so busy doing to distract yourself, and then demand to be faced and felt."
- "When you do face it, grief is a friend, offering so many opportunities to learn and grow."

From Francis Weller, "Creating a Companionship with Grief":[2]

- "Grief requires replacing the child-like strategies for dealing with loss that we initially use, with more useful and mature strategies, but that requires recognizing and embracing the origins of our instincts to respond as a child."
- "Society provides few communal opportunities to share and address grief, even though it is a universal human experience whose healthy resolution requires a community."

Think about that. Is there a larger purpose to this book of very personal essays?

Perhaps this book should motivate us as readers to use our influence to encourage organizations to invest in programs that teach these lessons to managers, employees, teams, students, and stakeholders. Should the next trend in "employee benefits" be a platform for collectively sharing and understanding grief and loss? Could corporations, schools, universities, and other organizations become a source of community for sharing, processing, embracing, and benefiting from grief?

The contributors to this book—and many of its readers—are influential coaches, executives, authors, and influencers. Yet, I suspect that without Ian's expert nudging and encouragement to contribute to this book, their conversations about grief, loss, and resilience would mostly happen informally and very personally with family, friends, and perhaps a few of their coaching clients. Could those lessons apply more broadly to the larger organizations and societies that these authors and their clients serve?

Perhaps the process that Ian used to create this book could serve as a template to encourage organization members to write and share their own experiences with each other. Our sadness, tears, intimate conversations, and need for community all connect in many ways with our daily experiences at work and in the broader world around us.

Radical Therapy

My coach/therapist, Beth Roy, is a pioneer in many arenas of personal and social health, including the concept of "Radical Therapy" (for more information, visit https://www.radicaltherapy.org/resources). **Radical Therapy** combines social analysis with traditional therapeutic practices. It starts with the premise that people are inherently good and do their best, given their circumstances, and focuses on understanding how the context of social conditions, institutions, values, and internalized oppression affect individuals' emotional and interpersonal lives. It suggests that you can't understand, diagnose, and help individuals without understanding the context that shapes them.

This book will remind you how to reap the significant lessons from grief and loss for yourselves and your family, friends, and colleagues. Perhaps it is also a call to action for all of us to extend those lessons and change the context.

For everyone reading this book, allow me to say, "Best wishes and thanks for all you do and will do!"

Notes

1. Tyler Perry, "Letting Go," *All There Is with Anderson Cooper*, December 11, 2024, https://www.cnn.com/audio/podcasts/all-there-is-with-anderson-cooper/episodes/ff041d56-7b6c-11ef-993b-b71fb105ae8d
2. Francis Weller, "Creating a Companionship with Grief," *All There Is with Anderson Cooper*, January 10, 2024, https://www.cnn.com/audio/podcasts/all-there-is-with-anderson-cooper/episodes/fe6aef5a-7b6c-11ef-993b-0fce69009d00

Part I

Why ... Write This Book?

Introduction—Friends for Life

In 2018, my business partner and friend Lacey Leone McLaughlin and I co-founded the Consortium for Change (C4C), which can be found online at https://www.consortium4change.com. C4C is a community network of independent coaches and consultants with expertise in leadership, talent, team effectiveness, transformational change, culture, DEI, innovation, and more.

While much has changed since C4C's inception, one core value remains fundamental to who we are: *The Spirit of Abundance*.

Our Guiding Principle

This principle is our shorthand way of saying that our purpose is to share business opportunities and referrals, competitive intelligence, learning and ideas, and best practices that allow us to collaborate on behalf of clients rather than to compete among ourselves. We are a community of colleagues in service of clients and one another.

The Spirit of Abundance also has personal resonance for each C4C member, including me, where it manifests itself in what I like to call my "friends for life" philosophy. It means that whether I meet you as a business colleague, coaching or consulting client, leadership development program participant, audience member at a speaking engagement, podcast host, student in my MBA course, friend, or friend of a friend, I consider you a friend for life. If I can help you, I will do my best. If you need something, just ask. If I can benefit from your support, I won't be shy about it.

This approach to life has served me well. It makes me a happier, more fulfilled person, even in circumstances where other people do not share my enthusiasm about being friends for life! It just works for me.

Special Somebodies

The Spirit of Abundance mindset and "friends for life" philosophy are also guideposts for me as lead author of this book, *Lives Lost and Leadership Found: Lessons from Special Somebodies*. My job has been to convene many smart and insightful

DOI: 10.4324/9781003585633-2

contributors, provide them a platform to share their stories about losing people important to them, and integrate their diverse views along with my own into what we hope is a coherent and holistic set of lessons about life and leadership.

Our unique twist is that these lessons come primarily from people we refer to as "special somebodies." They are mostly anonymous, unknown to you or me prior to writing or reading this book, yet they are pivotal and highly influential figures to our book contributors. These special somebodies were often quiet heroes during their lives and perhaps even more consequential silent leaders during and following their deaths.

To our book contributors, they were cherished loved ones who made a huge impact in teaching them about life and leadership. To you, they will become special somebodies. To me, they will be friends for life (even in their deaths).

A Wide Net

In keeping with *The Spirit of Abundance* and my "friends for life" philosophy, our book embraces perspectives from a wide range of people. Our contributing authors represent current C4C members, former C4C members, past and current CHRO and operating leader colleagues, current and former clients, board members, former MBA students, academics, founders/CEOs, long-time and more recent friends, and numerous others who became friends for life through this project. We cast a wide net, welcomed a multitude of viewpoints, and did our best to create a safe space for people to share intimate personal feelings about losing and learning from a loved one. Our book now makes you a friend for life, too.

What You Can Expect

As a reader, you can expect the following from *Lives Lost and Leadership Found:*

- Broad and diverse perspectives from people who have experienced loss and learned how to be a better person and leader
- Real-life stories and lessons from real personal circumstances packed with emotion, insight, and wisdom
- Practical translation into useful learning and action that will make you a stronger person and a better leader
- Confidence and inspiration that you are not alone—in loss of a loved one or in your role as a leader.

You can also expect one additional thing in accordance with *The Spirit of Abundance*. Proceeds from the sale of our book will be donated to The National Academy of Human Resources, a 501(c)(3) organization on whose board I serve (https://www.nationalacademyhr.org). We appreciate you taking this pay-it-forward journey with us!

Ian Ziskin
Sag Harbor, New York
(August 2025)

Author's Note: All essays included in this book by contributing authors were written in good faith and with the intent to learn from and honor those being featured. Should any reader have concerns, please contact Ian Ziskin at IZiskin@exexgroup.com

Chapter 1

The Presence of Absence

The Adam Bomb

My cell phone rang on a warm and sunny Saturday morning, June 10, 2023, just as I was about to begin my workout at home in Sag Harbor, New York. My 93-year-old mother was calling. Instantly, I knew something was wrong.

Most of us have experienced this kind of immediate and visceral sensation during a crisis. Something about the tone and intensity in my mother's voice, even before many words had spilled out, made me stop in my tracks.

"Adam thinks he is having a stroke and he's on his way to the hospital," she said. "He wanted to drive himself, but I told him he was crazy and to call an ambulance."

Hearing my 60-year-old younger brother's name, my first words were instinctively, "Did he?"

"Did he what?" my mother asked.

"Did he call an ambulance … and which hospital is he going to?" I replied.

I could hear my mother's breathing stop for a moment before she cried, "I don't know, I don't know. What if he collapsed at home and was unable to call an ambulance?" At this point, I don't think I was breathing much better than she was.

If there was any good news to be had on this day, it was that despite his apparent stroke symptoms, my brother did manage to call an ambulance from his condo in the suburbs of Atlanta, Georgia. And an hour or so later, my mother heard from the first responders telling her which hospital he was being taken to.

While all this was going on, I had already begun packing and making travel arrangements with my wife Sue's much-needed assistance. I was determined to get to Atlanta as quickly as possible. Before I left home, Sue put her hands on my shoulders, looked at me the way only someone who loves you can, and said, "Breathe." That turned out to be great advice.

To be perfectly honest, I do not remember much about my drive to JFK airport, my flight to Atlanta, or my drive to the hospital to meet my mother later that evening. It was mostly a blur and remains so.

DOI: 10.4324/9781003585633-3

What I do recall about my trip was repeatedly asking myself the same question: "Is this one of those strokes that are relatively mild, where the person is given some medication and physical and/or occupational therapy, and then goes on to live a relatively normal and healthy life? Or is this one of those strokes that are highly debilitating, where quality of life is significantly diminished, and the person requires constant care?"

It was neither.

By the time I arrived on Saturday night, hospital visiting hours were over and my mother was exhausted from a day of sitting with and worrying about my brother. So, despite my best efforts to get to him quickly, I was not able to see my brother until early the next day.

Arriving at the hospital Sunday morning with my mother, immediately we were accosted by two doctors at the doorway of my brother's room. One blurted out, "It's not a stroke. Based on the MRI we conducted of Adam's brain, he has at least two brain tumors and probably more throughout his body. We will need to confirm that through additional tests. Either way, he is terminal and likely has less than six months to live."

I remember thinking, "Well, good morning to you too, doctors."

Understandably, my mother did not take the news well and I did my best to keep her from collapsing next to her walker since the doctors did not have the common sense to invite her to sit down before dropping this "Adam Bomb" on us. Even though I thought my head might explode, I had two things to do first. One was to find a chair for my mother. The second was to say hello to my brother since I had not had the chance to see him prior to being intercepted by these two well-meaning but remarkably insensitive individuals.

The next five days involved a shitstorm of tests and more tests, followed by bad news and more bad news. As suspected, my brother had tumors throughout his body, including a very serious melanoma on his leg that had gotten out of control. The official diagnosis was metastatic cancer. The official prognosis went from less than six months to less than six weeks to less than one week to live. Thankfully, despite my brother's rapidly declining condition, he and our mother and I did somehow manage to share some laughs.

A few days into this ordeal, I had to do perhaps the most difficult thing I have ever done. I sat on my brother's bed, held his hand, looked into his eyes, and told him, "You are very sick, and you are not going to be with us much longer." To make matters worse, I think he understood me, but I cannot be 100% sure. The pressure on his brain from the tumors was causing him to go in and out of consciousness and he was beginning to suffer from periodic seizures. He was also being heavily medicated to manage the pain. (I choose to believe he heard me based on his reaction, but I also believe he already suspected what was coming.)

After five days in the hospital, as his life span shrank faster than a popped balloon, we decided, along with the doctors, to move Adam from the hospital to a hospice facility. There, over a three-day period, his life expectancy declined further from one week to a matter of hours. Adam died even more quickly than expected, shortly after midnight on June 18, 2023.

Here and gone.

The 30-minute drive to the hospice facility to say goodbye to my deceased brother on behalf of my mother and me felt like a trip to another planet. It was a mishmash of complete darkness endlessly interrupted by bright lights from oncoming cars. Normally, I would wonder why all these people were driving around at 1:30 a.m. on Father's Day morning, but my mind was otherwise occupied.

After arriving at my dead brother's bedside, I told him I loved him, forgave him for anything he might have felt the need to be forgiven for, kissed him, and said goodbye. I then drove to my mother's apartment to be with her until about 4:30 a.m., where we shared a lot of memories and asked one another endless unanswerable questions. After returning to my hotel room, I was greeted by my wife, Sue, and youngest son, Matt, who were waiting to support me after flying to Atlanta to be with my mother and me the day before. Their timing could not have been better, nor their presence more appreciated.

The six months that followed Adam's passing involved a whirlwind of dealing with emotions and realities for my family members and me: literally breaking into my brother's condo and tearing the security system off the wall with my bare hands because I didn't have the security code; cleaning out and selling said condo after 30 years of bachelor living; sifting through my brother's finances, debts, and other life surprises; discovering he had no will even though he had told me repeatedly in years past that he did; dealing with estate lawyers, creditors, the courts, and other bureaucracies too numerous to mention; frequently traveling to Atlanta to check on and be with my mother, who was handling my brother's death with amazing strength and resilience, but who also needed time to grieve in her own way while requiring support with certain daily chores; and continuing my own life running my coaching and consulting business and being a husband, father, and grandfather. It was a trying time, but we worked our way through it together.

Mom's Moment

Then, on December 24, 2023, after visiting my oldest son, Tyler, and daughter-in-law, Amy, and 10 minutes prior to Sue, Matt, and me boarding a flight home from Denver, my cell phone rang again. This time, the number on the screen was for the senior living community where my mother lived. I thought, "This cannot be good."

The facility was calling to let me know my mother had just been taken to the hospital with severe stomach pains (a condition she had suffered from multiple times in the past). That was all they knew, and they just wanted me to be aware of what was happening. Armed with this very concerning news but helplessly unarmed when it came to doing something useful in the moment, we decided to board our flight for New York after agonizing over the best course of action. We concluded that the logical, if imperfect choice, was to get home, learn more about my mother's condition, and then decide whether I should immediately travel to Atlanta to be with her.

Flying for four hours while not being able to do anything for my mother was excruciating to say the least. We landed at JFK airport in New York, and I immediately saw that I had several voicemail messages from the hospital. A doctor and nurse had tried to reach me while my flight was in the air. Again, I thought, "This cannot be good."

I dialed the hospital and a nurse answered. Once I identified myself, she awkwardly asked me to hold so she could get the on-duty emergency room physician on the line. An empathetic and respectful doctor-stranger then informed me how my mother's condition rapidly deteriorated after arriving at the hospital and that she passed away from cardiac arrest. While I was on my flight home, her heart had simply given out from all the trauma her body was experiencing.

Maybe, just maybe, the stress of my brother's death six months earlier had contributed to her sudden decline. Or maybe she was simply a 93-year-old woman whose time had come. Either way, I was not able to be there with her when she passed, and that feeling of regret will stay with me forever.

Fortunately, she died quickly and did not feel any pain thanks to the medications she had been given. My relatively healthy (for a 93-year-old) mother was fine until she wasn't.

Here and gone.

The silver lining with my mother's death was that, unlike my brother, she did have a will and I was familiar with all her finances. Happily, I also did not need to break into her apartment to clean it out. (We all can learn and grow from our experiences and be appreciative of small wins!)

The darker lining in this adventure was losing my brother and mother within a six-month period, barely allowing time to process one loss before having to face the next. However, I am not complaining. Please don't feel sorry for me.

My brother and mother did not suffer nearly as much as they might have. Many other people have had to deal with significantly more difficult circumstances (examples of which you will learn about in this book). By comparison, I was very lucky (and so were they), and I learned a lot about my brother, my mother, and myself in the process. (More about that learning journey later.)

The "Why" of This Book

At the time of this book's release, more than two years have passed since my brother died and it is nearly that long since my mother's death. That has been enough time to be well into the healing process but likely never enough time to fully accept that they are gone.

Their deaths and my father's passing at the age of 46 more than 54 years ago (see my last book, *The Secret Sauce for Leading Transformational Change* [Routledge, 2022], pages 6–7 for more on his story) have inspired—compelled—me to write this book.

But before we get too far along with the purpose and priorities of the book, there are some things you need to know about my brother and mother, and how I felt about them.

I want to acknowledge what I learned from them as well as their impact on others. You also need to know about them to understand me and where I come from as the lead author of this book. This level of disclosure about my brother and mother will also set the stage for many of the other stories you will read in *Lives Lost and Leadership Found*.

About Adam

Adam Brett Ziskin was born in Jamaica, New York, on October 13, 1962, grew up in Massapequa, New York until the age of 18, and lived the rest of his life in Atlanta, Georgia. He died unexpectedly and way too early at the age of 60 on June 18, 2023, of metastatic cancer. I am very grateful it took only eight days from diagnosis to death so that Adam did not suffer long.

He was simultaneously a very simple, straightforward, complicated, and multilayered person. Adam was extremely private yet incredibly giving. And he hated being the center of attention, which means he likely would not be thrilled to be so prominently featured in this book. (However, my mother would be ecstatic that I was bragging about her baby, Adam!)

Adam loved his family and friends and solving technology-related challenges of all kinds. In fact, he was a whiz who could fix anything with wires, buttons, switches, screens, or flashing lights. He also loved mashed potatoes, grits, meatloaf, chopped steak, pizza, and Mexican food. Adam enjoyed movies, TV shows, and music, and was an expert on news, current events, and weather (or thought he was). He took great pleasure in researching a wide range of subjects on his iPad and sharing what he learned. He had a great singing voice, loved to laugh, and regularly walked for exercise.

Adam was incredibly thoughtful, helpful, and polite. Even in his final days, when he could barely speak, he insisted on saying "thank you" to everyone at the hospital who assisted him. That was how he was wired and what he learned as a customer call center manager for many years.

Adam also had zero tolerance for stupidity, bureaucracy, bad customer service, laziness, and long lines. He was amazingly patient and impatient at the same time, depending on who he was dealing with and what issue he was addressing. While Adam was quite introverted and self-effacing, he took great pride in the success, happiness, and recognition of others, whether they were relatives, friends, work colleagues, or strangers. He never wanted to hurt anyone and often took the brunt of difficult circumstances, preferring to shield others from pain, discomfort, or inconvenience.

He had annoyingly neat handwriting and the world's most organized car trunk, yet his condo looked like a bachelor had lived there for 30 years. He saved mail, coupons, receipts, and advertising flyers forever. Like I said, Adam was a very simple yet complicated person.

I am a firm believer that every person has the capability to be truly great at one thing, yet very few people ever achieve greatness. While Adam had many talents, he was world-class as our mother's best friend and protector. He devoted his entire life to ensuring she was happy, healthy, safe, and well-fed with an impossible array of fat-free, taste-free foods. I will always marvel at the way Adam unselfishly dedicated himself to supporting her. That is Adam's greatest legacy.

Meet My Mother

Marilyn Joy Ziskin was born in Brooklyn, New York, on April 13, 1930. She lived her childhood and early adult years in Brooklyn and Queens, worked in office assistant jobs in Manhattan and on Long Island, took care of her husband (Ted) and raised two sons (Ian and Adam) primarily in Massapequa, and then spent her last 41 years living and working in Atlanta, Georgia. In her 93 years, my mother's experiences were filled with ups and downs, joys and worries, pride and pain, and never-ending laughter and love. She died on December 24, 2023, the same way she lived—in a hurry—after entering the hospital with severe stomach issues that ultimately led to cardiac arrest.

My mother divided her life between New York and Georgia, but she was 100% New Yorker through and through. Things had better be done fast and right. If she liked something, you knew it. If she did not, there was nowhere to hide! She was all about telling it like it is.

No matter her age or stage of life, my mother was defined by her resilience, toughness, directness, high standards, and love for the important people in her life. She was caring and supportive, and believed in people no matter their age, gender, race, religion, job, or socio-economic background. Once she liked you, she loved you. If she didn't care for you, you did not exist to her.

My mother battled through having an absentee father, becoming a widow at the age of 41, losing her mother and sister-in-law with whom she was very close, surviving cancer and other health issues, nursing her younger son Adam through a heart attack, and more recently losing Adam to cancer just six months before her own death. She loved life but it did not always love her back. My mother was very strong.

Likewise, she was uncompromising and unyielding in her quest to make issues, circumstances, and people better. At her core, my mother was an advocate … that was her superpower. She fought for her family, friends, and those less fortunate (even when those people may not have wanted someone to fight for them or possibly did not realize they needed someone in their corner).

When she was frustrated or dissatisfied with the level of service she was receiving (and to be honest, that was quite often), my mother would declare, "Are you kidding me?" or "I give up!" Adam and I would laugh at her because we knew two things about our mother … she was not kidding, and she never gave up. My mother had many layers, but she was fundamentally a very straightforward person. Don't lie, cheat, or steal. Do your best. Put family and friends above all else. Tell people you love them when you do. Tell people they are not meeting expectations when they are not. Set high standards and hold people accountable. Stand up for yourself and others.

On her worst days, my mother would complain—a lot. On her best days, she made everyone around her better. She had a lot more "best" days than "worst" days.

My mother had a great sense of humor and enjoyed making other people laugh. But she took her roles as mother, mother-in-law, grandmother, great grandmother, wife, sister, sister-in-law, daughter, aunt, friend, colleague, and neighbor very seriously. She loved sunshine, '50s music, exercising, walking, dancing, drinking cheap white wine with lots of ice, and eating a very short list of things—all of which had no fat or taste. And my mother gave my brother and me the greatest gift of all … she believed in us unconditionally.

Absence and Honor

The concept of "presence of absence" has been attributed to many people but it was brought to my attention by my mother-in-law during the process of losing my brother and mother. I think it sums up how life is without them. Every day, in every way, I feel the positive impact that Adam and my mother, Marilyn, had on my life. Every day, in every way, I also feel the emptiness and silence they leave behind. Their presence—and their absence—will always be with me.

After taking a few months in early 2024 to reflect on my brother's and mother's deaths and what they each meant to me, I decided to do two things, among many, to honor them and what they taught me. The first was to write this book to create a platform for myself and many others to share what we have learned about life and leadership in losing somebody special to us. The second was to write a song, "Here and Gone," to express my sentiments and gratitude directly to my deceased father, mother, and brother.

Even though I do not really believe they can hear me, I know you can. See Chapter 10 for the lyrics and for a link where you can hear me perform the song.

As you will note in Chapters 5–7, each essay in *Lives Lost and Leadership Found* concludes with three things the contributors learned about life and leadership from the loved ones they lost. In that spirit, here are the three most important things I learned from my brother's and mother's passing.

Three Things I Learned About Life and Leadership

1. Face reality and deal with it.
2. Advocate for the people, issues, ideas, and ideals you believe in, including for yourself.
3. Tell people that you care about, respect, and/or love them—then show them.

The "How" of This Book

While the idea for *Lives Lost and Leadership Found* came to me following my brother's and mother's deaths six months apart, that experience made me think about other people's experiences with loss and the leadership-related implications. Most of us have been affected by the passing of someone close to us. Even though there is pain and loss, as leaders we can also grow and learn from the life and death of someone we cared about deeply.

I therefore believe that people can benefit from the individual and collective experiences of others who have lost special somebodies in their lives—people they loved, respected, admired, and from whom they learned something about life and leadership. Accordingly, this book very intentionally incorporates views and experiences well beyond my own. I include the insights and perspectives of many other leaders and colleagues I admire greatly, who have themselves lost and learned from somebody special.

Before we address those special somebodies' stories in the soul of this book (Chapters 5, 6, and 7), Chapter 3 highlights perspectives from "famous" people who most of us know as public figures but who struggled privately with the loss of loved ones while continuing to make big impacts as iconic leaders and societal influencers. Then, Chapter 4 summarizes dozens of additional learnings and even more diverse thinking from more than 150 individuals who responded to a simple two-question survey we conducted in the fall of 2024.

Contributing authors include senior HR and operating leaders, academics, coaches, consultants, board members, founders/CEOs, clients, students, and others. Famous people include U.S. Presidents, CEOs, entertainers, sports heroes, and others. Survey respondents represent a broad array of leaders, employees, community and family members, and others. All the experiences, feelings, learnings, and stories they share are as different as the loved ones they lost. Yet, there are common themes that emerge from their ideas and insights.

Our book is first and foremost about leadership—informed and inspired by lessons learned from losing someone special. It explores four critical questions:

1. What did we learn from people important to us during their lives and deaths?
2. Can anything positive be gleaned from their passing?
3. How have these experiences of loss changed us as leaders and as people?
4. What can we *do* with what we have learned?

While our book is much more about leadership than loss, we do also use it to honor the important people we have lost. After all, they have inspired us and made us better people and leaders. That is their gift to us all.

If you are familiar with our last book, *The Secret Sauce for Leading Transformational Change* (Routledge, 2022), you can consider this book a follow-on because it explores leadership and transformational change at a very personal and individual level, namely, how the death of someone special affected and influenced us as people and as leaders, and how these difficult challenges changed us (hopefully for the better, but perhaps not).

Lives Lost and Leadership Found is intended to help you benefit from the diverse individual and collective experiences of the contributing authors. The book is uniquely positioned to focus not only on the personal impact the deaths of key people in our lives have had on us, but also (and as importantly) on the leadership impact and legacy they represent. It is not a book about grieving or feeling sorry for yourself, even though it reveals and explores raw emotions. It is a book about how we as leaders can, should, and will inevitably be influenced by what we have learned about life and leadership from people we loved who taught us valuable lessons through the way they lived and died.

The Structure of This Book

Our book is structured to allow for maximum variety of perspectives and lenses.

- Following Chapter 1 (this chapter), we provide relevant background research on the cognitive, physical, and emotional impacts of losing and grieving a loved one in Chapter 2.
- In Chapter 3, we address the loss experiences and leadership implications endured by "famous" people who had to overcome loss on the way to making significant contributions to society.
- Chapter 4 summarizes key themes from survey inputs offered by 150 respondents to two questions: (1) "If a person important to you passed away recently or a long time ago, what is the one most significant thing you learned from that person about life and leadership?" and (2) "What was that person's relationship to you (parent, grandparent, spouse, life partner, child, grandchild, sibling, friend, colleague, boss, mentor, etc.)?" The blend of insights from this crowdsourcing process is powerful and, in some ways, surprising.
- Chapters 5–7 feature 35 compelling essays written by our contributing authors, each with incredible poignancy and wisdom. These chapters highlight three essential life and leadership lessons including courage (and resilience), compassion (and relationships), and curiosity (and purpose). Each essay concludes with "Three Things I Learned About Life and Leadership," as a concise means of summarizing key learnings imparted from special somebodies to our contributing authors.

- Chapter 8 succinctly captures a series of "Tensions of Intentionality," making it as easy as possible for you, the reader, to understand the competing priorities that must be mastered because they make the biggest difference to your learning and success as a person and as a leader.
- Chapter 9 describes "The Smoothie Effect," my analogy to help you relate to the emotions and experiences reinforced throughout this book.
- Chapter 10 offers some conclusions and the song lyrics for "Here and Gone," my tribute to my father, mother, and brother who have all passed away but remain a part of me through the valuable lessons they shared during their lives and deaths. You can also access a link there to hear me perform it.
- In the Epilogue, contributing authors share how they and, in some cases, their family members, friends, and colleagues felt as a result of writing or reading their respective essays, including how feelings and emotions manifested themselves.
- The Appendix provides a framework for writing your own essay to honor your special somebody.

As you read our book, we invite you to think about and celebrate someone in your life who has passed away and has made you better every day through the life and leadership lessons they embodied. That person is one of the special somebodies. So are you.

Author's Note: In addition to the lessons described in Chapter 1 and throughout this book, I want to underscore something else very important I learned from my brother Adam's death. I have always known it, but his death served as a stark reminder. DO NOT IGNORE YOUR HEALTH OR TAKE IT FOR GRANTED! If Adam had undergone regular skin checkups and addressed related findings, he quite likely would not have died from an untreated, out of control melanoma that went directly to his brain. Physical and mental well-being are essential ingredients for life and leadership. Please consider this a free public service announcement.

Chapter 2

Neuroscience, Loss, and Leadership

There are literally thousands of books, articles, research papers, podcasts, blogs, YouTube videos, and other resources on the topic of grieving the death of a loved one and the psychological, emotional, spiritual, and/or physiological effects of such experiences. We cite a handful of useful resources in this chapter, but they are simply good examples among many.

These and other sources will help you understand the neuroscience of grieving in a more nuanced and thoughtful way than we can in this book. After all, our book is not primarily focused on grief or death. We are instead exploring the impact that losing somebody special can and does have on our perspectives as people and as leaders.

Can we *learn* something valuable about life and leadership? And will we *do* something valuable with those leadership lessons?

While writing this book, I became especially curious about the connection, if any, between Elisabeth Kübler-Ross's *Five Stages of Grief* concept introduced in her 1969 book *On Death and Dying*,[1] which includes denial, anger, bargaining, depression, and acceptance, and what leaders and organizations go through during large-scale transformational change. Spoiler alert ... there are overlaps, but that's another book!

I also wanted to learn whether grief and leadership are interconnected. They are, and that's in large part what this book is about. In service of this mission, this chapter touches lightly but directly on science-based findings about the impact of death and grief on human beings. This information will serve as relevant context for how and why losing a special somebody teaches us important lessons about life and leadership—if we allow ourselves to pay attention to, process, and put what we learn into action.

In addition to introducing the world to her *Five Stages of Grief*, Kübler-Ross also said, "The reality is that you will grieve forever. You will not 'get over' the loss of a loved one; you will learn to live with it. You will heal and you will rebuild yourself around the loss you have suffered. You will be whole again, but you will never be the same. Nor should you be the same nor would you want to."[2] If we accept this premise, we begin to understand the relevance of neuroscience to grief and leadership.

DOI: 10.4324/9781003585633-4

Impact of Loss #1—Brain and Body

Mary-Francis O'Connor is an Associate Professor of Clinical Psychology at the University of Arizona and the author of *The Grieving Brain: The Surprising Science of How We Learn from Love and Loss*. In her research, Professor O'Connor suggests that "a loved one's absence means a major disruption not only to our life but also within our brain."[3] She goes on to say, "Grief is the cost of loving someone. When a loved one dies, it can feel like we've lost a part of ourselves because their presence is coded into our neurons."[4]

This direct connection between loss and the brain got my attention.

O'Connor continues by outlining the emotional, physiological, cognitive, and other effects of losing someone. Examples include sadness, yearning, anger, blame, guilt, and panic; heart rate, cortisol levels, stress hormones, concentration, or remembering details; memory, decision-making, attention, speed of information processing, and brain fog; changes in behavior, sleep, and other patterns; and feeling waves of grief. She also reveals that grieving can be considered a form of learning.

In the November 3, 2023, edition of *Psychology Today*, Deborah L. Davis, Ph.D., builds on the idea that loss and the brain are inextricably intertwined. In her article, "How the Brain Rewires as We Grieve,"[5] she explains that there are neural maps in relationships. During the loss of a loved one, we must reconcile two opposing thoughts. We have conscious knowledge that the person we loved is gone. But we also have implicit knowledge (or belief) that our special somebody is everlasting.

Davis says, "Your brain requires ample time and a ton of rumination and lived experience to absorb the absence, update the predictions, and complete this enormous redraw. In the meantime, the still-outdated areas of your neural map make you think, feel, and act as if your loved one is here, now, and close. You grieve every time you confront an outdated prediction and update the neural map accordingly. You ruminate endlessly on what happened and what will become of you. You feel distracted and exhausted."[6]

As we will see throughout our book, different leaders respond to loss in different ways for different reasons. They handle loss using a variety of coping mechanisms and learn from loss through a wide array of approaches. But none of us, it seems, can escape the impact of a loved one's passing on our brains.

The negative impact of loss on the brain is further verified by Lisa M. Shulman, MD, in "How Grief Rewires the Brain." Dr. Shulman says, "Traumatic loss is perceived as a threat to survival and defaults to protective survival and defense mechanisms. This response engages the fight or flight mechanism."[7] Shulman goes on to say, "These defense mechanisms increase blood pressure, heart rate, and specific hormones, and can also cause changes in memory, behavior, sleep, and body function such as the immune system and heart, and lead to cognitive effects such as brain fog. The brain's goal? Survival."[8]

"When a brain circuit fires repeatedly," says Dr. Shulman, "it's reinforced and becomes a default setting. The long-term impact of grief is that it can disrupt the diverse cognitive domains of memory, decision-making, visuospatial function, attention, word fluency, and the speed of information processing."[9]

But wait, there's more!

In "Tragedy Assistance Program for Survivors: YOU ARE NOT CRAZY – YOU'RE GRIEVING – PART ONE," Dr. Alan Wolfelt indicates that, "After someone you love dies, it is normal to look for them or expect them to reappear. Every time you hear your front door or garage door open, your brain might catch and you might think, 'there they are!' This searching behavior is a sign that your mind is trying to process the reality of the death. It can also make you feel crazy because while you know that they have died, you don't yet fully know."[10]

But wait, there's even more!

"How Grief Affects the Brain," by Blossom Therapeutics reports that, "The prefrontal cortex is the part of the brain responsible for decision-making, problem-solving, and regulating emotions. During grief, the prefrontal cortex can become underactive, leading to difficulties in making decisions and processing information ... underactivity can also lead to mood swings and emotional instability."[11]

But wait, there's still more!

Christopher W.T. Miller, MD, a psychiatrist and psychoanalyst, argues in his article, "What Grief Does to Your Brain," that "In the brain, there can be a disconnect between 'episodic' or 'autobiographical' memory areas (which register factual events and are informing us the person is gone) and 'semantic' or 'conceptual' memory areas (which register contextual information about our lives and are informing us that this person has been, and therefore should continue to be, a predictable part of our day-to-day existence). This information paradox can lead to what has been termed the 'gone-but-also-everlasting' theory in grief."[12]

Loss and grief clearly have profound and lasting effects on the brain and body. What about their impact on leadership?

Impact of Loss #2—Leadership

According to neuroscience and leadership experts David Rock and Jeffrey Schwartz, "change is pain" and "focus is power." In their article, "The Neuroscience of Leadership," they argue that "organizational change is unexpectedly difficult because it provokes sensations of physiological discomfort."[13] Change is in fact pain.

Rock and Schwartz go on to explain that "... the brain sends out powerful messages that something is wrong, and the capacity for higher thought is decreased. Change itself thus amplifies stress and discomfort and managers (who may not, from their position in the hierarchy, perceive the same events in the way that subordinates perceive them) tend to underestimate the challenges inherent in the implementation."[14]

Change causes real pain and discomfort, and losing a special somebody is one of the most transformational—and painful—changes people and leaders can experience. Can leaders lead effectively while in pain?

Likewise, Rock and Schwartz assert that, "The act of paying attention creates chemical and physical changes in the brain."[15] Focus is in fact power. They explain that "neurons communicate with each other through a type of electromechanical signaling that is driven by the movement of ions such as sodium, potassium, and calcium. The brain is a quantum environment and is therefore subject to all the surprising laws of quantum mechanics."[16]

Rock and Schwartz further explain that "… the brain changes as a function of where we put our attention. The power is in the focus. Attention continually reshapes the patterns of the brain. Among the implications: people who practice a specialty every day literally think differently, through different sets of connections, than people who don't practice this specialty. In business, professionals in different functions—finance, operations, legal, research and development, marketing, design, and human resources—have physiological differences that prevent them from seeing the world the same way."[17]

Isn't the practice of leadership a "function" in many regards as well? Can a grieving leader be a focused leader? What are the implications for loss and leadership?

Consider the following questions as you continue to read *Lives Lost and Leadership Found*:

1. What are the risks of leading ineffectively during times of loss and grief?
2. How can we mitigate, manage, or overcome these risks?
3. Despite evidence of the negative impact of loss and grief on the brain and body, can leaders nevertheless maximize their effectiveness by learning lessons from the special somebodies they have lost?
4. What steps might you take to enhance your chances of learning something positive from a lost loved one rather than becoming debilitated as a result of the negative aspects of the loss?

Notes

1. Elisabeth Kübler-Ross, *On Death and Dying* (New York: Macmillan, 1969).
2. Elisabeth Kübler-Ross, *On Death and Dying* (New York: Macmillan, 1969).
3. Mary-Francis O'Connor, *The Grieving Brain: The Surprising Science of How We Learn from Love and Loss* (New York: HarperOne, 2022.)
4. Mary-Francis O'Connor, *The Grieving Brain: The Surprising Science of How We Learn from Love and Loss* (New York: HarperOne, 2022.)
5. Deborah L. Davis, Ph.D., "How the Brain Rewires as We Grieve," *Psychology Today*, November 3, 2023.
6. Deborah L. Davis, Ph.D., "How the Brain Rewires as We Grieve," *Psychology Today*, November 3, 2023.

7. Lisa M. Shulman, MD, "How Grief Rewires the Brain," *American Brain Foundation*, accessed October 2024, https://www.americanbrainfoundation.org/how-tragedy-affects-the-brain

8. Lisa M. Shulman, MD, "How Grief Rewires the Brain," *American Brain Foundation*, accessed October 2024, https://www.americanbrainfoundation.org/how-tragedyaffects-the-brain

9. Lisa M. Shulman, MD, "How Grief Rewires the Brain," *American Brain Foundation*, accessed October 2024, https://www.americanbrainfoundation.org/how-tragedyaffects-the-brain

10. Alan Wolfelt, Ph.D., "YOU'RE NOT CRAZY — YOU'RE GRIEVING — PART ONE," *Tragedy Assistance Program for Survivors*, accessed September 2024, https://www.taps.org/articles/29-2/you-are-not-crazy-you-are-grieving

11. Blossom Team, "How Grief Affects the Brain," *Blossom Counseling*, accessed September 2024, https://blossom-counseling.net/grief/how-grief-affects-the-brain

12. Christopher W.T. Miller, MD, "What Grief Does to Your Brain," *The Washington Post*, March 8, 2024, accessed October 2024, https://www.washingtonpost.com/wellness/2024/03/08/grief-brain-healing-coping-strategies

13. David Rock and Jeffrey Schwartz, "The Neuroscience of Leadership," *Strategy+Business*, accessed October 2024, https://www.strategy-business.com/article/06207

14. David Rock and Jeffrey Schwartz, "The Neuroscience of Leadership," *Strategy+Business*, accessed October 2024, https://www.strategy-business.com/article/06207

15. David Rock and Jeffrey Schwartz, "The Neuroscience of Leadership," *Strategy+Business*, accessed October 2024, https://www.strategy-business.com/article/06207

16. David Rock and Jeffrey Schwartz, "The Neuroscience of Leadership," *Strategy+Business*, accessed October 2024, https://www.strategy-business.com/article/06207

17. David Rock and Jeffrey Schwartz, "The Neuroscience of Leadership," *Strategy+Business*, accessed October 2024, https://www.strategy-business.com/article/06207

Part II

Who ... Were the Special Somebodies?

Chapter 3

Fame Ain't Fair Sometimes

If you have not yet figured it out, you will by the end of this book: I love a good quote. One of my favorites is by actress and comedienne Lily Tomlin, who is famous for saying, "I always wanted to be somebody, but now I realize I should have been more specific."[1] Since most of this book is dedicated to learning from special somebodies, Tomlin's quote resonates particularly well. However, it is even more meaningful in the context of this chapter.

Most of the stories and quotes in this book are about ordinary people who lived ordinary lives. They died in ordinary ways under sad but ordinary circumstances. But the examples they set and the lessons they taught us were anything but ordinary. After all, they were special somebodies.

Likewise, the people who loved and lost them—the contributing authors and survey respondents who have shared their perspectives in these pages—are (despite their many accomplishments in life) rather ordinary too.

I have obnoxiously but intentionally overused the term "ordinary" here to describe our special somebodies and book contributors to illustrate a point, not to offend. Specifically, by describing them as ordinary, I am suggesting they were and are just like the rest of us. They have lived, loved, lost, learned, and led. But they were not famous.

While most of our book will address the stories and lessons of life and leadership imparted by ordinary people (even though they were special somebodies to us), this chapter is different. It focuses on life and leadership through the eyes and experiences of famous people who lost loved ones. Why take this detour?

Despite the apparent glitz and glamour associated with fame and celebrity, people are people—famous or not. We all share the experiences of losing, grieving, and learning from special somebodies. Yet famous people have a much broader and more public platform from which life and leadership lessons can be shared. So, we will take advantage of our access to these insights as an important part of setting the stage to learn about loss, life, and leadership.

DOI: 10.4324/9781003585633-6

Loss and Achievement—Correlation or Causation?

Did you know that 19 (more than 40%) of U.S. presidents lost fathers when they themselves were relatively young (under the age of 30)? This list includes George Washington, John Adams, Thomas Jefferson, James Monroe, Andrew Jackson, William Henry Harrison, John Tyler, Andrew Johnson, Rutherford B. Hayes, James Garfield, Grover Cleveland, Theodore Roosevelt, Herbert Hoover, Franklin D. Roosevelt, Lyndon B. Johnson, Gerald Ford, Jimmy Carter, Bill Clinton, and Barack Obama.[2]

Were you aware 18 U.S. presidents lost one or more children, spouses, or siblings including John Adams, Thomas Jefferson, John Quincy Adams, John Tyler, Franklin Pierce, Abraham Lincoln, Rutherford B. Hayes, Grover Cleveland, William McKinley, Theodore Roosevelt, Calvin Coolidge, Franklin Roosevelt, Dwight Eisenhower, John F. Kennedy, Ronald Reagan, George H.W. Bush, George W. Bush, and Joe Biden?[3]

Interestingly, a few unlucky presidents experienced multiple losses.

Is there a direct correlation between loss of a loved one and these leaders becoming presidents of the United States, or their effectiveness in the office once they became president? That is unknowable and unprovable. Can we assume, however, that each of these presidents likely learned something useful from the experience of loss that made them better people and leaders? Quite likely.

U.S. presidents do not have the corner on this phenomenon. Lucille Iremonger found that 67% of British prime ministers from the beginning of the nineteenth century to the start of World War II lost a parent before age 16.[4] What is going on here?

What about CEOs, entertainers, sports heroes, artists, authors, inventors, societal icons, other politicians and government figures, and other celebrities and household names? What might they have in common when it comes to losing a loved one and learning life and leadership lessons?

Many such people of achievement share a common bond—that of losing a loved one and turning their negative experience into something positive.

In the early 2000s, author Malcolm Gladwell coined the term, "eminent orphans," defined as children who experience the loss of a parent before their eighteenth birthday.[5] In his book *David and Goliath*, Gladwell cites an encyclopedia review by psychologist Marvin Eisenstadt who researched biographies that merited "more than one column" (a proxy for people of achievement). Of 573 people, Gladwell reported, "a quarter had lost at least one parent before the age of 10. By age 15, 34.5% had had at least one parent die, and by the age of 20, 45%. Even for the years before the twentieth century, when life expectancy due to illness and accidents and warfare was much lower than it is today, those are astonishing numbers."[6]

In an NPR article, Robert Krulwich summarized Gladwell's book and findings by saying, "Gladwell doesn't come out and say that losing a parent early increases one's chances of success later. But in study after study, among those who have succeeded, the incidence of 'eminent orphans' is oddly high. The correlation shows up for scientists … It shows up in a study of 'father absence' among eminent poets."[7] Krulwich goes on to say, "Nobody wants to say that catastrophe is a career booster. But … kids with missing parents need extra muscle, grit, and self-reliance …"[8]

Losing a parent or any loved one is incredibly painful. Evidence suggests that how we cope with, learn from, and behave following the hurt is what makes the biggest difference. A huge part of success involves effectively processing the life and leadership lessons that emerge from losing somebody special to us.

Not-So-Ordinary People

Thousands of famous people have shared their views on the loss of a loved one via interviews, articles, blogs, books, social media posts, videos, shows, and other media. While their circumstances of loss are very unfortunate, we are quite fortunate to have public access to the lessons learned from their experiences. This considerable evidence is one reason, among many, to explore loss among famous people. It sets a strong foundation for deeper exploration later in the book.

We will focus a bit more in-depth here on a few representative examples of loss experienced by some highly visible and well-known leaders. Then, we will highlight some additional valuable insights from other famous people, but in a lighter fashion.

Sheryl Sandberg (Ride the Wave)

Sheryl Sandberg was COO of Facebook (Meta) until her departure on August 1, 2022. She is also the author of the book *Lean In: Women, Work, and the Will to Lead*[9] and the founder of Lean In, a nonprofit organization that helps women achieve their career ambitions, among other ventures. Her first husband, Dave Goldberg, CEO of SurveyMonkey, passed away unexpectedly at the age of 47 on May 1, 2015, while on vacation with his family in Mexico. Goldberg tragically suffered significant head trauma and blood loss after slipping and falling while exercising on a treadmill in the hotel gym.

Following her husband's death, Sandberg spoke and wrote openly about the "deep fog of grief" she experienced. She also co-wrote a book about the grieving process with University of Pennsylvania professor and psychologist Adam Grant entitled *Option B: Facing Adversity, Building Resilience, and Finding Joy*.[10] The book contains many valuable lessons for effectively dealing with adverse circumstances, including death, and building the resilience needed to cope and thrive.

For purposes relevant to this book, Sandberg and Grant mention three "convictions" to be addressed that I think are especially pertinent: personalization, pervasiveness, and permanence. Personalization is the worry that the situation or loss reflects personally on the individual. Pervasiveness is the concern that its influence is widespread. Permanence is the fear that the consequences will last indefinitely.

Applied to the loss of a loved one, these convictions can result in an endless loop of grief and the belief that it will never end. However, Sandberg shared a much needed and encouraging perspective in *Option B* when she said, "Grief is a demanding companion. In those early weeks and months, it was always there, not just below the surface but on the surface. Simmering, lingering, festering. Then, like a wave, it would rise up and pulse through me, as if it were going to tear my heart right out of my body … After a few months, I started to notice that the fog of intense pain lifted now and then, and when it rolled back in, I recovered faster. It occurred to me that dealing with grief was like building physical stamina: the more you exercise, the faster your heart rate recovers after it is elevated. And sometimes during especially vigorous physical activity, you discover strength you didn't know you had."[11]

Satya Nadella (Infuse Empathy)

Satya Nadella is CEO of Microsoft and among the most respected chief executives in the world. Microsoft is a company with $245 billion in revenue and 228,000 employees, but it appears Nadella's most cherished role is that of husband and father.

On February 28, 2022, multiple news sources reported that Nadella's son, Zain, died of complications from Cerebral Palsy at age 26. While learning to live with the challenges of a special needs child, Nadella had often talked of the joys and responsibilities of raising his son.

In a 2017 blog on the Microsoft Accessibility website, Nadella wrote, "As (Zain's) parents, it was up to us not to question 'why,' but instead to do everything we could to improve his life." Nadella continued, "I have learned that when I infuse empathy into my everyday actions, it is powerful, whether they be in my role as father or as a CEO."[12]

Nadella also used his son's health challenges and tragic death as a driver in Microsoft's business strategy and his priorities as CEO. He became insistent that technology become more inclusive and accessible to users with disabilities. In this way and others, being a father of a son with special needs transformed him.

"Becoming a father of a son with special needs … has shaped my personal passion for and philosophy of connecting new ideas to empathy for others," Nadella wrote on LinkedIn. "And it is why I am deeply committed to pushing the bounds on what love and compassion combined with human ingenuity and passion to have impact can accomplish with my colleagues at Microsoft."[13]

Anderson Cooper (Love More Fully)

Anderson Cooper is a world-renowned CNN news anchor. While he has traveled the globe reporting from dangerous places about the struggles of others, he has been very open about his own struggles with grief. Amanda Petrusich, a writer for *The New Yorker* magazine, wrote an excellent article on October 30, 2022, titled "Talking About Grief with Anderson Cooper." In it she profiled and interviewed Cooper about his family history, his views on grief, and his new podcast, *All There Is.*[14]

"When CNN anchor Anderson Cooper was ten, he lost his father, Wyatt, to heart disease; when he was twenty-one, his older brother Carter died by suicide. In 2019, his mother, the artist and clothing designer Gloria Vanderbilt, passed away at ninety-five of stomach cancer."[15] During the wide-ranging interview between Petrusich and Cooper, she asks him about grief, and he responds, "If you want to be the most human you can be, then this is part of that. Grief enables you to love more fully, to experience things more fully."[16]

Later in this interview, Cooper recalls a podcast interview he did with late night TV host Stephen Colbert who has also endured considerable loss in his life. Cooper says that he learned some very valuable insights about grief from Colbert who shared views including, "cultivating gratitude for loss" and "learn(ing) to love the thing you most wish never happened."[17]

Cooper also connects his views on grief to many of his career choices. For example, he admits, "It's clearly what motivated me to start going to places that were precarious, very real, elemental—where life and death were something that people wrestled with and spoke about … I did want to be around people I could relate to, who were in pain, and who understood pain …"[18]

About starting his podcast on grief, *All There Is*, Cooper acknowledges, "Doing the podcast has opened me up to other ways of looking at grief. Laurie Anderson (artist and composer and one of his podcast guests) pointed out that the little child I once was has died. I hadn't thought about it in those terms. There is no one left who really knew that little child."[19]

Reflecting on fond memories of his father and brother, Cooper recalls a memory that brings him joy, "My dad would always say to my brother, 'Carter, enjoy. Enjoy, enjoy.' I like that idea. I say it to myself because I know that is what my dad would say."[20]

Additional Celebrity Insights (Accept Joy and Happiness)

While we could feature many dozens of helpful insights on life and leadership from famous people who have lost loved ones, here are some that are particularly illustrative:

- "We all experience loss at some point in our lives. Loss of life or loss of love. Being able to really SIT in this grief allows you to feel the moments of joy and gratitude for having loved someone that deep. And we loved him deeply. He was such a part of our DNA."[21]
  - Actress Jennifer Aniston (about her fellow actor and friend Matthew Perry)
- "When she was in high school (my mom) wanted to be an actor, so I think I'm sort of getting to live this life for both of us in that way. And she was my best friend. So I think she'd be happy."[22]
  - Actor Austin Butler (speaking about his mother)

- "I hope this grief stays with me because it's all of the unexpressed love that I didn't get to tell her, and I told her every day, she was the best of us."[23]

  – Actor Andrew Garfield (about his mother)

- "One of the things that he always taught me is that you have to take a negative and turn it into a positive."[24]

  – NBA Hall of Famer Michael Jordan (about his father)

- "… I don't want to talk about it because it will make me sad, but once realizing that if I do talk about it, and I'm celebrating her life, then actually things become easier…You convince yourself that the person you lost wants you, or you need to be sad as long as possible to prove to them they are missed. But then there's this realization of, no, they must want me to be happy."[25]

  – Prince Harry (about his mother)

- "It's important to me to honor Ian in the totality of who he is, speak about him in the present, because he is always with me, the joy and happiness he gave all of us."[26]

  – Actress and Director Regina King (about her son)

- "When I was young, I told my dad, 'We are going to be rich and have a big house.' Then he said, 'Son, that is impossible.' Today I have what I said to my father … but I don't have my father."[27]

  – Soccer Superstar Cristiano Ronaldo (about his father)

Famous people grieve, love, learn, and lead—just like the rest of us. Now, let's see what we not-so-famous people have to say about loss and leadership.

Notes

1. Lily Tomlin, "I always wanted to be somebody, but now I realize I should have been more specific," *BrainyQuote*, accessed October 2024, https://www.brainyquote.com/quotes/lily_tomlin_109612
2. "Age at Father's Death," *Presidents of the United States (POTUS)*, accessed October 2024, https://potus.com/presidential-facts/age-at-fathers-death
3. Doug Wead, *All the Presidents' Children: Triumphs and Tragedy in the Lives of America's First Families* (New York: Atria Books, 2003).
4. "Eminent Orphans," *Eugenewei.com*, accessed October 2024, https://www.eugenewei.com/blog/2013/11/27/eminent-orphans
5. Malcolm Gladwell, "Getting In," *The New Yorker*, October 10, 2005, https://www.newyorker.com/magazine/2005/10/10/getting-in
6. Malcolm Gladwell, *David and Goliath: Underdogs, Misfits, and the Art of Battling Giants* (New York: Little, Brown and Company, 2013), Chapter 3.
7. Robert Krulwich, "What Makes Eminent Orphans Special?" *NPR*, November 5, 2013, https://www.npr.org/sections/krulwich/2013/11/05/243421304/what-makes-eminent-orphans-special
8. Robert Krulwich, "What Makes Eminent Orphans Special?" *NPR*, November 5, 2013, https://www.npr.org/sections/krulwich/2013/11/05/243421304/what-makeseminent-orphans-special
9. Sheryl Sandberg, *Lean In: Women, Work, and the Will to Lead* (New York: Knopf, 2013).

10. Adam Grant and Sheryl Sandberg, *Option B: Facing Adversity, Building Resilience, and Finding Joy* (New York: Knopf, 2017).

11. Adam Grant and Sheryl Sandberg, *Option B: Facing Adversity, Building Resilience, and Finding Joy* (New York: Knopf, 2017).

12. Satya Nadella, "The Moment That Forever Changed Our Lives," *Microsoft Accessibility*, October 21, 2017, accessed October 2024, https://blogs.microsoft.com/accessibility/satya-nadella-the-moment-that-forever-changed-our-lives/

13. Satya Nadella, "The Moment That Forever Changed Our Lives," *Microsoft Accessibility*, October 21, 2017, accessed October 2024, https://blogs.microsoft.com/accessibility/satya-nadella-the-moment-that-forever-changed-our-lives/

14. Amanda Petrusich, "Talking About Grief with Anderson Cooper," *The New Yorker*, October 30, 2022, accessed October 2024, https://www.newyorker.com/magazine/2022/10/30/talking-about-grief-with-anderson-cooper

15. Amanda Petrusich, "Talking About Grief with Anderson Cooper," *The New Yorker*, October 30, 2022, accessed October 2024, https://www.newyorker.com/magazine/2022/10/30/talking-about-grief-with-anderson-cooper

16. Amanda Petrusich, "Talking About Grief with Anderson Cooper," *The New Yorker,* October 30, 2022, accessed October 2024, https://www.newyorker.com/magazine/2022/10/30/talking-about-grief-with-anderson-cooper

17. Amanda Petrusich, "Talking About Grief with Anderson Cooper," *The New Yorker,* October 30, 2022, accessed October 2024, https://www.newyorker.com/magazine/2022/10/30/talking-about-grief-with-anderson-cooper

18. Amanda Petrusich, "Talking About Grief with Anderson Cooper," *The New Yorker*, October 30, 2022, accessed October 2024, https://www.newyorker.com/magazine/2022/10/30/talking-about-grief-with-anderson-cooper

19. Amanda Petrusich, "Talking About Grief with Anderson Cooper," *The New Yorker*, October 30, 2022, accessed October 2024, https://www.newyorker.com/magazine/2022/10/30/talking-about-grief-with-anderson-cooper

20. Amanda Petrusich, "Talking About Grief with Anderson Cooper," *The New Yorker*, October 30, 2022, accessed October 2024, https://www.newyorker.com/magazine/2022/10/30/talking-about-grief-with-anderson-cooper

21. Nora Dominick, "Jennifer Aniston Posted a Heartbreaking Tribute to Matthew Perry After His Death," *BuzzFeed*, accessed October 23, 2024, https://www.buzzfeed.com/noradominick/jennifer-aniston-matthew-perry-tribute

22. Austin Butler, quoted in "'Parts of Me Have Died': 15 Celebrities Who Have Talked Honestly About Living With Grief After The Loss Of A Parent, Child, Friend, And More," by Nora Dominick, *BuzzFeed*, July 12, 2024, from interview by Willie Geist on *Sunday Sitdown with Willie Geist*, accessed October 23, 2024, https://www.buzzfeed.com/noradominick/celebs-talking-about-grief

23. Andrew Garfield, "It's Okay to Miss Somebody," *Sesame Street*, aired October 2024, https://www.ew.com/tv/andrew-garfield-elmo-mom-grief

24. Michael Jordan, quoted in *The Last Dance*, "Michael Jordan's Grief Over the Death of His Father," *WRAL*, April 22, 2020, https://www.wral.com/story/Michael-Jordans-grief-over-the-death-of-his-father/19781098

25. Jack Royston, "Prince Harry Talks About Bereavement," *CNN*, June 27, 2024, accessed October 2024, https://www.cnn.com/2024/06/27/europe/prince-harry-bereavement-scli-intl/index.html

26. Nora Dominick, "Celebrities Talking About Grief," *BuzzFeed*, accessed October 2024, https://www.buzzfeed.com/noradominick/celebs-talking-about-grief

27. Cristiano Ronaldo, "...Today, I have what I said to my father and became rich, but I don't have my father," YouTube video, posted by silent, March 15, 2024, https://youtu.be/8VpRWASzzhY

Chapter 4

Notable Quotables

Author Jamie Anderson says, "Grief, I've learned, is really just love. It's all the love you want to give but cannot. All of that unspent love gathers up in the corners of your eyes, the lump in your throat, and in the hollow part of your chest. Grief is just love with no place to go."[1]

That quote deeply resonated with me as I read input from 150 survey respondents who we asked two questions in preparation for writing this book:

1. If a person important to you passed away recently or a long time ago, what is **the one most significant thing** you learned from that person about life and leadership?
2. What was this person's relationship to you (parent, grandparent, spouse, life partner, child, grandchild, sibling, friend, colleague, boss, mentor, etc.)?

People had a lot to share in their responses, covering a wide swath of life and leadership lessons—many of which are highlighted and summarized in this chapter. However, the power of the input we received went well beyond the words and themes addressed. I was quite struck by the raw emotional complexity that poured out via the replies to two very simple questions. I could read, see, hear, and feel people's pain, pride, and passion as they shared something important learned from somebody special to them. Jamie Anderson's positioning of grief as "love with no place to go" was on full display.

A Treasure Trove

Survey respondents seemed to realize that they were about to teach something incredibly precious and valuable to a bunch of strangers—the eventual readers of our book. Yet they felt compelled to share detailed stories, emotions, and memories with us. It is the ultimate example of transparency, vulnerability, and trust. And these survey inputs are now a treasure trove of insights from the crowd—colleagues, fellow leaders, and complete strangers—who told us stories about their loved ones lost.

DOI: 10.4324/9781003585633-7

So, let's absorb what they have so unselfishly shared with respect and empathy … and give their love someplace to go.

While, as expected, survey responses covered a very broad range of perspectives, three common and consistent themes emerged:

1. Cherish Relationships
2. Advocate for Yourself and Others
3. Dream Big and Go Bigger

In addition to summarizing these themes and featuring a sampling of specific quotes to reinforce each one, I am also taking some license as lead author of this book to include a fourth category which features other wide-ranging perspectives from survey respondents that I personally found highly impactful. This fourth category, "Seek Wisdom," features a small sample of additional inputs that did not fall neatly into the other main themes but offered practical and powerful messages as well as significant lessons.

We thank all our survey respondents and their special somebodies who have taught us so much, including what follows here.

Cherish Relationships

Not one survey respondent mentioned learning about the importance of power, money, fame, or possessions from a lost loved one. Nearly all focused on the value and quality of relationships, and the impact of those relationships on themselves and others.

The key life and leadership lessons most often surfaced through our crowdsourcing efforts included the importance of showing up, being present, serving and supporting other people, setting a good example, treating everyone with dignity and respect, listening deeply, making and maintaining connections, and giving and receiving empathy and love. There was a strong sense that family and friends come first and that deep personal relationships are everything.

According to survey respondents, the old expression "he (or she) who dies with the most toys wins" does not apply. Instead, they were inclined to say, "He or she who dies with the most meaningful relationships wins!" This was the single most powerful category of the survey themes that emerged from our analysis.

Here is a sampling of what our survey respondents (and I) learned about *cherishing relationships* from their special somebodies:

- "The most profound impact you can have on others is to live a life in service of those you love."

    – Katie Lopez, CHRO, Panavision Inc. (from her grandmother)

- "Life and leadership are about caring and showing up when caring and leadership is needed."

  – Susan Gebelein, President, Savannah Consulting LLC (from her friend)

- "Everyone deserves respect, and leaders care about people on a personal level."

  – Ted Forbes, Ex-Chief Learning Officer and CHRO (from his grandfather)

- "Treat others with respect and truly experience all the joys life has to offer knowing we all have a finite time on this great Earth."

  – Michelle Jansen, Vice President, Global Human Resources (from her mother)

- "The community should take care of each other, minimize drama, and see the best in everyone."

  – Andrea Bortner, CHRO, Grocery Outlet (from her grandfather)

- "Give people your full attention. Deep listening and being present."

  – Cher Murphy, Advisor/Executive Coach (from her mentor)

- "While integrity is the price of entry for effective leadership, connection is the real ticket that takes you far."

  – Jennifer McEwen, Vice President, Talent and Organization Development, Leidos (from her parent)

- "To be successful, we must rely on others."

  – Roby Hunt, Chief Transformation Officer, Kern Medical (from his father)

- "Integrity, kindness, and treating others with respect are the things that matter most in life."

  – Jodi Starkman, Executive Director, Innovation Resource Center for Human Resources (from her father)

- "Our emotions are pointing us to needs met or not met. Emotions are like a compass and should be fully felt instead of stuffed away … We are here to love and be loved. Loving yourself is difficult."

  – Denise Liebetrau, CEO, Prosper Consulting (from her spouse)

- "Where you spend your time tells people what is important to you. If you want to connect with people so that they trust you, you have to meet them where they are—emotionally and if necessary, physically."

  – Chris Palmer, former Chief People Officer and Founder, Chris Palmer Leadership (from his boss)

- "How you live and how you love is what matters most. The job, title, house, car, etc. you have (will be) gone, but the impact you had on others endures."

  – Judy Zagorski, former CHRO (from her grandmother)

- "Take care of the horses first. Before calvary soldiers were allowed to pitch their tent or eat, they were required to remove the horse's saddle, inspect their shoes, brush them down, and feed them. Only then could they take care of their own personal needs. Take care of people in the organization first."

  – Paul Russell, retired CEO, Stellant Systems (from his father)

- "How to recover from failure. First by admitting the truth about yourself and others, then, with humility, speaking candidly and courageously to stakeholders. Finally, trying again in a better way, while embracing gratitude."

  – Elizabeth White Sawyer, Talent and Organization Development Consultant (from her father)

- "I've come to realize that death is not separate from life but an inherent part of it, a thread woven into the fabric of our human experience ... I walked beside (a colleague and friend) as she faced death, and in those moments, I saw her confront it with humor, grace, and extraordinary courage. Our friendship and the grief of losing her gave me an unexpected gift, a profound lesson that must be applied to leadership. It is not about authority or accomplishments but the deeper connections we form, the empathy we extend, and the presence we offer to others in their most vulnerable moments. I learned that compassion, care, and being fully present are the essence of friendship but are also essential to leadership."

  – Adrianne Court Petruska, CHRO, Tealium (from her colleague and friend)

Advocate for Yourself and Others

Be who you are, with authenticity. Stand up for yourself, your beliefs, your ideas, your ideals, and your values. Do the same for other people. Fight for what and who you believe in. Advocate, inspire, and be a role model. Put the oxygen mask on yourself first so that you can then take care of others around you. Angela Davis, academic scholar and activist, captured these sentiments when she said, "I am no longer accepting the things I cannot change. I am changing the things I cannot accept."[2]

Here is a sampling of what our survey respondents (and I) learned about *advocating for yourself and others* from their special somebodies:

- "Bring your best authentic self every day ... never take a day off from your values."

  – Scott Burns, Founder, The Leader's Legacy LLC (from his grandfather)

- "Always do the right thing. Your character and reputation are worth more than any amount of money."

  - Rebecca Bagin, Founder and President, R Bagin Partners (from her parents)

- "Life is too short to not be yourself, show your emotions, and live by your values."

  - Henk-Jan Wesselink, Chief People Officer (from his mentor)

- "Build others up. Strong leaders don't push others down to artificially build themselves up. Insecure people do that."

  - Jamie Jacobs, Co-founder, Gig Talent (from her father)

- "Be an advocate for yourself. Unless you negotiate for yourself, give important feedback, and ask for substantive feedback, you will have a harder climb."

  - Deborah Walsh, Vice President, Enterprise Talent (from her parents)

- "Making mistakes happens and it's okay. What you do after a mistake is what matters, not the mistake itself. You have to own it, correct it, and never repeat it."

  - Rebecca Blucher, Owner, Pure Barre Eastern Shore (from her mentor/friend)

- "Life will always have setbacks, but it is how you come out of those setbacks that makes you stronger for the next challenge life is going to throw at you."

  - Anonymous

- "Be a maverick and do not worry about what people think of you."

  - Megan Burke, Head of Strategy, HumanThriving.ai (from her father)

- "Fight for what you believe in."

  - Edie Goldberg, Founder and President, E.L. Goldberg and Associates (from her friend)

- "It is not the job of leaders to make their people's lives or tasks easier. But it is the job of leaders to journey alongside in the process."

  - Lane Cohee, Project/Program Management Consultant (from his father)

- "Find talented people who don't realize how good they actually are, and either push or pull them into larger and more challenging roles."

  - Scott Bontempo, Principal and Founder, Bontempo Advisory Services (from his boss)

- "Leadership is about knowing yourself so you can be yourself."

  - Marybeth Gallagher, President, Insightful Leadership (from her father)

- "Each day provides us with opportunities to continuously improve, do good deeds for others, and choose the better path. Live and lead each day by trying to be a better person."

  - Karren Fink, Principal, KAF Human Resources Consulting (from her father)

- "Your true legacy is how you influenced and inspired others, not your personal accomplishments."

  - Wayne Davis, President, CDJr Consulting (from his friend)

- "The Dr. Seuss quote, 'Be who you are and say what you feel, because those who mind don't matter and those who matter don't mind.'"

  - Terry Gray, Senior Principal, Accenture (from his grandmother)

Dream Big and Go Bigger

Believe that you can and should try anything, do anything, be anything, and achieve anything. Take risks, work hard, persevere, be resilient, and overcome obstacles. Fail, and learn from it. Be bold, fulfill your potential, and do what you love. Take charge of your own destiny, with a sense of purpose. Sportscaster Jim Nantz summed up this point of view when he said, "People say 'dream big' … but I would dream hard, meaning I just wanted it so badly, I could feel it."[3]

Here is a sampling of what our survey respondents (and I) learned about *dreaming big and going bigger* from their special somebodies:

- "Tomorrow is not a promise. Live every day with intent and purpose and prioritize what is really important. No regrets."

  - Anonymous

- "Persevere, be resilient, and do not back down from challenges."

  - Barbara Goretsky, retired HR Leader and Consultant (from her mother)

- "Don't sweat the small stuff. It's all small stuff."

  - Joan Hynes, Executive Director and Global HR Business Partner (from her father)

- "Live every day with passion and grace and do what you love."

  - Mary Olson-Menzel, CEO, MVP Executive Development (from her mother)

- "Be not afraid, take risks, step into the unknown with courage."
    - Brad Neary, Director, The Saint John's Bible Heritage Program (from his parents)
- "Believe in myself and assume I can do anything I want."
    - Alessandra Yockelson, CHRO, NetApp (from her father)
- "Care to make a difference and do not fear failure, rather, learn from it."
    - Rick Brady, Advisor, The Brady Advisory Group (from his father)
- "There is no greater burden than great potential."
    - Sarah Wendt, Chief People Officer, Asset Management Industry (from her mother)
- "If I didn't think you could do it, I would not have suggested it."
    - Heather Coleman-Otuyelu, Project/Program Manager, HLC Career Support Services (from her mentor)
- "Make the first move. Ask the question. Take the action. Be responsible for the outcome."
    - Amanda Sullivan, People Management Director, The Aerospace Corporation (from her grandfather)
- "You are in charge of your own destiny, so reach for the stars!"
    - LaTonya Groom, Founder, Talent IQ Partners (from her grandmother)
- "Everything is possible, I just need to figure out how … I look at life as only hindered by my own will and action."
    - Suzanne Levy, President/Executive Coach, Bolder Leadership, Inc. (from her mother)
- "Where there is a will there is a way. A can do, no excuses approach to life. Every problem has a solution."
    - Larry Senn, Founder, Senn Delaney, and Partner, Heidrick Consulting (from his father)
- "If you are unhappy, change it! Get clear on what you want out of life and go for it!"
    - Anonymous
- "You can do anything you want to do and be what you want to be. Just go after it, work hard, believe in yourself, and persevere. Never give up and set an example for others."
    - Vicki Cansler, retired CHRO, Piedmont Health Care (from her grandparents)

Seek Wisdom

From understanding lifelong impact to being curious and humble, to laughing and assuming positive intentions, the below list includes some of my favorite survey responses that did not fit with the previously discussed survey themes, but which were every bit as enlightening to me. Artist and inventor Leonardo da Vinci said it best, "While I thought I was learning how to live, I have been learning how to die."[4]

Here is a sampling of what our survey respondents (and I) learned about *seeking wisdom* from their special somebodies:

- "I learned the love of reading and the value of questioning."
  - John Sigmon, CEO, Sigmon Leadership Solutions (from his mother)
- "Humility and quiet charisma."
  - Karen Zupanic, Chief Executive, Heard-Craig Center for the Arts (from her father)
- "You only have so many arrows in your quiver, so use them wisely."
  - Virginia Means, Chief People Officer (from her mentor)
- "Be curious."
  - Sheila Alishouse, Founder and Chief, Client Services, Levata Human Performance (from her grandfather)
- "Don't judge. Everyone has a story."
  - Lauren Doliva, Partner Emeritus, Heidrick & Struggles (from her boss)
- "You are only as good as your team."
  - Michelle Jansen, Vice President, Global Human Resources (from her mother)
- "Grace, impact, and joy in the moment. Brief touch lasts a lifetime."
  - Liz Huldin, Chief People Officer, Great Day Improvements (from her father)
- "The most critical aspect of leadership is demonstrating unconditional positive regard. It costs nothing and reaps huge rewards."
  - Dr. Lois Frankel, President, Corporate Coaching International (from her boss)
- "If you make good people decisions, good mission decisions, and good business decisions, all the metrics and KPIs will take care of themselves. If they don't, they were stupid metrics."
  - Edward Swallow, Senior Vice President, COO, CFO, and Treasurer, The Aerospace Corporation (from his boss and mentor)

- "Never take yourself too seriously. Take time to laugh and enjoy the moment."

  – Betty Click, Board Member, Coca Cola Beverages NE and retired CHRO (from her boss and friend)

- "Assume positive intentions."

  – Orly Maravankin, President, Edge Consulting (from her mother)

- "The people around you must know that you are willing to do the same hard work you expect them to do."

  – Alexis Cogar, Manager, Talent Management, BAE Systems, Inc. (from her great grandmother)

- "You don't have to do some macro project or be a member of a huge organization to have a tremendous impact on people's lives."

  – Steve Milovich, President, Milovich Partners (from his cousin)

- "Never forget where you came from."

  – Lynnette Woodbury, CHRO, The Wilhite Law Firm (from her parent)

- "I have learned that parts of you that were influenced by (lost loved ones), stay with you long after they are gone … Over time, you have less pain and more gratitude for what they gave you."

  – Rebecca Feder, Principal Consultant, Princeton HR Insight (from her grandmother)

With the themes of *cherish relationships*, *advocate for yourself and others*, *dream big and go bigger*, and *seek wisdom* yielding an inspiring array of insights from survey respondents and their lost loved ones, we will now turn our attention to the central core of this book, Chapters 5–7, which features 35 essays written by our contributing authors. All have remarkable stories to tell in connection with lessons learned about life and leadership from their special somebodies.

Notes

1. Jamie Anderson, "Grief, I've learned, is really just love. It's all the love you want to give but cannot. All of that," *Goodreads*, accessed October 2024, https://www.goodreads.com/quotes/9657488-grief-i-ve-learned-is-really-just-love-it-s-all-the
2. Angela Davis, "I am no longer accepting the things I cannot change. I am changing the things I cannot accept," *Goodreads*, accessed November 2024, https://www.goodreads.com/quotes/7767240-i-am-no-longer-accepting-the-things-i-cannot-change
3. Jim Nantz, "People say 'dream big,' … but I would dream hard, meaning I just wanted it so badly, I could feel it," *BrainyQuote*, accessed December 2024, https://www.brainyquote.com/quotes/jim_nantz_410400
4. Leonardo da Vinci, "While I thought I was learning how to live, I have been learning how to die," *BrainyQuote*, accessed December 2024, https://www.brainyquote.com/quotes/leonardo_da_vinci_104789

Essays Introduction

The Power of Yet

"'The Power of Yet' is a concept popularized by the psychologist Carol Dweck in the context of a growth mindset. It refers to the idea that adding the word 'yet' to a sentence can transform a statement from a line of failure into one of potential. The addition of 'yet' implies that although you may not have achieved something right now, there is still room for growth and improvement in the future."[1]

Prepare for growth and improvement.

You are about to meet dozens of absolutely incredible people and one dog. (Yes, you read that right.) They were special somebodies, one and all, but you don't know them … yet!

We will also introduce you to the contributing authors who have honored these lost loved ones by telling their stories in powerful ways. They will tell you about real people who lived real lives and who made a real impact on those around them. Essays run the gamut from tragedy and triumph to pain and pride to insecurity and inspiration.

In addition to more traditional references such as Mom, Mum, Dad, Daddy, Grandpa, Grandma, and the like, these special somebodies were lovingly referred to by nicknames and terms of endearment such as A^2 ("A-squared"), Hawkeye, YLP (Your Loving Padre), Iye Mobi, Mechi, The Giant, Scouty, Pop, Baba, MaMa, and many others. They held jobs including lawyer, teacher, scientist, engineer, pharmacist, government official, accountant, politician, business owner, entrepreneur, salesperson, professor, hotelier, homemaker, office assistant, executive, CEO, nurse, military officer, project manager, and more. Their hobbies, skills, passions, and life histories were as diverse as fresh snowflakes—each one beautiful and unique but none lasting beyond its time.

The 6Ls

Chapters 5–7 can best be characterized by what I am calling the "6Ls": Life and Leadership Lessons Learned through Loss and Love. These essays are that simple, and that complicated.

DOI: 10.4324/9781003585633-8

Each essay teases out multiple layers of wisdom learned from and inspired by one or several special somebodies. However, every story emphasizes a leaning toward one most important lesson. These primary lessons are the basis for the way Chapters 5–7 are organized.

I will introduce you to each special somebody and contributing author according to three unifying themes:

- Chapter 5—Courage (and Resilience)
- Chapter 6—Compassion (and Relationships)
- Chapter 7—Curiosity (and Purpose)

While every essay highlights a primary theme as outlined above, they also teach us a varied menu of life and leadership lessons. We hope you find the structure of Chapters 5–7 a helpful framework for reading and digesting key lessons, but please feel free to read these essays in any order you prefer. The essays reinforce one another without being dependent on one another. Therefore, read them as you wish. Focus on some that interest you most. Skip others that interest you less. And come back to read others later.

These essay chapters are the soul of this book and the heart of your leadership journey, so we encourage you to take control and make the learning process your own. As Sir Richard Branson, Founder of Virgin Group, says, "You don't learn to walk by following rules. You learn to walk by doing, and by falling over."[2]

Notes

1. Carol S. Dweck, *Mindset: The New Psychology of Success* (New York: Random House, 2006).
2. Sir Richard Branson, *Business Stripped Bare: Adventures of a Global Entrepreneur* (New York: Virgin Books, 2010).

Chapter 5

Courage (and Resilience)

This chapter contains 12 essays that combine the powerful forces of courage and resilience. You will read stories that focus primarily on the determination and fearlessness needed to overcome adversity, hardships, and obstacles, as well as the strength required to challenge, push back, and bounce back from difficult circumstances.

Frontier Tough: Lessons in Love, Resilience, and Leadership from My Mother

by Shelley D. Dionne, Dean and Professor of Management, Binghamton University School of Management

My fervent wish would be that I were not in the position to write this essay—that I have not had to experience profound sadness over the loss of my mother, Mary Ellen Golan Wilson, six years ago from metastatic breast cancer.

Raised on a dairy farm in Binghamton, New York, my mother received her teaching degree from Marywood University in Scranton, Pennsylvania, and became a kindergarten teacher in the school district where her family farm was located. She married another teacher, my father Stanley Wilson, and then left teaching in the mid-1960s to raise their family, which included my four siblings and me.

Dedicated to all things "family first," she had a farm-girl work ethic that never left her, not even at the end of her life. She honored her own parents and siblings, was an amazing neighbor, and never had a jealous day in her life. She kept a secret and did not engage in gossip, and she was always the first person to help whenever anyone needed anything. She was quick to laugh and always smiled—which is an important characteristic for a mother of five children. And I remember being proud of her, even before I knew what being "proud" really meant, because she seemed to create this incredible, loving family effortlessly, providing a safe space for all of us to be our authentic selves.

DOI: 10.4324/9781003585633-9

Love Is a Learning Process

The most important gift my mother gave me was the understanding that love is a learning process, which is a bit strange because we were not an "I love you" kind of family. We weren't about words; we were about actions, and my vicarious learning began at a young age.

We often spent weekends on my grandparents' farm, where my mother would hop on a tractor and hay fields or help in the dairy barn or help her mother cook for the hired hands. She would never complain that her weekends were taken up by work. In fact, she seemed energized by spending time with her parents. We would play all day at the farm while she and my father worked. Looking back, I can't imagine how tired she must have been, but she would do anything for her parents or brother and sisters.

I remember once in the early 1970s when we drove to Rhode Island to help my aunt when she entertained her husband's extended family from Iran. My mother didn't want my aunt working so hard by herself, so we went to help. Other times, because my mother was keenly aware how overwhelming it was to have five children under the age of seven pour out of the family station wagon—even if we were all there to help—she would drive there herself: six hours one way in the morning and six hours back home at night after the last dishes were cleaned!

She put family first and loved being able to help. We might not have talked about what love means, but I saw it every day in her priorities. Through experiential learning and observation, I realized that love is bigger than self, and that putting other people ahead of you, especially family, builds a dependable and enduring love.

My first love was for my parents, followed by a different kind of love between siblings that was grounded in friendship and respect. Later, I experienced romantic love that didn't diminish anything I felt for my family but was unique to my husband and me. Eventually, I felt another kind of love—the love for my child, a love that my entire family shared with us, and which extended to the love we felt for their children.

Through it all, my mother was always there—still caring for me, my siblings, and our growing families. I believe the way she mothered and loved us evolved over time. If possible, I think she may have loved us more as adults because the feeling was mixed with a pride she probably didn't feel when we were throwing board games at each other after a heated game, arguing over toys, or dunking each other in the pool.

She never smothered us as we grew into adulthood, which always amazed me. She never discouraged us from moving away after college. She never suggested how we should parent, and she never asked for anything. I realize now that's because she already had what was most important to her: family who loved and supported each other.

I know it's uncommon to have all your siblings move back home after spreading their wings, and I remember everyone always asking my mother how she did it. She always said she was just lucky. But it wasn't luck. It was love, imperfect at times and continuously learned and relearned over the years, yet always strengthened by the tests of its foundation.

Peer Mentoring and Resilience

Somewhere along the way, my siblings and I learned that "family" is the foundation of all happiness, a loving bond that would keep us closely knit together over time. While it probably helped that we were all so close in age, my mother worked hard to make sure we valued the family. One tool she used quite effectively to teach us to be kind to each other was "peer mentoring" (long before it was ever a fad). This is how it worked: two Wilson kids started arguing, and then five Wilson kids stood in their respective corners of the living room as punishment—often for what seemed like days (but was probably just a few hours). I definitely learned early on that life wasn't always going to be fair, but my mother's take on peer mentoring helped make me resilient, which has served me well.

I specifically remember being constantly annoyed by my siblings, having no space in a small home that wasn't shared by at least another brother or sister, and having to eat really fast if I wanted seconds on any meal. But respect in our home was expected, and the message that the family came first above any individual was at times subtle and at times overt, but it built resilience.

My mother used to say, "Someday your brothers and sisters will be the most important people in your life, so the sooner you learn how to be kind to each other, the better your life will be." Her wisdom was a gift!

All five Wilson kids left home for college and then for graduate school. We started careers all over the U.S., but slowly we realized we were so much happier when we were together. Eventually, we all returned to Binghamton, New York, to build our lives and our families, enjoy fulfilling careers, and invest in each other.

We learned resilience again through the complexity of marriages and children and competing priorities. Then we experienced the biggest test of resilience to date: the sadness of losing our mother, and then this year, my father and brother.

My family has always centered me, and nearly half of them have now left me forever. My remaining siblings and I all grieve differently, which at times has been a hardship and caused conflict. But resilience is helping us out of this painful place and teaching us even more about each other.

Developmental Leadership

Resilience, kindness, work ethic, and understanding that love is a learning process were just some of the amazing characteristics my mother modeled for us throughout her life. More than anyone else, she believed in each of us, but there was never pressure for us to have any kind of life other than the one that would give us the most joy. She never said, "I think you should be a ..." Instead, she just listened, day after day, to all of our ideas and dreams.

She gave us the confidence to choose the best path for ourselves. She taught us to love ourselves. She was as proud of me and my choices as she was of my siblings' choices. She truly was the first person who taught me how to be a developmental and individually considerate leader. Each person is not treated the same but rather encouraged to take an individual path to success. Along the way, the leader is there to help, but not to decide or tell you which is the right path.

Frontier Tough

My mother was 60 years old when she had her first bout of breast cancer. She had avoided going to the doctor for years, always busy with everyone else. She had cancer in both breasts and the tumors were fairly advanced. She had ignored some breast cancer signs for quite a while.

On the day of her double mastectomy, just out of recovery and moved to her hospital room, she told me she was leaving. I didn't even know what she meant, but a few hours later, against the better judgment of just about everyone involved, I wheeled her out of the hospital and into my car. That was the day my father coined the phrase "your mother is frontier tough," which was probably still an understatement.

In the 20 years following this first bout of cancer, she broke her back jumping from high bleachers at a grandchild's baseball game, had uterine cancer and subsequent treatment, provided daycare for all 10 grandchildren, shoveled snow from all her neighbors' sidewalks and driveways during the winter, and provided whatever else her friends needed. Then life as we knew it changed forever. Two decades after her initial breast cancer detection and treatment, she developed an aggressive metastatic cancer. It took her life in a matter of months.

Never, not even a single time, did I hear her ask, "Why me?" or complain that she was ill. Never. She only cared about everyone else: her family, her neighbors, her friends. She faced adversity head-on, and she was literally the hardest working, toughest person I've ever met.

On the morning her doctor came to her hospital room to suggest we consider hospice, I was trying not to cry in front of her because she was always so strong for us. She knew I was struggling. He finished talking, asked if she understood, and she said "Yes." She then turned to me and said, "This muffin is delicious."

I see greeting cards that make fun of women becoming their mothers— as if it's a bad thing. I'd be honored to become my mother. I miss her every day.

> ### Three Things I Learned About Life and Leadership
>
> 1. Love of family is a gift that teaches resilience, teamwork, kindness, and sacrifice, as well as the gift of knowing, at a very young age, that life isn't always going to be fair.
> 2. Leadership means seeing people for their unique potential and then having the good sense to listen and nurture in such a way as to build confidence in followers, allowing them to own their successes and mistakes.
> 3. Facing adversity with courage and toughness helps everyone around you manage a crisis more effectively.

***

Work Hard, Play Hard

by Connor Muldoon Forte, MBA Student, Binghamton University School of Management, New Professional

Joseph Forte was born in Westchester, New York, on August 17, 1966. He grew up in Ossining and attended SUNY Oneonta. He was father to triplets: my brother Declan, my sister Kileen, and me; a lifetime partner to my stepmom, Dorothy; and stepdad to my stepsister, Shannon. He made sure to live every day to the fullest and loved many deeply.

Who My Dad Was

My dad used to take us hiking to a spot near our hometown called Bear Mountain when we were kids. He loved to travel and would take me and many others with him on his adventures. His favorite place in the world was the small town of Marmora in Ontario, Canada, where my great grandmother (and then my grandfather) had a cottage on Crowe Lake. My dad would tell us stories of spending entire summers there when he was young, either bringing his friends up there to drink or enjoying the lake with family. He loved being able to bring us up there with him once we were born—and the first time my stepmother remembers him being truly sad was when the cottage was sold. (My siblings and I still visit Crowe Lake every summer.)

My dad was the biggest history buff I knew. He could talk for hours about former presidents, and he made sure we all knew our facts about the different branches of government. A huge cinephile, one of his favorite hobbies was going to Redbox at 7-Eleven to find a new action movie for us to watch and make fun of—or rewatching *Lord of the Rings* for the sixth or seventh time.

When we weren't watching a movie, we were watching *Cops*, and Dad would sing loudly along to the theme song, "Bad boys, bad boys, whatcha gonna do, whatcha gonna do when they come for you?" I guess he wanted to be sure we kids got the message!

He was also obsessed with the New York Giants. Every Sunday during the NFL season, you could guarantee they'd be on the TV. When the Giants won the Super Bowl in 2008, he surprised my siblings and me by taking us out of school to go to the Giants Super Bowl parade.

My dad definitely wasn't setting any fashion trends. We would always tease him about his big white Oakley sunglasses with purple lenses, bright orange Hollister shorts, or red shiny Nikes. Of course, that only meant he would be sure to wear these items even more.

Each Sunday, he would make breakfast for us: waffles, bacon, eggs—all just the way we liked them. He would also take us for walks with the dogs, and if we were lucky, he would treat us to ice cream at Carvel. My stepmom would say, "Any excuse to get Carvel with his kids is a good one."

During his career, my dad worked in IT project management for many companies. His most recent title was Director, Infrastructure Architecture Programs at Atlas Air. Before that, he worked for IBM, PepsiCo, Stanley, Black & Decker, Westin Hotels, and others. To be entirely honest, I never fully understood exactly what he did for work while he was alive—I just knew it had something to do with computers.

Dad was "Mr. Talkative." My stepmom used to call him the "Mayor of Yorktown," our hometown, because he talked to everyone all the time. No one was off limits. If someone was nearby, then there was someone to talk to. He would make jokes with random strangers all the time and was always a positive, uplifting person whose company everyone enjoyed. He lived every day to the absolute fullest.

My Dad's Passing

My sister woke me up in my bed on the morning of March 27, 2020, to let me and my brother, who was in the room with me, know that Dad had died. It was the day before our nineteenth birthdays.

A few days earlier, we had been planning to go to Dad's house for dinner, but he told us not to since he wasn't feeling well and didn't want to get us sick. He was only 53 and wasn't experiencing any major health problems except for asthma, a condition he'd had since childhood. He passed from COVID-19— one of the earliest cases of the pandemic.

Obviously, Dad's death was a complete and immediate surprise to all of us. It was difficult to believe. Even to this day, more than four years later, his loss still hasn't fully sunk in for me (I don't think it's possible for any change of such significance to sink in right away). Hearing the news, I had absolutely no idea what to do or how to react. Already separated from everyone I knew due to the pandemic, I had now lost my dad for good.

At the onset of the pandemic, I was at college and had been pledging my fraternity the entire semester before being sent home by New York State. I had been calling Dad a few times a week, but I hadn't seen him for a while before he passed. While I was devastated, my siblings and I were lucky enough to have supportive family and friends for the tough times that followed.

Dad always gave us specific instructions on what to do when he passed. He did not want a funeral or a wake; he thought they were sad and depressing, and not how he wanted to be remembered. He specifically instructed us to have an event at a local venue or bar where everyone could have a good time and share stories and happy memories. We were lucky enough to do this in his honor a few years later, once the pandemic ended. He also told us to cremate his body and spread his ashes in Crowe Lake near the old family cottage, which we did.

His passing was extremely difficult for us. I've had to accept there are some things in life I can't control. I do the best I can each day to improve and be someone who would make him proud.

Lessons from My Dad

Dad taught us not to take life too seriously. My stepsister, Shannon, said it best: "Dad was never afraid to be himself, no matter where he was or who he was with—whether it was doing his famous gopher dance or picking me up from hanging with friends (which often included him reclined in the driver seat in his green Dodge Caravan), wearing white framed Oakley sunglasses with a sideways baseball hat, or waving the peace sign out the window yelling 'yo, yo, yo' and trying to be cool. He didn't care what anyone thought about him because he was the one having fun. It's one of many things I miss most about him."

Dad taught me to do my absolute best for the ones I love, all the time. Although we never lived with him full-time, we would see him every Tuesday night for dinner and then either Friday or Saturday night (whichever worked better for our schedules). When he lived in an apartment, he was never more than 10 minutes away from me and my siblings so he could be involved and available as much as possible. When he bought a house the year before he passed, he made sure it was just as close, even though he knew we'd be in college soon. Anytime there was ever an event through school, sports, or clubs, we could count on Dad to be there to support us. He loved going to all our games, especially baseball. He would put a spare jersey on our dog and make the dog be the team mascot.

My dad always had a great time, regardless of the location or situation. You might see him in Canada having a beer and cigar with his cousins, at the town tennis courts running with the dogs to get their energy out, or in the car singing "Clocks" by Coldplay extra loud since he knew we hated when he did that. He had a special energy to him which radiated positivity and left no room for moping around or being sad. The last thing he said to me before dropping me off at college my first year was, "Work hard, play hard."

Dad always motivated us to be the best possible version of ourselves. He would never make you feel judged if you underperformed or didn't get the result you wanted. He was the first person to brush your worries away and help you focus on improving. He constantly let us know he was proud of us. He would celebrate our accomplishments more than we would ourselves (even if this included posting an embarrassing picture of me on Facebook when I got my first lifeguard job).

Dad also taught me that the people we love aren't around forever. As difficult as it has been to come to terms with his passing, he helped teach me to appreciate my family and friends more than ever. He loved his family and friends so deeply and I hope to be able to make others feel even half as loved as he made us feel every single day.

Three Things I Learned About Life and Leadership

1. Don't take life too seriously.
2. Take care of the ones you love.
3. Work hard but have fun.

***

Resilience Without Regret

by Lori Heffelfinger, Executive Coach and Founder, President, and CEO of The Heffelfinger Company

I dedicate this essay to my mother and life mentor, Gladys Lorene Heffelfinger Close, of Sioux City, Iowa, U.S.A. She had a hard life until she hit her fifties, but she learned to enjoy life and made good choices regarding friends and family, which she nurtured.

Early Days

My mother was born in 1933 on a farm in Nebraska, the youngest of six in the heart of the Great Depression. In 1935, she lost her father, and her mother made ends meet for her six kids through welfare payments and working as a midwife. My mother lived in a small town and was frequently called upon to play piano at church and community events. She had a beautiful voice and was musically talented, but she let it go in later years, perhaps because it was such an obligation when she was a child. Her mother was strict and had high expectations; my mother later developed these traits.

My mother attended a two-year college to obtain a teaching certificate. Shortly after, she met my father at a YMCA dance. They were engaged within three months and married soon after. The happy marriage yielded two children, my brother and me. But their marriage was not long lasting. It ended when my father suffered a fatal heart attack. At the time, my mother was 33 years old and I was seven. My mother took my father's passing very hard but ultimately pulled herself together, went back to college, and accepted the support of her siblings. We started traveling across the country to meet family members.

Modeling Key Qualities

My mother was a model of strength and humility. She never gave up. She knew how to tap her resources, whether it was family, friends, the community, or her college education. Her married friends shunned her as a single mother, so she found a community of "parents without partners." In this way, she ultimately met more lifelong friends and my stepfather.

She went back to college while my brother and I were in grade school. I remember summers of intense study and closed bedroom doors while he and I were playing with friends, wondering what our mother was up to.

As a result of her additional education, she returned to work part-time and later full-time. Thus, we learned the importance of education and building a career to support ourselves financially, even though we had a small inheritance from my father. As a woman, I learned that I could not depend solely on a man and must take care of myself, because one day, I may have to. Whether intentional or not, this modeling instilled a strong sense of agency, career ambition, and a desire to fend for myself financially.

My mother also set great examples of the importance of friends, family, and a good marriage. When she spoke fondly about my father, I saw she knew what was important in a marriage and how to keep it healthy. When I was 12, she met and married a man who made some promises he could not keep. He never moved in with us, and my mother profoundly "let him go" after a year of trying to make it work.

Later, when I was 15, she met the man who became my stepfather. This marriage lasted until they both died in 2011. In him, she found the "perfect husband." She always said that my biological father was a workaholic, and she wanted something more. While my stepfather worked hard and made a good living, he also knew how to enjoy life. What I remember about my high school years are great family camping trips to the Rocky Mountains.

My mother was very strict with my brother and me. I suppose she felt she had to make up for the absence of a second parent. Much was expected of us. She modeled openness in communication, not letting issues fester, voicing your opinion, taking a stand for what is right, having a sense of humor, the importance of family, being resilient, earning your keep, having a strong work ethic, and a desire for continuous learning. I have a great career and husband because of the model she set.

I left home right after high school because she set the independence model. As a woman, she modeled the capability of strong women. As a young single woman/mother in the late 1960s and early 1970s, she took over contentious business partnerships that my father had left behind, raised two kids, went back to college—ultimately receiving a master's degree plus certifications—and worked part-time. She took us traveling so we wouldn't "miss out" by not having family around us.

Time for Enjoying Life

What I loved about my mother most is that she encouraged debate and discussion and never stopped loving us, even when we, perhaps, took the debate too far.

As strong as she was, my mother also knew how to have a good time. In her seventies, she went off-roading, biking, hiking, and was president of the American Association of University Women (AAUW). She had many long-time friends and was close to her siblings, nieces, and nephews. In fact, she was the favorite aunt amongst many.

My mother enjoyed life. She took vacations and had lifelong friends with whom she spent regular time, enjoying bridge club and potluck dinners. She was active in service organizations, Eastern Star (a Masonic organization open to both men and women), and the AAUW. No matter where we went, it seemed she always met someone she already knew.

My parents "retired" early; my stepfather got a package at age 62, and my mother took early retirement from her teaching job at age 57. They bought an RV and cruised for 20 years, meeting with friends at long-term stay campgrounds and visiting family. They also traveled the globe, visiting Alaska, Australia, New Zealand, and Europe. My mother started family reunions with her siblings and their kids. This was always part of their annual adventure. Around the holidays, they would visit Arizona, New Mexico, California, or wherever else we lived. We always saw them three to four times a year.

What a great role model—to retire early and travel with your partner to see friends and family. They were so happy!

All Good Things ...

Both died in 2011, which was far too early for such active human beings. Mom was 77, and my stepdad was 82. They had both been healthy until the last minute. My stepbrother died unexpectedly of pancreatic cancer in late 2009. This seemed to cause a downhill slide from which my stepfather never recovered. He died of chronic obstructive pulmonary disease (COPD)—yes, grief is held in the lungs—on March 3, 2011. My mother followed him in death on

June 27, 2011, succumbing to an untreated bowel obstruction. Her death was so unexpected that the State of South Dakota decided to look into her case, just to make sure something unusual hadn't been the cause. In all likelihood, had my stepfather still been alive, he would have taken her to the hospital, she would have had surgery, and she probably would have been fine.

Mom died alone, very close to a phone in her apartment. I had talked to her the Friday before, and she had told me she wasn't feeling well. She promised to see a doctor soon. She had sent my brother, stepsister, and me an email in May. When I read it to some friends to get their opinions, they felt I should head home immediately. After receiving the email, I called Mom from dinner, but she dismissed my concerns (perhaps, a little foreshadowing).

My brother-in-law was supposed to go over to her apartment on Saturday night before her passing, but it was storming so he did not venture out. She died the next day, and he found her. He called to tell me. My husband answered the phone and then handed it to me.

"Lori, your mother is gone," my brother-in-law said.

"Where has she gone?" I asked in all sincerity. I absolutely had no inkling that she would die so suddenly. My brother had a similar reaction. He was unable to accept the news.

I tried to process how it happened for up to a year afterward. Why had God taken her and my stepfather and left a bunch of other "assholes" behind? When people around me were happy or unhappy, it all seemed so trivial and overly dramatic, given what I had just gone through. I also found that many were uncomfortable talking to me about her death. They would change the subject, walk away if the topic came up, or say, "How old was she? She had a good life." It was a very, very lonely time. Her apartment of 14 years, with carpet the landlord wouldn't change, was rented out within two weeks.

After her passing, I did a ton of reading about death and grief. I attended two grief support groups for other adults who had lost their parents. I found solace in talking to my brother and my husband, who had lost his father the same year. To this day, people tell me they remember when my mother died and the effect it had on me. I guess I was fairly open about the experience. Yet life went on … business continued.

Prepared for the End

Looking back, my parents were well prepared for death. They had detailed wills, detailed lists of who got what, and had worked out a way of selling their assets through a bank so there would be no fighting amongst their children (as they both had experienced with the loss of their parents). Additionally, my parents had good relationships with all of their family and friends.

Any issues they may have had seemed to have all been worked through and resolved. Of course, there may have been issues unknown to us, but I honestly think they both were able to die peacefully and quickly because of their lack of unresolved issues and their relationship with God. My stepfather died immediately after a minister visited, and my mother died alone in her apartment, close to the phone. She had no meetings or appointments and no expected visitors. When we finally got to her apartment, everything we needed was laid out for us. She was either ready to die or move or both—there had been significant flooding from the Missouri River just before her death, and she was prepared to move as a result.

A Lifetime of Relationships

My mother had great relationships with her siblings and their kids. She was seen as a favorite among my cousins. She had close relationships with her sisters and sisters-in-law from her early days as a mother to the end of her life. She started a twice-yearly family reunion so my brother and I would continue to benefit. After my father died, the family provided a lot of support for her and us.

My mother had lifelong friends from teaching days to Eastern Star, from parents without partners to couples' friends. These friends all assembled at our weddings and her funeral. She was so loved, but she never left these friendships to chance.

My mother was understated, and she expected the same of my brother and me. She also had high expectations of us regarding education, work, family, and contribution to society. She both stated these expectations and modeled them for us.

Three Things I Learned About Life and Leadership

1. Never forget your family.
2. Nurture lifetime friends.
3. Be humble, work hard, and be of service.

✳✳✳

Walking with Wisdom: Life and Leadership Lessons from My Father

by Salima Hemani, PCC, SHRM-SCP, Founder and CEO, SZH Consulting

This essay is in honor of my dad, Zul Hemani, who passed away on February 17, 2020, after a long and hard-fought health battle.

Early Memories

One of my earliest memories of my dad, who I called "Daddy," is going on long walks with him through the dusty streets of Karachi, a port city in Pakistan by the Arabian Sea where I was born. I was seven or eight years old, and despite my aching legs and feet, which were starting to develop sores from the too-tight shoes I insisted on wearing, I remember being completely enthralled by Daddy's stories.

During our walks, he would share stories of his life, growing up first in Sanjan, India, and then spending his teenage years in Uganda, Africa. As we walked, the city buzzed around us with its vibrant smells of spices and sea breeze. We would pass by various bazaars, shanty towns, and neighborhoods where kids played cricket as we made our way to my grandmother's house on the other side of the city. As we walked, Daddy would weave in the history of the city and the country, his life lessons on ethics, our responsibilities as humans, books by his favorite authors—Somerset Maugham and Mark Twain—and everything that fascinated him about the broader world. From my end, I would offer a constant supply of questions and opinions about everything I heard. It was no surprise, then, that our five-to-six-mile walk would often end up taking almost half the day.

Loving Remembrance

Forty-some years have passed, and those times remain some of my favorite memories of Daddy because they beautifully encapsulate the journey of growth and guidance that he provided, shaping my understanding of life and leadership. Daddy was a man of profound depth, whose presence commanded both admiration and respect. His personality was a blend of unwavering resilience and deep kindness, making him a figure I looked up to and cherished deeply. He possessed immense strength of character, an unyielding sense of fairness, and a deeply rooted sense of responsibility and faith that guided his every action.

He profoundly believed that my sister and I, his two daughters, could do anything we wanted, and he pushed us to understand and think beyond the confines of the narrow part of the world we were born in. He instilled in us the courage to stand up to the traditional norms of an often narrow-minded society that surrounded us and not to be afraid of taking a less-traveled path in life.

Daddy was, however, not without his imperfections. His drive for excellence often led to moments of impatience with both himself and his family. His strong sense of right and wrong sometimes led to rigidity in actions and decisions.

He grew up poor and worked incredibly hard to be the first in his immediate family to get a graduate degree from the University of Minnesota, helping to elevate his family's economic status. This background left him uncomfortable with social pretenses and hierarchies.

Despite this, his innate gifts shone brightly. His passion for family, learning, and helping others were the anchors of his life, and they played an essential role in shaping my worldview. Daddy was my mentor, my compass, and my greatest supporter.

What made him special to me was not just what he did but who he was—a man whose integrity and love knew no bounds. I love him for the unwavering support he provided, for the values he instilled in me, and for the lessons he imparted, both intentionally and unintentionally.

The Power of Giving

In his professional life, my father was an accountant, a problem-solver who was brilliant with numbers and thrived on finding solutions to complex challenges. Beyond his career, he had a passion for community service, which was instilled in him from a very young age by my grandmother—who was a community leader—and my grandfather, who dedicated his life to teaching in underprivileged areas.

Daddy loved mentoring young professionals in our community. His volunteer work often revolved around providing guidance and even financial support for the educational aspirations of those in need, instilling in them the confidence to pursue their dreams. This dedication to others left an indelible mark on me; it taught me the power of giving back and the importance of leadership that is rooted in service.

Strength, Resolve, and Embracing Change

Daddy's approach to life was defined by his strength and resolve. He was no stranger to change, having lived across five countries and three continents. No matter the challenges he faced—growing up in humble circumstances, navigating life's ups and downs, adapting to a new country and culture in mid-career to give his daughters access to the best opportunities, and facing serious health issues—he approached them all with humor and determination that were both reassuring and inspiring.

His impact on me is profound. He taught me to approach life with courage and tenacity. He instilled in me the capacity to welcome change as an opportunity to broaden my horizons. Our relationship was enriched by countless Socratic conversations that taught me the power of critical thinking and reflection on the complexities of human nature, the importance of questioning assumptions, and the pursuit of truth in understanding myself and the world around me. Through his actions and words, he taught me respect for integrity, persistence, and hard work. I never saw him compromise on his ethics and principles, even when doing so would have led to an easier road and career advancements.

Daddy's influence extended beyond our immediate family to countless others who saw him as a mentor and role model of strength in the face of adversity. Whether through his words or deeds, my father taught me that leadership is less about being in charge and more about how you make others feel seen, supported, and capable. His lessons were not always explicitly stated but woven into his actions—showing me that to lead well is to live with integrity and empathy.

Watching him lead by example, I understood that effective leadership is about humility, resilience, and a deep sense of responsibility to those you serve.

The Last Act: Death with Dignity

Daddy passed away after a long, hard-fought health battle just before the coronavirus pandemic hit us full force in February 2020. His passing was not sudden. We were by his side through his tough battle that he valiantly fought.

Around mid-January 2020, Daddy was admitted to Fair Oaks Inova Hospital in Fairfax, Virginia, with severe symptoms of an infection. After many tests, doctors determined that the infection was due to his body's inability to respond to dialysis treatments. After almost 18 long years of enduring painful hemodialysis, which is almost unheard of, his organs could no longer tolerate the pressure. Doctors saw no value in extending his hemodialysis treatments, as they would continue to be ineffective and cause him more pain.

Daddy's last act of incredible courage before his death was accepting that his body had reached its physical limits and giving his consent for hospice care. He understood clearly that once the dialysis treatment stopped and hospice care began, he would not have much time before losing consciousness as the pain management medication took effect. He demonstrated resilience and strength even in his final days, telling childhood stories, inquiring about the lives of the many family members and friends who visited, bonding with the nurses, and even teasing my mom in a playful manner.

Through his actions, he showed that despair is never an option, no matter how hard life gets, and that the meaning of life and leadership is to be a beacon of hope for others.

My last words to Daddy before he started losing consciousness due to morphine were, "Thank you and bon voyage, Daddy. This is not a goodbye. Till we meet again. I love you."

Daddy's last words to me were, "You are strong. I know that you will go very far in life but never forget your faith and your responsibilities toward your family and your community. I love you."

The day of Daddy's death, I remember the numbness I felt as reality sank in, and the wave of sorrow that engulfed me as days turned into months. My father had been at the heart of our lives—a constant, unyielding presence even in sickness. His absence left a chasm that was difficult to fill. In those moments of sorrow, I found myself reflecting on what he must have experienced in those final moments—how he, a man who set an incredibly high bar for courage and strength, met death with dignity.

A Powerful Legacy

The way Daddy faced life, even until its end, taught me something invaluable about resilience. He had always spoken of accepting life's unpredictability and adapting to circumstances beyond our control. The way he lived his life prepared me to find strength amid loss. I learned that in life and in death, we must hold on to what is most essential: love, kindness, and the legacies we leave behind in the people we touch.

Daddy's lessons resonate with me still. From him, I learned to lead not just with intellect but with heart. I learned the importance of presence—of truly being there for those you love and lead. I have realized that leadership is also about leaving behind a legacy that others can carry forward.

The values he embodied, such as integrity, empathy, tenacity, faith, and fairness, guide my interactions today. His life taught me the power of perseverance, and his death reinforced the importance of living authentically and never giving up.

Three Things I Learned About Life and Leadership

1. Never compromise on your values—always live and lead with empathy, integrity, and authenticity.
2. Facing adversity with courage and humor is essential, and true strength is found in refusing to give up, even when things get hard.
3. True leadership is about making others feel valued and understood.

***

Be Fearless and Be You

by Susan Kelliher, Retired CHRO of The Chemours Company

My special somebody is Wally Luthy, former President and General Manager of Mobil Natural Gas. To tell this story, I need to provide some context for how Wally came into my life.

My first job out of graduate school was with Mobil Oil, specifically Mobil Exploration and Producing U.S., which managed all the company's oil and gas fields in the United States. In the early 1990s, it was a tough time in the oil and gas sector—one of those cycles where lots of people were losing their jobs, many in places where opportunities were slim.

I worked with a sophisticated and caring group of tenured leaders who had been through many downcycles and knew how to run the play. For me as a newly minted 25-year-old human resources professional, the pace was exhilarating, the amount of learning daunting, and the realization of the human impact of everything I was doing terrifying.

On the day of one particular restructuring and lay-off announcement, I felt so proud that we had executed a plan to ensure a fair selection process, communicated with courage and compassion, and committed to supporting people through the transition to what was next. I was still green in my profession, but I felt good about what we had done and had an extra level of confidence that comes from "not knowing what you don't know."

The Rules Apply to Everyone, Even Leaders

Soon, it was my time to move to an assignment as the new human resources partner for Wally, which put me on the palatial ninth floor for Mobil Natural Gas in Mobil's Greenspoint office in Houston. Wally had a storied reputation at Mobil. He grew up in the oil patch and had climbed the ladder for 30 years to become the President and General Manager of Mobil Natural Gas. He was kind of a big deal and an intimidating character. He was a chain smoker, avid golfer, and a non-nonsense tough talker. He swore when he was mad and had an utter disdain for weakness. He was a short and slender person but had a giant presence. When Wally spoke people listened, and they did what he said.

My first assignment on my first day was simple: let Wally know that the "no smoking policy" adopted the prior year did, in fact, apply to him. My boss, George Bourgeois, coached me in advance (and that's a leadership lesson all by itself). He let me practice and tested some likely objections.

Afterwards, I marched myself up to Wally's lair—a whole corner of the ninth floor. He was enjoying a cigarette, and I suspect he knew why I was there (maybe George tipped him off). I launched with, "So Wally, you know everyone stopped smoking in the office last year, and you know that everyone knows you are still in this office smoking. It's a bad look and I need you to stop."

Wally appeared annoyed. "I'm in here with my door shut. I have extra venting and air cleaners so there's no odor or smoke, and I CANNOT go outside and huddle under the eaves with everyone else. I've worked more than 30 years to be a senior executive and I've been smoking for longer than that. If I ask, I know Allen (as in Allen Murray, Mobil's CEO and occasionally Wally's golf partner) and Paul (Paul Hoenmans, Executive Vice President Exploration and Producing Worldwide and Wally's boss) will be fine with making an exception."

Ouch! He was pulling rank, which was not unexpected. So I tried to appeal to his sense of fairness and leading by example. We went back and forth for a while. He cursed and banged his desk a few times.

That's when I realized Wally was testing me. He was probing to see if I was tough enough or if I would slink back to the HR floor to get reinforcements. I wouldn't budge on "no smoking," but I could give him something—a little privacy and dignity. I knew there was an outdoor covered area on the opposite side of the building where no one went. I asked him to come downstairs with me and I showed him his new "private" outdoor smoking area. He relented and, bless his heart, he would take his smoke breaks down there even in the swamp that is Houston in the summer.

Passing the Test

Wally and I had many table-banging moments over the course of our partnership. I did not win every battle—plenty of times he was right and I was wrong. My epiphany that day was that Wally wanted to see me stand up, push back, and hold my ground. It was an important test of my mettle, and the experience taught me that I could and should never be afraid of a fight.

Finding Strength in Differences

Wally was a leader who took chances with talent. One time, as we were putting together talent development and succession plans, Wally identified a mid-level natural gas sales manager. Her name was Kim, and though she had strong results, she was seen as a bit of a lightweight as a people leader and a negotiator. Senior managers felt she was too soft: "She doesn't hold people accountable." They criticized her methodical focus on data: "She's slow to make decisions." And they viewed her as too much of an engineer to progress in the sales culture: "She isn't one of the gang."

Wally saw Kim's "weaknesses" differently. He liked that she was different from the typical people (men) who were often promoted into sales leadership. So, while Wally remained quietly in the background, he put Kim into a Director role over a large sales region, giving her room to grow and fail. Wally checked in on Kim, sent her private notes to acknowledge her successes, and invited her down to his private smoking area to give her critical feedback. He never overrode her direct manager or gave her special treatment in front of others. However, he provided essential wind under her wings so she could take flight.

As I think about how Wally treated me, I see that he behaved the same way. He liked that I was different from many of my other, more experienced HR colleagues. I think he enjoyed the fact that I was too young and brash to follow all the well-worn ways of working at Mobil. He saw me differently and he helped me succeed in ways that were uniquely me. It is no accident that when I left Mobil, he got me a silver platter inscribed, "Wacky and Wonderful."

Investing in Excellence

Wally believed in spending money to get the right people and create a great environment that would keep them performing at a high level. One of his favorite sayings was, "A spendthrift may never be rich, but a miser will never build a quality organization."

Although the industry was in the doldrums in the early 1990s, Wally insisted on giving outsized pay increases and special bonuses to recognize performance. He was ALWAYS overspending his compensation budget, which drove me nuts trying to make things balance! He made sure the Mobil Natural Gas offices were more than utilitarian and beautifully decorated, and that individual offices were inviting and spacious. Wally simply would not compromise on those things, and I know his CFO had many sleepless nights trying to make it all work.

The Rest of the Story

When I left Mobil in 1995, Wally flew me back to Houston and threw a huge party for me. Two things about that trip stand out: (1) I still have the napkin he made me sign with "Nothing said will offend" when the whiskey and cigars started flowing; and (2) he insisted I stay at his home with him and his wife, Jan (where, by the way, Jan made him smoke outside on the lanai).

A few years later, when I was living in San Diego and Wally had retired from Mobil, he had his former Mobil Executive Assistant call up and arrange for me to meet with him and his golf buddies. After dinner, they wanted a ride back to their hotel which was barely two blocks away. So, I loaded the four of them into a Nissan 300ZX. (I will never forget the sight of Wally scrunched up in the front seat on Al Byington's lap!)

When I got married in 1998, Wally and Jan sent me a huge Armetale platter. I use that platter every holiday.

After a few more years, I did not hear from Wally, so I looked him up and was sad to find his obituary from July 30, 2005. The obituary details his storied career from University of Pittsburgh Petroleum Engineer to the Board of Directors at Energen Corporation. In it, I found two sentences that sum up why Wally is my special somebody, "Throughout his career and life he was known for his strong character, integrity, and leadership. His fair and common-sense approach earned him respect and admiration from the many he cared for and mentored."

Indeed.

I am eternally grateful that I was one of those people "he cared for and mentored." The lessons Wally taught me and seeing him lead formed the foundation of the leader I have become.

Reading his obituary, I made myself promise to always—ALWAYS—celebrate and thank the people who shaped me before all that's left is their story in a newspaper and memories in our hearts. Thank you, Wally. I hope I make you proud.

Three Things I Learned About Life and Leadership

1. You don't have to win every battle, but you must get into the fight, have a position, and stand up fearlessly.
2. See and celebrate the uniqueness of individuals, and invest head, heart, and hands to allow them to do their best, be their best, and proudly and happily be who they are.
3. What you put into creating a great place to work gets returned a thousand-fold in the quality and performance of the enterprise.

***

Cherry Trees and Refugees

by Simon King, BSc Hons, Chief People Officer,
Daiichi Sankyo Inc.

"Hurry up, they are coming!" shouted several family members from the farm ahead. They were urging a four-year-old child and her mother to pick up their pace as they made their way through the sleepy village of Rossbach in Sudetenland.

Hearing the shouts, mother and child began to run toward the nearby farmhouse.

"The soldiers are coming. You need to hide. Quickly, come this way."

The neighbors hurried them to their old wooden barn where, breathing heavily, the girl and her mother climbed several steps to the loft.

"Hide yourself under the hay in the far corner … now!"

The girl and her mother crawled through the hay as instructed and lay absolutely still.

Knowing her daughter was always full of life and curious, the mother put her fingers to her mouth as a sign not to make a noise and held her close. "Stay absolutely still and calm," she whispered. "No matter what."

Trusting her mother, the girl lay completely motionless—even though she was terrified. They heard the sounds of heavy boots climbing the stairs to the loft. They heard voices and the sound of soldiers stabbing the haystack with bayonets.

Eventually the sounds receded and mother and daughter were left trembling in the darkness. After what must have seemed ages, they carefully crawled from under the hay to take a peek. Silence. Emptiness. The Russian soldiers had gone.

They felt relief; they had survived.

Happiness in the Face of Adversity

The year was 1944 and the young child was Gerlinde Hoefer, my mother. To me, my mother has always stood for love and kindness—a lifelong, conscious choice she made despite childhood experiences that would have defeated so many others.

My mother had a unique ability to make every person she encountered feel loved, as though they were the only ones who truly mattered. Her story is one of choosing kindness, displaying extreme courage, and helping others become greater than they ever thought they could be, including me.

Her story starts in Rossbach, which is now in the Czech Republic. There she was born, to Herbert Höfer and Erna Gemeinhardt. At the beginning of World War II, the family had moved to Posen in Poland to work on the railways to avoid her father being drafted into the German army. He was drafted anyway and sent to the Russian front.

Gerlinde and her mother moved back to Rossbach, where they lived in a typical farmhouse of that era. The living room was in the front of the house, the kitchen at the back, and the stables directly connected to the living area and a loft.

Mum loved that house and had such happy memories of it, despite the war. In the back garden there was a cherry tree in which her grandfather had hung a swing. My mother was a bit of a "tomboy" who was always looking for adventure. I am told that she would swing as high as she could to try to snatch cherries from the tree! In the winter, her grandfather would create a sledge run in the deep snow. It would start on the roof, wind through an open field, and end in the orchard. Mum used to tell me how much she loved sitting on the sledge, zooming down through the orchard, and then running back to the house to do it all over again.

A Childhood Shaped by War

My mum used to sleep on a bed in the front room of the farmhouse. One night, toward the end of the war, she heard a knock on the window. Terrified it was the police, she shrank back into bed trying to hide. But the police were not at the window. It was her father, looking hungry and disheveled. (Later, Mum learned that he had decided to leave the German Army and somehow made the thousand-plus mile journey back home.)

Her mother boiled water and filled the copper bath for her husband so he could get warm and have a good meal. The three of them spent the night together, talking and wishing the time would never end. However, before dawn her father left again. He gave himself up to an allied prisoner of war camp where he spent the next few years.

The end of the war was a very confusing time for my mother. One night, the family carried a heavy sewing machine through the forest and left it there. On another night, her mother, who was a talented seamstress, told my mum to get up, grab her clothes, wrap towels and tablecloths around her body, and walk through the dark forest to meet friends. She was doubly confused when they did not return to their warm and happy farmhouse that night but instead moved to a single room above a school in a new town.

There, she and her mother had no friends. People in the town called them "Flüchtlinge" (refugees). My mother later realized that this was the time when the German speaking citizens fled Sudetenland as it was taken over by the Russians and became the Czech Republic.

In her new life, my mum would go to school until about 2:00 p.m. while her mother worked as a seamstress for families in town. Mum would wait in the town square until her mother had finished and then walk home. There was never enough food, bread was non-existent, and they would live off potatoes. Her mother often went without food to make sure my mum had something to eat.

Despite such hardships, Mum told me stories of her family asking her to do made up errands such as go to the corner shop to "buy some elbow grease!" Of course, the shop owner was in on the ruse and there would be much laughter. Even with so little, they made the best of the situation. It was a family full of love.

At the age of nine, Gerlinde's darling sister Renate was born. Sadly, Erna passed away 10 days after "lying in" following the birth, during which time she developed a blood clot that killed her.

A New Beginning

The next nine years for Mum were very challenging. Her father had returned from the prisoner of war camp and re-married. My mum told me snippets of both the verbal and physical abuse she and her sister endured.

She was forced to leave school at the age of 12 to help earn a living for the family, working in a department store. After four long years, my mother had reached her limit and decided to leave.

On the day Mum went to the department store intent on not returning one way or another, her manager noticed she was not being herself. "Is everything okay?" she asked. Out of concern, the manager called the Head of Social Care, Herr Otto Reincke. Herr Reincke took immediate action and had my mum brought to his office. Herr Reincke told my mother she did not need to go home. Instead, she was to come to his house that afternoon following work.

Nervous and scared, Mum showed up at Herr Reincke's house, where he lived with his wife, Gerda. That evening they took my Mum in as their own daughter. The year was 1957, which Mum always recalled fondly as one of her best years ever.

Gerda and Otto took care of Mum their entire lives. Later in life, one of my mother's favorite activities of the week was her 6:00 p.m. calls on Sunday evenings with Gerda. Apparently, Gerda had the talent to really "hear" my mum and provide the most profound and wise advice.

100% There

Over time, my mother came to trust others and live her life again. She moved to Paris to be an au pair and then returned to Stuttgart. There, she decided she wanted to continue to learn, so she took English lessons at the same school where the man who would become my dad was teaching. There are many stories I can tell, but the short version is that they fell in love, and Mum moved to the UK and married my dad, Brian. After 25 years, Mum and Dad ended up going their separate ways, but their parting was amicable (they still always asked about each other).

Annette (my sister) and I were born shortly after my parents married, making our family complete.

What was remarkable about our childhood was that Mum was always there for us. She walked us to school, somehow made our household work on five pounds a week, made my sister and me walk two miles to the supermarket and then carried us and several heavy bags back (and still made us laugh), took us on vacations, and made every day seem magical. When we moved from London to Norfolk, she was there for us as we struggled to make new friends.

Even as Annette and I became adults, married, and had our own children, my mum did the same for our families. My son Sam is now 33 and a physician, and my daughter is 30 and has her dream job in sustainability in Colorado. If you ask them about some of their happiest childhood memories, without doubt they'll mention summers with my mother—their grandmother—and the adventures she would take them on. No matter the circumstance, she was always 100% there.

Lifelong Learning

As an adult, I realized that my mother was resilient. No matter the challenges she faced, my mum would rise to overcome them. She was a lifelong learner who excelled at whatever she chose to study.

She learned English, adapted to life in the UK, and learned lots of "DIYs" to continuously decorate and improve the homes we lived in. She proved herself to be deeply intellectual when she went to the University of East Anglia to do a Bachelor of Arts in German history in her forties.

Mum was an avid reader. She read German classics, including Goethe, and was a huge fan of Stefan Zweig and her former tutor, W.G. Sebald. She taught herself to spin woolen fleeces and was incredibly creative in her knitting. To earn a living, she set herself up as a freelance translator and did the most complex translations.

My mum was also a prolific correspondent. She kept all of her letters and wrote her thoughts and reflections with creativity and fluency that amazed me. Later, she mastered the technology of the iPhone and iPad and continued her fascinating correspondence in lengthy texts to my sister and me—always full of what was happening around her and hungry for our news and that of her grandchildren.

Mum combined her penchant for learning with the knack of meeting and making close friends to create a new business. She would spend time on the Isle of Muck, off the west coast of Scotland, teaching residents there to spin the wool of their many sheep. Mum would design and knit hats, socks, sweaters, and gloves, and send them exclusively to her friend Jenny's shop on the island. Jenny was married to Lawrence McEwan, who owned the island—quite literally, Lord and Lady Muck. Throughout her entire life, Mum could never knit enough because as soon as her new items reached the shop they sold out.

Mum was also an amazing cook who made the most delicious jam and cakes. She would feed everyone to bursting with delicious food, even mailing Victoria sponge cakes to her grandsons while they were at university to make sure they were eating enough! She always had treats for the family and even the postman was rewarded with chocolate or jars of jam. Her generosity and warmth were legendary.

Gerlinde Hoefer was the rock of my life. Sadly, she passed away at the age of 83. Her funeral was reflective of her life, with so many close friends sharing stories of what she had meant to them. Hers was a life well lived.

Three Things I Learned About Life and Leadership

1. Live your values—no matter the hardships you face, you can choose to stay true to your values.
2. Courage—you will be faced with many challenges, which may not be fair or just, but face them with courage and the unbendable spirit to overcome them.
3. Generosity of spirit—choose to understand and get to know your friends and colleagues deeply; be fully present with each person; and use every ounce of your energy and insight to help others be their best "selves."

***

Barb: Still with Us Today

by Lacey Leone McLaughlin, President, LLM Consulting Group, and Jamie Snyder Smith, SAHM, Program Manager and Consultant

Barbara Snyder was born in 1948 in Chicago, Illinois, to a first-generation American from Germany. She was known to her friends and family as "Barb." Barb received a Bachelor of Science in Nursing from St. Olaf University. Upon graduation, she was commissioned as an officer in the U.S. Navy, which was not common at the time for a woman. She advanced to the rank of Lieutenant Commander and earned a Master of Business Administration from Pepperdine University during her career.

My name is Jamie Smith. I'm Barbara's daughter. I'm a mother of three, a wife, and an MBA-educated professional. My mom not only had a dramatic impact on me, but also on my best friend, Lacey Leone McLaughlin, who co-wrote this essay with me.

My name is Lacey Leone McLaughlin. Jamie Smith is one of my dearest friends. I joke with her often that we are only friends because once Barb knew she was sick and would be passing on, she made me promise to be Jamie's friend. I would never want to disappoint Barb by not fulfilling that promise (or risk being haunted by her). Together, we will share why Barb was so amazing and how she impacted us as young adults, women, mothers, and working professionals.

Who Barb Was and What She Embodied

Barb was raised in a city surrounded by her extended family. Being surrounded by "real" family and "chosen" family made her realize its importance and what it meant to be there for others. Barb was a fiercely loyal friend, daughter, sister, mother, and leader. Once you were part of her life, it didn't matter if you were actually related; you were family. That's how she showed up for you and treated everyone. Barb was someone you could always depend on. She demonstrated selflessness by putting the happiness of others before her own, and she found such joy in making others happy. She was always strong, confident, and independent in her daily life.

Barb was more than my mother. She was the person I (Jamie) could lean on in any situation, guiding me to be the person I am today. She always seemed to have the answers when I did not and knew precisely how to handle every situation. She was the type of person who would face a situation head-on until a solution was found. No matter what I was going through, she was my True North and the calming presence in my life, which has been irreplaceable.

In her free time, Barb found relaxation in reading and learning from books. Sometimes, she would devour two or more per week. If she wasn't reading, she was watching baseball and football. She would cheer the Bears on no matter how bad (or good) they were doing. The only thing she loved more than sports and reading was travel. She was always about her next adventure and what new place she would get out and see.

In addition to her love of reading, she knew the importance of formal and informal education, so she invested her time earning her degrees and passing the significance on to the next generation.

After 20 years of service and several duty stations later, Barb's focus shifted to that of her family. She took a job in the local school district so she could be at every event and available for every non-school day. Her love and support for her kids was evident by the amount of time she devoted to them. For example, she would attend weekly games an hour away from their house when other parents did not. Her love of sports continued with her kids. You could always count on Barb to be in the stands cheering them on. If she wasn't cheering them on, she was always helping them be the best versions of themselves through their education and social development.

Barb's Impact During Her Life

Looking at her life through the eyes of her daughter and her daughter's best friend is cathartic, healing, sad, honest, and just another way Barb continues to bring people together. Each time we come together, we talk about Barb. Clearly, she continues to influence us in her own way.

Barb's life has affected us both in many ways, specifically through her confidence, loyalty, and the sheer horsepower she showed throughout her career and personal life. As two professional mothers with advanced degrees, like all women, we have both wondered why things seemed harder for us compared to our male counterparts and colleagues. You can't help but wonder how hard it must have been to be a commissioned officer in the 1970s and 1980s, but she was able to be tough, self-sufficient, and deliver.

Barb was committed to ensuring that future generations of women leaders had an easier path forward than she did. One of the reasons she valued higher education was that she believed it "got her in the room," and that once she was in the room, she could demonstrate the value she added. This continued expectation of self-development and growth was a key value she passed on to everyone she managed, as well as her daughter and her daughter's best friend. This extended to professional learning, college degrees, teaching Jamie how to be independent and manage a household, and giving Lacey lessons on baking. While she might have gotten some good laughs at a few areas of growth (Lacey's cooking and Jamie's DIY skills, for instance), her loyalty and commitment to others were genuine and impactful.

Lessons Learned During and After Death

When I (Lacey) met Barb, I had just recently met Jamie. Soon after, Barb was diagnosed with cancer and she realized her daughter needed a support network—a person who could fill some of the void left by her passing. It was a hectic time: Jamie had just gotten married, was about to have her first child, and now her mother was sick. So, in addition to fighting to get well, Barb planted seeds and made promises to ensure her daughter would be all right. Knowing how ill Barb was, I was still surprised by her passing because each time I saw her, she was powering through and focused on her family. She had a way of never really letting us know how much she was suffering. Her focus and concern for everyone else—even as she was dying—was a continuation of the way she lived: loyal, selfless, and determined to get it right.

Within a year of her diagnosis, Barb lost her battle—though she was not one to give up and she fought every day to stay with those she loved. She knew when the time was close and instead of thinking of herself, she thought of her family and friends, taking one last trip back to Chicago to say goodbye. She wanted to spare them the trip to her funeral and the painful memory of her frail, weakened state at the end of her life.

This action reinforced for me (Jamie) just how much my mother valued the time and feelings of others. She never wanted to be a burden; her intention was always to be a benefit to the lives of others. In that same spirit, at the time of her passing she requested there not be a funeral—which many of us found hurtful because it took away a chance for loved ones to gather and mourn her passing. Now I can appreciate how it was just another example of her trying to save others from experiencing more pain from her loss.

She's been gone for 13 years, and I still find myself longing for her knowledge and wisdom. At the time, she was the person I could talk to about anything, learn from, laugh with, and love more than anyone else. The impact she had on me and the tragedy of losing her early in my life has affected who I am today more than I will ever truly know.

As we reflect on the memories, stories, joys, and grief of Barb's life and her passing, it's clear that we "show up" for our families, kids, and work in a way that's intended to make her proud. When we are worn out because we're trying to do it all, her memory surfaces and reminds us that this is what it's all about: balancing the roles of mother, coach, friend, professional, boss, leader, and more. Though challenging, these are the "things" that drive our growth, forge meaningful friendships and connections, and create the challenges that inspire us to set and achieve our goals.

We recognize that these roles are tough, but they were tougher for her. She did it all before many women did. She paved the road by challenging us and proving that it was possible. She pushed us not to compromise our approaches to life, work, family, and death. Her legacy challenges us to make all aspects of being a wife, mother, and professional meaningful, to create memories, and to do it with vigor.

Three Things We Learned About Life and Leadership

1. Growth, goal setting, and trailblazing are the cornerstones of personal and professional success.
2. Regardless of your role, gender, and education, there is no substitute for loyalty and accountability.
3. Sheer will and horsepower DO matter. The ability to work your way through something without giving up, no matter how difficult, is the essence of resilience and determination.

***

Lessons in Leadership and Resilience: A Tribute to My Mother and Sister

by Cheryl Perkins, CEO and Founder, Innovationedge

Losing a loved one is an experience that reshapes our lives and perspectives in profound ways. It transforms the way we see the world, what we hold dear, and how we choose to spend our remaining days on this planet.

For me, the losses of my mother, Clare Louise Gump, and my sister, Caryn Therese Sudduth, to breast cancer have been particularly transformative.

My relationship with my mother was deeply meaningful. She was more than just a devoted mom who always went above and beyond for her children. She was also a cherished friend and guiding light whose unwavering faith and love left an indelible mark on me.

Of course, she also shaped my sister, Caryn, whose radiant smile and caring nature were a constant source of joy and support. Together, they created a nurturing environment filled with laughter and love, reinforcing the importance of strong relationships.

After losing both of these incredible women to the same awful disease, I've had time to reflect on the many ways they influenced me, both in my personal and my professional lives. Whether you've recently lost a loved one or are facing another challenge in your life that feels impossible to overcome, with this essay I hope to share some of the invaluable lessons my mother and sister taught me about leadership, resilience, and relationships.

Embracing the Non-Obvious: Lessons from Artistry to Innovation

My mother and sister were both remarkable women who had a lasting impact on everyone around them. They were loving, caring individuals who were deeply devoted to their faith and family. My mother, in particular, was a beacon of strength and inspiration. She was a devoted homemaker and talented painter who won numerous awards for her work.

As an artist, my mother had an exceptional ability to guide viewers to see the world through a different lens. Her paintings were not merely images but invitations to explore the hidden layers of reality. She had a gift for reframing the ordinary, encouraging others to find beauty and meaning in the overlooked. This talent was more than artistic expression. It was a way of thinking that extended into her role as an informal teacher and philosophical guide. Her discussions often challenged us to reconsider our assumptions and approach life with a fresh perspective.

I have many fond memories of my mother taking on the role of "teacher" at home to help me with my schoolwork. As with all things, she encouraged me to push the envelope and dig deep to find answers that other students easily overlooked. Caryn also embodied this curiosity for life, fostering a family environment that valued learning and exploration.

"Don't focus on the obvious," I can hear my mother say. "Focus on the non-obvious." Her encouragement to always take things a step further sparked my curiosity and has fueled my career.

In my role as a business leader and innovator, I find myself echoing her approach. Much like how my mother would shift perspectives through her art, I strive to push boundaries by asking out-of-the-box questions and seeking solutions that others might overlook. This process of reframing and creating new ways of understanding is central to my work with clients and when interviewing fellow business leaders. It's about putting things in perspective and uncovering insights that can lead to groundbreaking solutions.

The lessons I've learned from my mother's artistic and philosophical approach are now woven into my daily life, especially my mentoring and coaching efforts. Just as she guided others to see things differently, I aim to give back by helping others find new perspectives and solutions. This feels like a full-circle moment, honoring her legacy by embodying the principles she cherished most.

Her influence continues to shape my approach to leadership and innovation, ensuring that her legacy lives on through the ways I support and inspire others. Her love for family and her nurturing spirit motivate me to invest in my relationships and connect with others on a deeper level. And isn't that one of the most beautiful tributes we can pay to those who have passed—to live our lives aligned with the virtues and values they held dear?

Reflections on Death, Resilience, and What We Leave Behind

Throughout their lives, my mother and sister gave so much of themselves to others that it was often at the expense of their own well-being. They touched the lives of many, and their impact was frequently spoken of by those who had the privilege of knowing them. Their unwavering commitment to family and friends was a testament to their remarkable and resilient nature. Both my mother and sister were incredibly strong-willed and determined, pouring their entire hearts and souls into everything they did. Even as they battled cancer, they fought with unyielding resolve until their very last breaths.

My mother's death is a poignant reminder of the importance of cherishing the time we have with our loved ones. Her legacy extends beyond the art she created—it lives on in the lessons she imparted and her steadfast dedication to nurturing genuine relationships.

She lived by the golden rule: *treat others as you would like to be treated.* Through this principle, she emphasized that relationships should never be transactional but rather about authentic care and connection. Her resilience in facing her illness while continuing to focus on the well-being of those around her was a powerful example of this commitment.

During the five years my mother battled cancer, she remained focused on preparing us for life without her. She worked tirelessly to ensure we were all taken care of, both during her illness and beyond her passing. Similarly, my sister embodied these values with grace and determination. Even as Caryn faced her illness, she remained dedicated to maintaining strong relationships and ensuring her loved ones were supported.

Caryn's unwavering strength reminds me of the importance of resilience, even in the face of unimaginable circumstances. Her focus on others, despite her own challenges, reflects the strength and resilience she shared with my mother. Both of their lives are reminders of the importance of looking outside of ourselves to overcome the challenges we face.

In the face of adversity, our focus should be on moving forward with purpose and compassion, continuing to build and nurture meaningful connections. Sometimes the best medicine is finding ways to support and uplift those around us. By leveraging our experiences and the lessons learned from our loved ones, we can move on with a sense of determination. It's this resilience that helps us bounce back from hardships and reminds us we are always growing.

Living with Compassion: Making Every Moment Count

If there's one thing I learned from my mother, it's that being a leader is not about going it alone. Being a leader requires the courage to be vulnerable and to lean on a support system when needed. This can be incredibly challenging, but it is essential for personal and professional growth.

While my mother was used to putting others first, as she battled cancer she allowed herself to rely on the support system she had nurtured throughout her life, showing that strength also includes the ability to seek and accept help when we need it.

Managing multiple aspects of life, especially during challenging times, can be overwhelming, but this was an area in which my mother and sister both excelled. I've found that compartmentalizing—focusing on one area of your life at a time, whether it's work or personal matters—can help you maintain balance and productivity even in the worst situations, giving you space to address your immediate needs while preventing burnout. My mother's ability to compartmentalize her concerns and focus on what was most important at any given time was a testament to her remarkable organizational skills and emotional resilience.

Ask yourself, what do you need to get done in the next two days? The next hour? Focus on that thing, then move on to the next.

My mother's battle with cancer and her approach to it also taught me the importance of resilience. Despite the physical and emotional toll, she remained steadfast and focused on what she could control. She embraced challenges and used them as opportunities to create something positive. Her resilience left a mark on her loved ones—a reminder that whatever challenges we face in life, we can find strength in our relationships and learn to navigate through adversity together.

Resilience empowers us to view setbacks as setups for a comeback, helping us emerge stronger than we were. I encourage you to look beyond the obvious to find opportunities waiting to be uncovered, even in the hardest moments. They will fill your cup and propel you forward.

In moments of profound loss, it becomes especially clear that the time we have with our loved ones is precious and unpredictable. Cherishing those moments, remembering the laughter, the joy, and the love shared, can help us see things from a different perspective. Rather than dwelling on the pain of the past, let us leverage our experiences to create positive change.

I believe the lessons my mother and sister shared during their time with us offer valuable insights for anyone navigating the rocky road of leadership and personal growth. By building community, compartmentalizing challenges, and cultivating resilience, we can all find a way to face adversity, form deeper connections with those around us, and continue growing.

As you move forward, consider how you can apply the lessons below to your own life. Reflect on what you can do to honor the legacy of those who have influenced you and make the most of the time you have with your loved ones. By focusing on what truly matters and nurturing relationships with compassion and strength, we can all build a more meaningful and resilient path forward. Isn't that a beautiful way to commemorate those who go before us—to live in their likeness and treat others the way we would like to be treated?

Three Things I Learned About Life and Leadership

1. Rely on your community—it's okay to be vulnerable.
2. Compartmentalize and focus on the most essential tasks.
3. Build a framework of resilience by focusing on the good.

***

Lessons Learned from Loss: A Journey Through Compassion, Transformation, and the Practice of Letting Go

by Adrienne Shoch, Founder, 5 to 1 Consulting, LLC

The following reflections stem from the profound loss of my parents, Ann and Roger Shoch, in 2024 and 2022, respectively. Both journeys ended in hospice care—my mother's spanning three weeks, while my father's was a brief but intense 24 hours following a 10-day hospital stay. Their final weeks provided me with life-changing insights into humanity and the nature of suffering, compassion, resilience, and renewal.

These lessons, however, are not confined to the recent past. They are the culmination of an eight-year chapter in my life marked by relentless waves of loss and transformation. From the upheaval of a divorce after 25 years of marriage, the challenges of empty-nesting, and a significant job loss, to caring for parents as they battled cancer and Alzheimer's, experiencing the devastation of Hurricane Helene, and navigating the complexities of running a business amidst chaos—each experience has deepened my understanding of human connection, leadership, and the capacity to endure and let go.

Life, it seems, has been preparing me for an extraordinary journey through the realities of human suffering, change, and renewal. While these events were personal, they reflect the broader human experience: we all face loss, we all encounter uncertainty, and we all must navigate the space between endings and new beginnings.

In the face of such profound loss, there were moments of doubt, devastation, and fear. But these were always accompanied by unexpected miracles, compassion, durability, and freedom. These events, though heartbreaking, have shaped me, deepened my understanding of leadership, and transformed my approach to change management. Through the lens of grief and transformation, I have discovered that loss, while a constant, is not only inevitable—it can be a powerful catalyst for renewal and profound human connection.

Loss as a Practice: Awareness and Participation

Loss is often viewed through the lens of something that happens to us—a crisis, a sudden event we have no control over. However, over the years, I've come to see loss as a practice of presence and a process that invites us to participate fully. It's easy to think that we can simply endure loss, checking it off as something we've survived. But sustainable transformation, I have learned, doesn't emerge without intentional, active participation.

In our fast-paced, results-oriented world, we are often taught to avoid pain and suffering. We seek quick fixes, outcomes, and "closure." We want to move on, to finish, to check off the box. But in my experience, loss is never a one-and-done event. It is a process that requires us to show up fully present and wholly engaged. When we rush through the process, we miss the learning, the evolution, and the connection that can transform us. We miss the opportunity to really see what's beyond our knowing.

In the final days of my mom's hospice stay, I witnessed something extraordinary. The week before she passed, she began to experience random apnea, a form of irregular breathing. It wasn't until the day of her death that I realized what I thought had been happening all along: she was practicing. Her body was preparing for the final transition, not in some dramatic, theatrical fashion, but in a gradual, organic way. Similarly, life requires us to practice—whether it's preparing for the unknown, leaning into pain, or responding with compassion. Without this practice, life becomes more difficult, and transitions become more burdensome.

Loss is a process that requires participation. Without full participation, we remain detached from the wisdom and growth that can emerge from the experience. The invitation to us is clear: lean in. The more we lean into the pain and uncertainty, the more we discover about ourselves and others—the deeper our capacity for empathy, and the richer our leadership becomes.

The Practice of Compassion: Responding to the Pain of Others

Some of the greatest lessons I've learned through loss involve the profound power of compassion. When my parents passed away, I was forced to confront the raw, vulnerable nature of human suffering. Watching my mom in her final days, surviving without food or water for more than 12 days, was a humbling experience. Despite the immense pain, she remained present and connected to her journey. The human spirit, in its most vulnerable state, exhibited a strength that defied reason.

In the final hours of my dad's passing, I received an extraordinary act of compassion when the hospice nurse asked me, "What is it that you would like from this experience with your dad?" In that moment, I became aware of my deep connection to humanity and the magnitude of the journey I was sharing with my dad. Despite the disorienting reality, in my deepest level of despair, I was seen by someone else. I was not alone. It was a defining moment.

Compassion, when we lean into the suffering of others, can transcend the physical and emotional dimensions of life. The act of showing up for someone in their most vulnerable state requires us to sideline our own fears—fear of death, fear of pain, fear of loss—and be fully present. It is in this space of deep presence that healing can begin, not only for the person suffering but for those of us accompanying them through their journey.

In the field of change management, we are often required to help others navigate pain, uncertainty, and loss. But how can we support and lead others through these difficult transitions if we haven't learned to lean into pain ourselves? When we sidestep discomfort and avoid suffering, we miss the opportunity to truly connect, learn, and evolve.

Throughout my career, I've observed that the most effective leaders are those who have a high capacity for empathy and compassion. They don't shy away from the difficult moments; they face them head-on, supporting others with authenticity, grace, and presence. In doing so, they create an environment where growth and healing can occur, not only for individuals but for families and organizations as well. When we embrace the suffering of others, we create space for them to heal—and that, in turn, heals us.

Resilience vs. Durability: Navigating the Storm

The final week spent in hospice with my mom brought an emotional and physical toll on me that was immense. The weight of grief was compounded by external pressures—strained family dynamics, damaged relationships, and damage to my home sustained from Hurricane Helene. In the midst of this storm, both literal and figurative, I was forced to find a way to hold myself together, not just for my family, but also for my own mental and emotional well-being.

In these moments of intense pressure, the difference between resilience and durability became clear to me. Resilience is often understood as the ability to bounce back from adversity or recover from hardship. But in this situation, it was not just the act of bouncing back that mattered—it was the ability to endure, to persist, to stand firm in the face of relentless strain and uncertainty. This durability is what allowed me to get through each day's storm of emotions, physical exhaustion, and unrelenting stress; durability is what allowed me to lean in and be of support to others.

That being said, the true foundation of resilience is durability. Whether we are guiding a team through a major organizational change or supporting a colleague through personal hardship, our ability to remain durable, steady, and grounded is essential. Durability—the capacity to withstand and navigate the inevitable storms of life with conviction, clarity, and focus—is the bedrock from which resilience can emerge.

The Role of the Appropriate Response: Mastering the Art of Compassionate Leadership

The essence of compassionate leadership lies in our ability to recognize and choose the appropriate response. It's not about being right or fixing everything; it's about being fully present and offering what the moment requires.

Life, particularly during times of grief and loss, presents us with countless opportunities to choose our responses. I've learned that the quality of our response in difficult situations is what determines the outcome, not the situation itself. This truth became a constant reminder throughout my journey, as I navigated the complexities of FEMA processes, hospice care, family dynamics, burial arrangements for both parents, and my own emotional turmoil.

Amid exhaustion, stress, and confusion, I discovered that the most powerful response was a simple, gracious phrase: "Yes, thank you. That would be lovely." Words I previously struggled with and rarely used became my lifeline, opening doors to unexpected support and grace.

The hospice staff who cared for my parents were masters of the appropriate response. They weren't fixers, but facilitators, creating an environment where the transition could happen with ease, grace, and dignity.

Similarly, in leadership, we are often tasked with facilitating change while guiding and leading others through difficult transitions. Our response to the chaos, the uncertainty, and the pain of others can either exacerbate the situation or create space for healing. The appropriate response is a practice and a skill, one that requires deep awareness, empathy, and courage to be present. It's the glue that holds moving parts together during times of loss and transformation.

Final Reflections: Embracing the Unknown and Letting Go

In the end, my experience with loss was not about fixing things or achieving outcomes; it was about embracing the unknown, letting go of control, and responding to fear with compassion.

Life is full of unexpected transitions, and it is through the practice of embracing these transitions that we cultivate the strength, durability, and compassion needed to build resilience so we can transition into what's next—all while supporting and leading others through the process.

Whether in our personal lives or professional roles, we are all navigating loss and change. But when we lean into the process, show up with grace, and respond with presence, we open ourselves up to the extraordinary transformation that lies on the other side of suffering. The result is not just about reaching the finish line; it's about being fully present in the journey. And in that journey, we discover the power of love, peace, and ease—the true markers of leadership in times of loss.

In the words of the ancient Zen master Yunmen, when asked what the teaching of a lifetime is, he replied simply, "An appropriate response."[1] The invitation, then, is clear: lean in, participate fully, and respond appropriately with compassion. Only then can we truly learn from the experience of loss and emerge stronger, more connected, and more capable of supporting others through the inevitable transitions of life.

Three Things I Learned About Life and Leadership

1. The "appropriate response" requires our full presence and offers what the moment requires.
2. True resilience is built on durability—the ability to endure and persist through relentless strain and uncertainty.
3. Leaning into the pain, suffering, and uncertainty of others enriches our ability to lead with authenticity, empathy, and compassion.

✳✳✳

Pop: He Lived and Died on His Own Terms

by Scott Span, MSOD, CSM, ACC, Leadership Coach, Transformation Specialist, and CEO of Tolero Solutions

Norman Rothstein. My grandfather. He was affectionately known to his family as "Pop" or "Big Poppy," except to his wife, Nan, who just called him "Norm," her sweetheart.

Pop was a role model for me, his youngest grandchild. I often think that if it was not for the relationship I had with Pop my life would have turned out quite differently. I may never have graduated college or purchased my first home. I certainly never would have become an entrepreneur. And I probably would not have learned strategies to handle the adversity life has tossed my way or developed some of the values that are so important to me.

Once, Pop shared with me that, of all his grandchildren, he was the proudest of me for becoming a success because I battled the most adversity and kept on going. After he delivered those heartfelt words, he handed me a small piece of paper that he kept on his fridge. The quote on it read as follows:

> In battle or business, whatever the game, in law or in love, it is ever the same; In the struggle for power, or the scramble for Pelf, let this be your motto—Rely on yourself! For, whether the prize be a ribbon or throne, the victor is he who can go it alone!
>
> (John Godfrey Saxe)[2]

For Pop, this quote was less about having to do everything on your own and more about preparation, strong will, and the determination to tackle anything life may toss at us. All those are traits I got from Pop.

He Was a Fighter

When Pop was diagnosed with bladder cancer, he beat it. When he was diagnosed with prostate cancer, he beat that too. When he almost had a heart attack and needed a stent put in, he made the changes to his lifestyle suggested by his doctors and kept on going strong. And that was all just in the later years!

One thing he didn't give up, though, was his daily cocktail hour with Nan. Pop was fond of saying, "Suck up, you're behind!" (This actually became a family motto we still laugh about today when making toasts at family events, or for me when I toast Pop after a Philadelphia Eagles win.)

Pop worked until age 89. He sold candy in the 1930s, built ships during World War II, sold vending machines, and owned a pizza shop and a couple of bars. His last job was as a financial advisor. Pop liked to stay busy. He was as determined in life as he was in business, which is another trait I am grateful he passed on to me.

He also passed on to me many leadership lessons about preparation, determination, transparency, accountability, communication, the importance of building quality relationships, presence and charisma, strategic thinking, problem solving, and more. The list is not short. All are important lessons, traits, behaviors, and characteristics that I practice and continue to develop daily. Each helps me to be successful in my business and in life.

On His Own Terms

Pop loved his sports. As I got older, we used to chat after every Philadelphia Eagles game. He said he refused to die until he saw his Philadelphia Eagles win a Superbowl. At 100 years old, while screaming at the TV surrounded by his family, he finally saw that happen. He was a force to be reckoned with. Pop hung on to the age of 102, still sharp as a tack, before his body just gave out due to old age in early 2019.

His last few weeks he was in hospice care. I was lucky enough to have a client 15 minutes away which provided me the opportunity to visit Pop frequently. It was tough to see such a strong and steady figure in my life become so weak and frustrated in his final days. But I never let him know I noticed. I just sat with him, cracked some jokes, and got some smiles.

Before leaving, I'd always give him a kiss on the head and say, "Don't worry Pop. It'll be okay. We'll take care of Nan." Then I'd put his wool Philadelphia Eagles hat on his head, which he always wore to bed to keep his bald head warm because Nan liked to sleep with a window cracked.

Pop and Nan were married for almost 80 years. When he knew the end was very near, he insisted he be moved home to die in the company of his "honey" and his companion since age 17. After some family drama, his wishes were honored and he was transported home.

That's the thing about Pop, he was quiet but firm, even until the end. When he spoke, the family listened.

He died at home two days later holding the hand of his "honey." Pop died the way he lived, on his own terms—a trait I will always respect about him and one I've proudly inherited.

A Legacy of Values and Lessons

Pop passed on values and lessons that helped shape my way of being and informed how I handle certain situations in leadership—professionally—and in my personal life. He was very much a "You live your life and do no harm; I will live mine" kind of guy. He didn't always have to agree with a person or a situation, and he didn't push his own views and perspectives. It's a value I also hold.

I recall being afraid to come out to Pop in my late twenties because I didn't want it to change how he viewed me or change our relationship. I had a plan to tell him at a Father's Day barbecue at my parents' house. But my dad, in his ever-caring way and thinking he was doing me a favor, beat me to it. He told Pop after I went into the house to get something. When I walked back outside, I remember being nervous.

Pop looked up at me and smiled. He said, "We all knew anyway. We love you and wish the best for you. As long as you're happy that's what matters." Then he joked, "But choose your partner wisely or they may nag you the rest of your life!" Nan shot him some side-eye, and we all laughed.

Understanding, acceptance, empathy, and a dash of tough love and humor—that was Pop.

Pop even insisted that he be part of my wedding and graciously supported the union. It's a memory I cherish. I got to watch my 93-year-old grandparents walk down the aisle at my wedding, participate in the ceremony, and dance at the reception. Pop was always up for a good party. Especially when it involved celebrating family.

Preparation was another lesson Pop taught me. Pop was always very deliberate and measured. He never acted in haste or without having all the information available to him to inform his decisions and actions.

He was also determined. Pop was no quitter. I can't recall one time when he didn't try to conquer a situation head on. When he was given bad news, he would ask what he needed to do to try and get through it, and then he'd do what was needed.

As for transparency, Pop was big on sharing what was on his mind in a direct yet non-confrontational or upsetting way. He may have taken some time to think about what he wanted to say, but then he said it.

Accountability was also important to Pop. Sometimes he would even take accountability for things not in his control.

Pop was also a great problem solver. He would think of multiple solutions and ways to handle things, sometimes while tossing and turning in bed, and often in creative ways. Then he would weigh the options and act.

Quality Over Quantity

Pop valued his relationships with friends and family. He wasn't one for shallow or superficial. He didn't have lots of acquaintances. He valued quality over quantity. He had a close group of lifelong friends, and he outlived them all.

When it came to family, Pop always had a "family first" mentality. He also taught me the importance of authenticity.

Authenticity is such a strong core value of mine that in my work as a leadership coach, I strive to help others define what it means to them and explore how they can access their own authenticity and live an authentic life.

Pop also taught me some lessons I choose not to emulate but sometimes find myself guilty of doing anyway. For instance, he would often quietly stew and let his mind spin over things, often overthinking to the point of frustration. He also had an old-school, generational mentality when it came to gender roles. He wouldn't let my mom and her sister take care of anything related to business, despite my mom having life experiences and a graduate degree.

Pop also had a somewhat "hierarchal" mentality. As the oldest male grandson, my cousin who was 15 years older than me, was designated to handle business and legal matters. Despite the fact that I ran my own business, dealt with legal matters frequently, and had many business-related discussions with Pop in my adult life, I was not allowed to take the lead on certain family matters.

Pop was also the peacekeeper to an extent. He would squash family issues before they were really resolved. He kept family secrets hidden, many of which I only learned about after he died.

Precious Time

I miss Pop. I will always cherish the time we had together.

His death hit me hard. I handled the situation the way he would have. I stayed strong, supporting my mom and Nan. I compartmentalized my feelings until all was settled. Then I cried it out, laughed it out, took some time to reflect and grieve, and went right back to living my life.

I like to think that's just what he would've wanted. As the youngest grandchild, I do feel I lost out on precious time with him. He was the patriarch, the glue, the boss.

Certain family relationships changed dramatically after he died. Many other things haven't been the same either. Football certainly hasn't been the same. And I miss our deep conversations, our laughs, and his no BS advice and insights. I still often stop and think in certain situations, "What would Pop do or say?"

Three Things I Learned About Life and Leadership

1. Never give up—Pop's determination in life, his ability to face challenges head on, tackle adversity, and keep on going, is something I'm glad I learned from him. It's a core part of how I try and live my life.
2. Suck up, you're behind—one of Pop's mantras, which has become a family mantra to live life to the fullest (and a great toast).
3. You do you and I'll do me—always strive for understanding even when common ground can be tough to find or differences are plenty. Do no harm and live and let live.

***

Reality Stinks So We Might as Well Laugh

by Jill Wrobel, Executive Vice President, Chief Human Resources Officer, Brunswick Corporation (and my dad's "ylnod")

His name was Julius Keresztes, but to me he was always "Dad," though I occasionally called him "padre," which started sometime in grade school after a basic Spanish lesson. Later when I was in college, he elected to sign off emails to me as "ylp," short for "Your Loving Padre." The brevity was both sweet and a necessity given his poor finger dexterity derived from a neurological autoimmune condition called Multiple Sclerosis (MS). In return, I started signing my name as "ylnod," which was for "Your Loving Number One Daughter." This stuck as a term of endearment in every email he sent me until he died.

Insights into My Dad

My dad was incredibly smart, and when he physically felt well, he was also wickedly funny. He loved storytelling, landing jokes, his career as a director of pharmacy at a local hospital, and he loved being a dad to my sister and me. He also had diverse hobbies that included prime-time TV watching, swimming, technology, listening to investing strategies on talk radio, home improvement projects, and occasional kitchen experiments like homemade popcorn and meticulously researching bread machines to concoct the perfect dense breakfast treat.

He grew up in South Bend, Indiana, the youngest child and only son in a proud Hungarian family. He was diagnosed with MS at a very young age, receiving the tough news at age 17.

After my dad's death, I gained a new awareness of how deeply he revered his parents. Home videos from the early '90s show him setting up the perfect scene to record my grandfather singing the Hungarian National Anthem. This was also a convenient excuse to test out my dad's latest tech toy, a handheld recorder. My grandfather was a bit reluctant at first, but with Dad's lighthearted convincing he swiftly moved to a booming rendition of the anthem, his eyes bright with pride for his birthplace and love for his son. They both laughed and clapped at the end, recognizing joy in the simple moment. I've watched that clip hundreds of times and tear up every time I see it. I love that it illustrated my dad's essence: a son who cherished his parents, simple moments, and a fun memory enabled through a personal desire to try something new. Their frequent but simple interactions imparted valuable lessons, emphasizing the importance of consistent and intentional time together … and laughter.

A Most Unique Opportunity

My dad and I grew closer during my high school years, bonding over chats served alongside home-brewed Folgers coffee and day-old chocolate cake donuts. Our conversations spanned current events, school updates, and basic finance, with him always valuing my thoughts and encouraging my opinions.

This early practice in forming viewpoints from the direct question "What do you think?" became an invaluable life skill. He cared about my opinions and, even more importantly, my thoughts about how I arrived at the conclusion. I always felt seen, valued, and loved.

Other than coffee chats, our time together often included a request to borrow my hands to help with tasks he couldn't complete alone. Shouts from another room would usually begin with, "Jill, I need you for a minute." Invariably, this would lead to me learning something new, and often not in line with traditional gender roles. Tasks included learning how to change oil in a car, rototill the soil in our family garden, re-route home electrical wires, install wood floors, and fix computer motherboards.

His instruction was always slow and deliberate, allowing him time to verbally coach me and my novice hands since he couldn't show me through example. I'm aware that if his hands had worked easily, I may have lost the opportunity to learn a breadth of skills that were quite unique for a young girl to acquire.

Looking back, how lucky was I that his disease became a teacher to us both? Throughout his life, we silently acknowledged his limitations, we enjoyed our time together, and in the meantime, he helped me build capability and confidence to feel like I could "do it all."

Adjustments

Though a great dad, he struggled as a husband, leading to my parents' amicable divorce in my early twenties. My father, already a retired pharmacist since age 47 due to his worsening condition, moved to a two-bedroom apartment at the young age of 50.

MS is a cruel and relentless disease, slowly eroding physical health in microscopic nibbles until they become big bites of daily living. Each day of completing ordinary tasks was a marathon that required energy, patience, and grace—especially when he did everything on his own. Despite his challenges, he found pride in living independently, mastering grocery shopping, doing the laundry, and car tinkering.

However, the divorce and his declining health foreshadowed a time when he would need more help, a responsibility to coordinate his care that I knew would primarily fall to me.

My dad's decline started with minor changes to our father-daughter routines, such as swapping lunch outings for takeout. By age 57, he required full-time care. He still had energy spurts that allowed him to leave the home, but they were far more limited.

Acceptance

Despite the challenges, Dad faced everything with acceptance and a resolve to live on his own terms. He continued to watch TV, tinker on his computer, and delight in simple phone calls and visits—notably when my sister or I would tote our children along. He would try to make the visit fun for the grandkids. While he was limited in his ability to move around with them, he would create joy by ordering a clown wig and putting it on to invoke giggles when the grandkids toddled into his bedroom.

I marvel that Dad never denied his disease or showed visible anger. He lived a full, active, joyful, and joke-telling life with MS for more than 50 years after being first diagnosed. While extreme fatigue may have shielded depression, he always remained in acceptance. "Bunky, I am doing fine. It is what it is, and thanks for asking," he often said during our visits.

His decline was both anticipated and surprising. In the last year of his life at age 68, his health unraveled quickly—his legs became immobile and his hands would flail with tremors. He required help eating at every meal. Despite the hardships, he stayed positive, often saying, "Looks like I'll need some help today, Bunky." Feeding him turned into a shared joke, lightening the mood with playful antics such as pretending to be a bird or assuming the utensil was an airplane.

Amid the challenges, his breathy laugh reminded us all that even in tough times, we were living life right, choosing joy over misery, while simultaneously accepting reality.

His decline came swiftly due to a bed sore that rapidly worsened when his air mattress malfunctioned in late summer 2019. What was at first a small spot the size of a pencil eraser quickly became the size of an 8x10-inch picture frame—a gaping wound that was impossible to keep clean in his bedbound state. Despite frequent hospital visits and delirium from the infections, he never lost hope or his will to live. His acceptance of reality was matched with incredible courage and resilience. He was always ready to tackle each challenge, share something funny he saw on television, or attempt to find a more comfortable position with a determined "Ok, let's give it a try."

Peaceful Transition

Before he lost the ability to speak and respond, we exchanged a few heartfelt sentiments really hoping they were not the dreaded final last words. Within a few days, and after he lost the ability to remain lucid or awake, the doctors presented two paths: several grueling surgeries with a long uncertain recovery or the comfort of hospice. My sister and I chose the latter, knowing it was time. The wounds were too severe and his discomfort too great for any viable alternative.

We spent a week by his side in the hospice facility, holding hands, talking to him over hospital-brewed coffee, filling the room with laughter, reminiscing over the silly memories he created for us, and listening to his favorite music. As he transitioned peacefully, I imagined him reuniting with his parents, free from the constraints of his illness, running to them with arms wide open while my grandfather belted the Hungarian Anthem as they hugged and laughed.

A few days after my dad passed away, I saw a van like his parked outside my house. The large size and light brown color were a unique combination, not often seen on the roads. It belonged to Larry, a family friend, who had unexpectedly come by to help with some projects. His story about buying the van to help his daughters with cross-state moves and teaching them home maintenance struck a chord with me.

"Kids need to know how to do basic home maintenance, Jill, especially girls. My daughters love it when I'm there, even if they are embarrassed when I pull up in that monster van in that crazy color," Larry explained with a laugh. I laughed too, and then I cried. The laughter came from seeing the ridiculous van and still being able to squeak out a chuckle despite my deep grief, and the tears came from realizing that my dad sent a sign.

I was reminded of the life lessons he taught me: the value of simple conversations, the confidence that comes from learning new skills, and the importance of finding joy and laughter even in tough times. He was my ylp, and I am so proud of the lessons his life and struggles imparted to me, his ylnod.

> ## Three Things I Learned About Life and Leadership
>
> 1. The best relationships are built through consistent and simple conversations.
> 2. Competency builds confidence. Always say yes when someone you love says, "I need your help for a minute," especially if it means you'll learn something new.
> 3. Accept reality and find joy and laughter even in tough times.

***

Lessons in Leadership and Love from Grandma Lori

by Jackson Yaeger, MBA, "Favorite Grandson"

In 1998, the world-stage was introduced to a sport where precision, strategy, and teamwork came together in unexpected ways. The sport required both mental and physical labor and rewarded participants with crowds that would erupt into thunderous applause as teammates guided objects perfectly to their targets.

Curling's Olympic debut revealed the true thrill of this unique, stone-sliding sport. It's not the high-speed drama of figure skating or the intensity of downhill skiing. Instead, curling's most thrilling moments emerge from subtle, calculated moves and collective effort.

Central to every curling team are the "Sweepers." Their job is to sweep the ice in front of the stone as it slides toward its target. The sweeping warms the ice, making it smoother, and helping the stone reach its mark with precision. For sweepers, timing and coordination are crucial. Their efforts can mean the difference between a successful shot and a miss. In essence, sweepers are the unsung heroes, guiding the stone exactly where it needs to go.

In many ways, Loretta Fleiss was my family's sweeper. She held many titles to many people: mother, wife, sister, friend—the list goes on. To me, she was Grandma Lori.

Meet Grandma Lori

A devoted family woman, Grandma Lori embodied love, connection, and unwavering support. Born in the Bronx in 1941 to immigrant parents, she was the middle child of three. She and her older sister served as caregivers for their much younger brother.

Grandma Lori was raised in a traditional Jewish home, celebrating holidays with extended family. Summers were spent at sleep-away camp and that is where Grandma Lori met Grandpa Izzy. As the story goes, Grandma fell down the stairs and Grandpa caught her. He later told a friend he was going to marry her, and the rest is history.

When I was little, Grandma Lori playfully dubbed me her "favorite grand-child," even though I was one of many. Though she didn't truly have favorites, this special title strengthened our bond and made me feel unique. Grandma Lori had a remarkable ability to make everyone feel special, loved, and part of something greater. Her warmth reflected her upbringing, her life with Grandpa, and her lifelong devotion to family.

Commitment and Resolve

Grandma Lori wore her role as a homemaker with pride. She raised four children, one being my mother. Grandma Lori managed her household and stayed deeply involved in her children's lives. She was active in the PTA and was a class mother for a number of years. She also volunteered at Temple, setting up for various holidays and arranging for hamantaschen on Purim, apples and jelly apples for Sukkot, and Simchat Torah. Her devotion to her children was unwavering.

When she was younger, Grandma Lori went to PS 76, a K-8 school at the time, and she often told the story of how, at the start of junior high, she was transferred to JHS 113. When her mother learned of this, she marched straight to the principal's office at PS 76 to question the decision. The principal told her there was no longer a seat available for Grandma, and that her new school was JHS 113. Without missing a beat, her mother responded that she had bought a house right next to PS 76 for a reason, and that Grandma would be there the next morning—folding chair in hand—if there were no more seats. Needless to say, Grandma never went to JHS 113, even though many of her friends and neighbors did. She inherited her moxie from her mother, and that fierce determination became the foundation of her own commitment to family.

One of Grandma Lori's most admirable qualities was her determination. A lifelong smoker, she quit cold turkey after her mother voiced concerns about her smoking around her children. She did it without programs or patches. She simply stopped for the sake of her family. This resolve, despite decades of habit, showed her strength and commitment. When Grandma set her mind to something, she could accomplish anything, no matter the challenge.

Family Ties

At 13, I became curious about our family history. Exploring online, I discovered our heritage, including my great uncle Joe, the former head of the Division of Biostatistics at Columbia University, and a distant cousin, Mike Fleiss, the creator of *The Bachelor*.

I turned to Grandma Lori for more stories, discovering a family tree connecting Fleiss relatives around the world. Our heritage traced back to Poland, linking family members in Israel, Brazil, and beyond. Grandma's stories emphasized the power of connection and unity—qualities she embodied throughout her life—reminding me that family ties extend beyond names and locations, weaving an interconnected legacy.

One of Grandma Lori's ways of keeping our family connected was taking my sister and me out to lunch on days when we were off from school. Before the COVID-19 pandemic, our lunch outings were filled with lively conversation, laughter, and stories from the past. I can still vividly remember one of our first meals together after the dining restrictions were lifted. The dynamic had shifted: the animated conversations we once shared were replaced with long silences, with Grandma quietly sitting through the meal. It was a bittersweet moment, one that underscored the rapid decline in her health and served as a poignant reminder of how much had changed, and how much more was yet to come.

Lasting Legacy

Grandma Lori passed away on September 13, 2024, marking my first experience with such profound loss. At her funeral, I saw the far-reaching impact of her life, as people traveled from across the country to pay their respects. Though her passing was not unexpected, her final months were difficult, with dementia gradually taking its toll.

Despite her fading memory, her commitment to family remained unwavering. I believe it was for her family that she stayed as strong as she did in her final days. Through it all, she never forgot her "favorite grandchild," and even in the toughest moments, her spirit continued to be a source of strength.

Like curling team members who carefully guide their stone to its destination, Grandma's life was dedicated to guiding us through the obstacles of life, smoothing our path with her unwavering love, practicality, and determination.

Reflecting on Grandma Lori's life and the values she embodied, I realize how deeply her lessons have shaped my approach to leadership and life. Her resilience taught me the importance of perseverance and selflessness, as seen in her decision to quit smoking for the sake of her family. She exemplified courage and determination through her devotion to family, creating traditions and fostering connection even in difficult times. Grandma's unwavering commitment to her loved ones serves a constant reminder that true leadership is about building trust, offering support, and leading with love.

Grandma Lori's legacy lives on in these values, ones I hope to pass forward as she did for me.

Three Things I Learned About Life and Leadership

1. Resilience showcases the value of persistence and perseverance. Keep moving forward, even when things get tough.
2. A pioneering spirit drives us to overcome challenges and uncertainties with courage and determination.
3. Commitment to family is vital for creating traditions, providing support, and leading with love.

Notes

1. Stephen Batchelor, "Stephen Batchelor on the Prajna of an 'Appropriate Response,'" *Upaya Zen Center*, May 14, 2014, accessed December 2024, https://www.upaya. org/2014/05/stephen-batchelor-need-discernment-prajna
2. John Godfrey Saxe, "Rely on Yourself," *Poems of John Godfrey Saxe*, edited by Sophia Newell Sollace Saxe (New York: Houghton, Mifflin, 1884.)

Chapter 6

Compassion (and Relationships)

This chapter features 13 essays that blend the essential ingredients of compassion for others with the ability to cultivate and nurture relationships. You will read stories that reinforce behaviors such as assume positive intent, don't judge, be empathetic, be emotionally and physically present, recognize that everyone has a story, listen, treat others with kindness and respect, foster a sense of belonging and safety, and accept that people give and receive love the best way they can.

In addition to all the essays in this chapter that honor lost loved ones and lessons learned, one essay takes a slightly different twist. It includes lessons from a special somebody who has not yet passed but who is expected to do so soon. We have included it with our book because it speaks so poignantly to the grieving and learning process leading to the inevitable: we are losing someone we love, know it is coming, and are powerless to stop it—yet we do have the power to learn life and leadership lessons from the moment.

The Matriarch Who Shaped My World—A Legacy of Leadership

by Ekhoe Ame-Ogie, HR Leader and Executive Coach

In southern Nigeria, amid the warm vibrancy of Benin City, lived a woman who was more than just my grandmother. Kehinde Eke, known to everyone as "Iye Mobi," was a true matriarch, a constant source of strength, and a beacon of wisdom for many.

She embodied resilience, compassion, and an unwavering spirit that shaped my understanding of family and deeply influenced my approach to leadership, resilience, and service. Her story is not just about overcoming obstacles but about the incredible impact of creating opportunities for others.

DOI: 10.4324/9781003585633-10

Defying Limitations Set by Others

Iye's beginnings were modest. Unlike her brothers, who were educated and became lawyers, she was denied the same opportunities simply because she was a girl. Despite this, she didn't let those limitations define her. What the world refused her, she created within herself. She confronted life's harshest realities head-on. By sheer will and determination, she built her own home, literally laying the bricks with her hands in a part of the city where land was affordable.

This was more than survival; it was an act of profound leadership. Iye showed me that true leaders create safe spaces for others to grow and thrive, even in the face of overwhelming odds. She was a living example of resilience, never yielding to the restrictions others tried to place on her. In a society where women were often expected to play supporting roles, she stood as a pillar of strength and independence, building not only her own life but creating a foundation for the generations to follow.

Safe Haven: Lessons from the Elekwukwu

One of the most memorable stories from Iye's life was the arrival of the elekwukwu—doves that nested in such great numbers on her roof that it eventually collapsed. These birds, symbols of peace and tranquility, seemed drawn to her spirit. They stayed with her until the end of her days, as if to honor her presence.

This story, though simple, taught me a vital lesson about leadership. People, like the doves, are naturally drawn to those who offer peace, strength, and refuge. Iye showed me that leaders don't lead by force but by creating environments where others feel safe, valued, and at peace. She transformed her home from a mere shelter into a sanctuary of hope, a demonstration of her leadership in the most tangible way. In a world where leadership is often defined by ambition and competition, Iye taught me that leadership is about nurturing and inclusion. She created a space where people could come together, feel supported, and be inspired.

This lesson is something I carry with me, especially in today's frenetic world. Whether in business, community, or family, I've learned that people are more engaged, more productive, and more loyal when they feel safe and supported.

Seeing the Good, Spreading Kindness

Despite the many challenges life threw at her, Iye never allowed bitterness to take root. Instead, she saw the good in people and situations, building a life not just for herself, but for others. Her home was always open—a sanctuary for family, neighbors, and even strangers. Her generosity extended beyond the material; she had a special gift for helping women struggling with fertility, using her knowledge of herbs and traditional practices to offer comfort and support.

Through her, I learned one of the most powerful leadership lessons: leaders don't just lead, they lift others up. It's a lesson I hold dear—true leadership is measured not by personal achievements but by the impact we have on the lives of others. Iye's compassion and dedication to others showed me that seeing the good, even when it's difficult, is the foundation of a meaningful life. Her kindness was not just a virtue but a form of strength that inspired those around her.

A Gift that Sparked a Business

One pivotal moment in my life, which I now realize was another example of Iye's subtle, empowering leadership, came when she traveled outside Nigeria for the first time. She returned from her trip with a makeup set for me—a beautiful collection that would go on to change the course of my life. To others, it may have seemed like a simple gift, but to Iye, it was a strategic way to empower me. She saw potential in me and wanted to give me something that would put money in my pocket and provide a skill.

This makeup set marked the beginning of my journey as an entrepreneur. With it, I started a small business, providing makeup services for brides and clients for special occasions.

Iye's gift was more than just makeup, though. It was a tool for independence and growth. She had given me an opportunity to build a career, start something of my own, and gain confidence in my abilities. In my work today, I now realize how vital it is to identify people's potential and give them the tools to unlock it. Just as Iye's thoughtful gift empowered me, I strive to empower those around me in meaningful ways, believing in their potential even before they see it themselves.

Embodiment of Servant Leadership

Iye also showed me that leadership is about service. Long before "servant leadership" became a popular management term, she lived it. Her door was always open and her wisdom available to anyone who needed it. She treated everyone who sought her help with the same respect and care, regardless of who they were.

She taught me that to lead is to serve, and that service is a strength, not a weakness. Leaders gain trust, loyalty, and respect not through power but through service to those they lead. This is a principle I strive to uphold in my own life—leading with a servant's heart, making time for those who need guidance and support, even when life gets busy. Iye's servant leadership taught me that no act of kindness or service is ever wasted, and that these small, everyday actions are the building blocks of a legacy.

Leadership Presence: Accessibility over Authority

Iye's leadership was never about authority or control—it was about care and accessibility. In today's world, where efficiency often trumps accessibility, Iye's example reminds me that effective leadership requires presence. It requires leaders to show up, listen, and be emotionally available.

As a leader, I've learned that accessibility doesn't always mean being physically present—it's about being there emotionally, understanding the concerns of the people around me, and building trust through consistent, compassionate actions. Iye's presence in my life was a quiet yet powerful reminder that true leadership isn't about the title but about the relationships you build along the way.

Leadership Grounded in Empathy and Spirituality

One of the qualities that set Iye apart as a leader was her empathy. She wasn't just a grandmother to me but a leader who led with love, compassion, and tough lessons when needed. (I remember her dance of joy when I told her about my first internship, celebrating it as though it was her own victory.)

Iye taught me that true leadership is about acknowledging and uplifting the efforts of others. Whether in the workplace or at home, I have learned that empathy is essential in leadership. It fosters a culture where everyone feels seen and appreciated. Iye's spirituality grounded her leadership; she had a remarkable ability to see into people's hearts, offering wisdom and peace in even the most difficult situations. Her perceptiveness taught me the importance of being attuned to the needs of those I lead. Anticipating challenges and addressing concerns with empathy and tact—these are lessons I carry with me in my own leadership roles.

Passing the Leadership Torch

On my birthday, January 3, 2009, Iye passed away at the age of 86. The significance of that day is not lost on me. Each year, as I celebrate another year of life, I reflect on the values she instilled in me. Her passing on my birthday feels like a symbolic passing of the torch, a reminder that her legacy of strength, compassion, and leadership is now mine to carry forward. Her life didn't just end that day; it continues to guide me and influence the lives I touch.

The impact of losing her on my birthday, a day usually filled with joy, was profound. Her death felt like a marker, urging me to honor her legacy not only through memories but through my actions—as though the universe had chosen that day to challenge me to become the kind of person she always believed I could be. It was a bittersweet moment, one that deepened my resolve to carry on her principles and values. Losing her was not just the loss of a grandmother; it was the loss of a mentor, a guide, and a steady source of wisdom and strength. In many ways, her passing became a call for me to embody her values and share them with others, to honor her in the way I live and lead.

The resilience and compassion that defined her life became my foundation, teaching me to approach challenges with grace and to find purpose in uplifting others. Iye's life taught me that true leadership doesn't come from titles or authority; it comes from the quiet strength of service, the courage to create opportunities for others, and the compassion to see the good even in the hardest moments. Her values are now woven into every part of my life and work, reminding me daily that the legacy of a remarkable person lives on in the lives they've touched.

> **Three Things I Learned About Life and Leadership**
>
> 1. Create safe spaces for others to grow and thrive, even in the face of overwhelming odds.
> 2. Lead by serving, knowing that service is a strength, not a weakness.
> 3. Show up, listen, and be emotionally available to those who need it.

The Imprints We Leave

by Bill Baker, Chief HR Officer, Wolters Kluwer

Leadership lessons are everywhere. In most every interaction, there is something to learn if we pay attention. What did that feel like? What impact did it have? What imprint did it leave?

When I think about what knowledge and experiences I draw on as a leader, they seem random as a collection. They aren't, though. The common thread is that these experiences, these lessons, impacted me in ways that left enduring imprints—imprints with legacies that shape how I think, feel, and experience situations.

Meet Myrtie "MaMa" Smith

I grew up knowing and being close to three of my grandparents—both of my father's parents and my mother's mom. My mother's dad passed away the year before I was born when my grandmother was in her fifties, one of many moments that defined her long life, but more on that later. Myrtie Smith—no, that's not a typo, M-Y-R-T-I-E (can't get much more southern than that)—was born in South Carolina in 1909. She lived a small-town life, grew up on a farm, knew everyone in the community and who "your people were," and lived with her faith and her family at the center of her life.

In our family, she was a daughter, sister, sister-in-law, wife, aunt, mother, grandmother, and great-grandmother. She found love in all of those roles and loss in some. She was gentle and soft-spoken, yet strong and determined. To me, she was "MaMa," and to her, I was "Billy," even when I traded "Billy" for "Bill" as an adult—and that was fine with me.

She was my refuge. Her home was peace and love to me. Her presence brought out my best because she was proof that difficulties and loss don't have to define you—that you can decide to focus on kindness, grace, and love to fuel a determined spirit and work your way from darker days toward the sunshine.

MaMa loved her church and while she drew on her faith to guide her life, it was her guide, not her judgment. She didn't drink, but for whatever reason had space in her refrigerator for some homemade wine if someone "happened" to bring her some, and a hot toddy for when you were under the weather (all medicinal, of course). Once in a while, I wondered with a smile about her definition of "under the weather." She loved a good joke, including "off-color" ones, which she deemed okay if you whispered the "off-color" parts.

When I was a child, time with MaMa Smith was always special. My cousins, my sister, and I would spend a week in the summer at her house without our parents. We would make ice cream (yes, with the hand crank ice-cream freezer) and go to drive-in movies where we put a big blanket on the hood of MaMa's blue Ford (that car was a tank). She would lie in the middle, back against the windshield, with the rest of us gathered 'round eating stupid amounts of popcorn—generally enchanted by everyday things that didn't seem so "everyday" because we were with her. As I got a little older, and so did she, my time with her became even more special.

Some of my most treasured memories from the last several years of her life center around the Christmas holidays. She always had the family at her home for Christmas, and in later years, the family had gotten pretty large. Getting ready was a lot of work. She used to say "many hands make light work," so off I would go from New York City to South Carolina to help clean house, decorate, shop, wrap gifts, cook—eat!—breathe, learn, love, and just be in the moment.

Treasured Takeaways from MaMa

Looking back, there are several key takeaways from those days that I continue to hold close.

First, Rummikub is not to be taken lightly. If you don't know the game, it's a tile/board game and MaMa loved it. If you wanted to see the steely side of her genteel soul, Rummikub was your ticket. Always gracious whether she won or not, make no mistake, she intended to win … and she usually did. But it was the time between the plays that meant the most, when she'd share stories about happy times and sad times, about love and loss, and about people I knew and some I didn't.

She told me what it was like when my grandfather, her husband, died of cancer when they were in their fifties, and how she had no idea how to manage the "business" of life. Typical of the era, she had always taken care of the home while my grandfather took care of the rest. When he knew he was going to pass, he called on his sister to look out for MaMa and take care of her. And while Mama was grateful, she wasn't having any of that. She set her mind to learning what she needed to know to take care of herself. Her firm resolve and determination was not to be underestimated. She got a job and made it her business to reshape her life in a way to find happiness again. In her words, "I didn't know what I was doing. I just knew I had to do it."

Between these poignant stories, there would be belly laughs—and she had a belly laugh that on its own would make YOU laugh—and sometimes a few tears. I learned the power of being in the moment, really listening and being connected to others, and taking the time to just have some fun. I have her Rummikub set to this day.

Imprints.

Next, cake baking at 1:00 a.m. is not for the weak. This was especially true in MaMa's house. For special occasions, she always made a coconut cake and a banana cake (among others), but these two were particularly special. In fact, as I write this, I can almost taste them even though I haven't had either since she passed. For some reason, she was most inspired to bake after the clock struck midnight. Funny thing is, my mom is the same, and I suspect I will follow that pattern too.

I vividly remember the first time helping to bake the coconut cake. We'd been playing Rummikub for a couple of hours—yes, she won—when she said, "Well, that cake's not going to bake itself, but wouldn't it be something if it did?" Cue the belly laugh. She got up, went to put on one of the light, flowered house coats she always wore when she cooked, and started pulling the ingredients from the various places in her cozy kitchen.

I was a dutiful set of hands as she got the cake batter going—there was no box of mix in sight—and into the oven. Then came the coconut and the hammer. Yes, hammer. We cracked the shell, she saved the coconut milk for later, and I started peeling as she gave me instructions so I wouldn't cut off a hand. As we chatted, I asked her why she didn't just use the shredded coconut you could get from the store. With a quick, sideways glance and a bit of a disapproving smirk, she said, "Not in my house, not for this cake."

And in that small moment, a lesson. The standards were clear: know what's important, set those standards high, and never compromise quality for ease.

Imprints.

Her Final Lesson: A Legacy of Love and Grace

As her last years ticked by, I treasured the time I had with MaMa, often asking her to repeat stories I already knew just for the comfort of hearing her tell them. She always told them as though it was the first time.

In 1999, she left us as she lived—with grace and determination. Toward the end of her nearly 91 years, she had health issues and was in and out of the hospital. I would get a call, go down to see her, and she would work to recover and keep going until the time came when she couldn't any longer.

The last time I got one of those calls, she had just come home from the hospital and she was calling for her children, grandchildren, and great-grands to gather around. She told us she had some things to say. I was the one farthest away and she said she would wait.

The memory of that trip is still like a slow-motion movie. I picked up and left the office as soon as I got the call. My partner arranged for my flight while I gathered a few things at home, and my dad met me at the airport in Greenville, South Carolina, which was the best flight I could get even though it was a bit of a drive to her house. Dad was not someone who talked about emotions and feelings with me, but it was clear that this was not easy for him, and I think he fully understood how hard it was for me. He shared stories with me on that drive and we smiled and even laughed a bit.

When we got there, she was sitting up in her bed. We all gathered around. She spoke from her heart—humbly and softly as was her way—expressing gratitude for all she had, the life she lived, the love she had known, her love for all of us, and then said simply that it was her time, that our job was to care for one another and to be good. It was the last she spoke. A few days later, her presence in our lives became her legacy and our memories.

It's been a lot of years now since I could sit with her or hug her, and stretches of time do go by without her being present in my thoughts, but then there comes a day when I feel her presence as though I could talk to her.

I have a picture of her in my office—one I have carried with me from office to office over the years. It's one she didn't hate, which is saying a lot, because there was never any danger of her photobombing your picture. I keep it where I can see it. There are days when the swirl of life's emotions and events, for whatever reason, can make it tough for me to maintain a positive or calm disposition. When that happens, I glance at her picture and am reminded of all she is to me—all she taught me in her gentle and humble way, the legacy of her imprints, and that grace is a gift we give to ourselves and to others.

Three Things I Learned About Life and Leadership

1. Small actions can have big impacts, and those impacts leave imprints.
2. You won't always know how but figure it out anyway.
3. Standards and character are defined by what you do, not by what you say.

***

Hawkeye's Heart: A Legacy of Integrity, Family Devotion, and a Generous Spirit

by Gina Collins, J.D., Healthcare Executive

My father, Carmine, was born in Rhode Island to the parents of second-generation Italian Americans. He lived a full, rewarding, and happy life until his passing at the age of 82.

Carmine was highly intelligent in a way that comes from a formal education combined with experiential learnings gained through living life to its fullest. He was a highly positive person. He was honest, kind, straightforward, and had a great sense of humor. My father captivated everyone by telling stories of people he met, places he visited, and events he experienced. We would all listen attentively even if it was the tenth time we heard the same tale.

As a devoted son, husband, brother, father, grandfather, colleague, and friend, he was always ready to help others, whether through personal support or financial assistance. His genuine happiness and zest for life were evident in his constant smile. Friendly and welcoming, he could strike up a conversation with anyone, anywhere, about anything.

Education, Service, and Family

Carmine was a civil engineer, having completed part of his education at the Massachusetts Institute of Technology. He served as a sailor in the U.S. Navy and later worked for the U.S. Air Force Army Corps of Engineers, where he traveled and lived in places such as Paris and Germany. After retiring from federal service, he joined the Rhode Island Department of Environmental Management, where he worked in the Wetlands Division.

During his years of service, he earned the nickname "Hawkeye" due to his exceptional eyesight, remarkable analytical ability, and attention to detail. Ironically, when he suffered a stroke at age 80, his only lasting impairment was tunnel vision.

When my father married my mother, he was in his early thirties and she was in her twenties. This made him an older father than was typical for his generation. (One of my greatest regrets is that my daughters were only six and three when he passed away, so their memories of him as a loving grandfather who lit up whenever he saw them come mostly from family photos.)

He was a devoted husband, father, and grandfather. Sadly, several children and grandchildren of my siblings were born after his passing and never got to experience his deep love and generous spirit as their grandfather and great-grandfather.

Balancing Work and Personal Time

Carmine embraced life with the same passion he brought to his work, always finding pride and balance in whatever he was doing. He never missed a school, sports, or personal event for me, my siblings, or his grandchildren. In his free time, he was an avid boater, golfer, and fisherman—hobbies requiring patience and commitment.

He valued family deeply, spending quality time with his siblings, their families, and his friends—frequently calling or visiting to maintain these connections. He enjoyed building and fixing things, taking pride in doing the work himself. Learning from any mistakes, he experimented with new approaches or solutions, never showing frustration. His curiosity and patience made him a lifelong learner who inspired others by example.

Carmine was a self-starter with a wealth of worldly experience. He taught my siblings and me to persevere, pursue our dreams, and value a day's work. His government roles sometimes placed him in situations where integrity, ethics, and confidentiality were paramount. He always chose to do what was right, not what was easy or self-serving, avoiding politics in decision-making while demonstrating diplomacy.

Our family took many memorable vacations, often by car. My father preferred road trips because he valued the experience of getting there as much as the actual destination—a perspective he passed on to me. With his joy of driving, he talked about owning a fast sports car but never bought one. When I asked him why, he simply said, "You can only go as fast at the car in front of you," which summarizes perfectly his pragmatic style.

Carmine had a passion for travel within the U.S. and abroad and encouraged my siblings and me to explore new places and experience diverse work, life, and community environments. He and my mother often visited us in the various states where we lived, taking pleasure in exploring each new area.

The Collision of Happy and Sad Events

A family vacation in 2006 marked the beginning of a difficult two-month period leading to my father's passing. While the earlier stroke left him with reduced vision, he remained active and eager to travel whenever possible. On this particular trip, my family joined my parents in Florida at their timeshare properties. There we met up with my brother and his new girlfriend who were traveling from California (they are now married with three children).

After a very happy and memorable week together, during the night before we were to leave, I received a call from my mother saying that my father wasn't feeling well. I went to their room and found him experiencing symptoms that necessitated an emergency room visit and subsequent hospital admission. The next day, I stayed in Florida with my mother while the rest of the family flew to their respective homes, thinking he'd be discharged in just a few days. Instead, days turned into weeks.

Weeks 1–7

My father had experienced a cardiac event that required ICU observation and monitoring. After several days, the doctors recommended implanting a pacemaker to regulate his heart. The pacemaker helped and he was eventually moved from the ICU to a general cardiac unit. Once stable, he was transferred to a rehabilitation facility, where he was expected to stay for a short time to stabilize enough for travel.

With each transfer, our hopes grew that he would soon be discharged and able to return to Rhode Island—either by plane or car—to be near family and his personal doctors. Unfortunately, before that could happen he took another turn for the worse and was re-admitted to the ICU.

Throughout his time in the hospital, my father was alert, talkative, happy, and optimistic—his usual self. The nurses often remarked about what a wonderful patient he was. Even in his challenging situation with a weakening heart, he never lost his sense of self or joyful attitude. Each conversation began with him asking how I was and how others were, never focusing on his own feelings or deteriorating health.

During this time, my mother stayed in Florida while my siblings and I took turns, at times overlapping our visits, to ensure someone was always with my parents and available to speak with the medical staff. Fortunately, we had family nearby for support, including access to an apartment owned by one of Carmine's brothers, just a short drive from the hospital.

Week 8

With my father back in ICU, discharge without risking his health was not an option. Our family discussed the importance of safely returning him to his home state and ways to do so. After many conversations among ourselves and with his doctors, we determined the only feasible approach was to personally coordinate with an air ambulance company willing to make the trip. We also needed to find a hospital in Rhode Island willing to accept his transfer from Florida.

I traveled to Florida once arrangements were finalized and remember a conversation with my father at his hospital bedside. He was aware of our plan and was visibly relieved and grateful to be returning home. During our talk, he told me he didn't expect to have much time left, but that it was okay—he had done everything he wanted in life. True to his nature, he was more concerned about how everyone else, especially my mother, was holding up. This was the last one-on-one conversation I had with him.

The air ambulance transport was successful, and we remained optimistic that my father would bounce back. Sadly, within two days, he died at the hospital late one night. Earlier that same day, during visiting hours, he had known where he was; his siblings, children, my mother, and other family members had been able to visit him; and he had been alert and talking. It was as though he was waiting for an opportunity to be surrounded by loved ones before passing on.

My father was the rock, glue, and strength within our family. His tremendous loss is a void we still feel. In his final days, he epitomized the qualities he displayed throughout his life—strength, putting others first, selflessness, and positivity. This is his legacy and serves as my role model for life and leadership.

Lifelong Memories

During times with unique challenges, I find myself asking, "What would my father do?" I step into his shoes—big ones to fill—and draw on his example to guide how I live and lead. The lessons that stand out most are to be pragmatic, tenacious, genuine, kind, and joyful.

When faced with a stressful situation, acknowledge it emotionally, but then focus on actions to make it better. Be persistent in your goals and explore different ways to achieve them, taking the high road and staying true to yourself. Make time for family, friends and colleagues, checking in and helping whenever possible. And laugh and enjoy life.

Three Things I Learned About Life and Leadership

1. Act with integrity—let your principles guide you in situations where your values and morals are tested.
2. Persevere—you can achieve your goals if you have the personal commitment, drive, and positive attitude to work through challenges along the way.
3. Show kindness and respect—people will remember how you treat them and the feelings you inspire in both work and life.

***

A Tribute to My Mom's Strength, Kindness, and Teachings

by Jack Dickson, MBA Student, Binghamton University School of Management, Early Professional

Many people have strained relationships with their parents, leading to problems they carry into adulthood. This was not the case for me. I am privileged to have been raised by compassionate, loving, and dedicated parents. Because of this, I have been able to overcome life's obstacles with ferocity and determination, although this was severely tested in the spring of 2024, when I lost my mother, Joan Ruddy.

I was in the last semester of my MBA program at Binghamton University. Every week I travelled home to visit her in the hospital. Seeing the strongest woman I know in that state was traumatizing to say the least, but it also offered me a new outlook on life.

Meet My Mom

My mom was truly the most caring person I have ever met. I could provide countless examples of her putting the needs of others before hers. I don't know of any time when she acted selfishly or failed to consider others.

My mom was an incredibly accomplished and respected lawyer. She spent her entire career as a medical malpractice defense attorney, working tirelessly for the doctors she represented in ways that showcased her intellectual prowess and unquestionable determination to help others. I have spoken with many of her colleagues, who, to a person, noted the exceptional quality of her work and the lasting impression she made on anyone fortunate enough to cross paths with her. She had an undeniable light to her, brightening people's days effortlessly.

My mom also had a remarkable personality and joie de vivre. She rode a motorcycle throughout her twenties, trekking across the country and experiencing life in a unique and fascinating way. She even spent months backpacking and hitch-hiking through Europe, creating experiences that she later used to impart wisdom to my brother and me.

With the ability to live from just a backpack for months at a time, it goes without saying that she was not a materialistic person. A favorite gift my mom received was from one of her nieces, who made her an almost distractingly large ladybug-shaped necklace. Having been made by a seven-year-old, it was not exactly fashion-forward. Yet, my mom called it her "vacation necklace" and wore it during every vacation regardless of venue or attire. It was just one of the lessons she taught me from a young age: getting caught up in material possessions is a mistake; instead, live to make memories with loved ones.

Mom Strong

My mom was a very tough woman. When hoverboards were trending a few years back, she got on the one that my brother and I shared (against our better judgment). She fell off very quickly, and as we helped her up, she said, "I think I broke my arm."

My brother and I shrugged it off, thinking she may have just landed wrong. Then she lifted her arm, showing off a limp wrist that was clearly badly broken. I jumped at the sight and exclaimed, "Let's go to the hospital!" She calmly stated she was okay and would go the following day. Then she used the situation as an opportunity to teach us a new word. "Boys, my wrist is undulating," she said, asking us to guess what it meant. We both looked at her as though she was crazy. Her response was, "Now you will never forget what that word means." Even in pain she would always stay strong and maintain her undeniable intelligence and humor. This stayed with her through her battle in the live to make memories with loved ones.

My mom was a big proponent of advocating for those less fortunate. Originally, she wanted to practice law in the field of international women's rights but eventually decided to defend doctors. She would sometimes say she wanted to get into politics after she retired as a lawyer.

While in law school, she was brave enough to fly into Cuba during a trade embargo that prohibited travel there for Americans. She was able to get in via a third country, flying on Air Haiti. My mom did not enjoy flying, so this was not a pleasant experience for her. She described the plane as "a bus with wings." Nevertheless, she loved her time in Cuba, coming back with numerous memories, including several that involved armed soldiers.

Mom was fearless, and I always try to reflect her courage in everything I do. She did more in her 57 years than most people do in 10 lifetimes. Now that she's gone, not being able to hear her stories and lessons—and just never hearing her voice again—is heart-wrenching.

Leading by Example

My mom led by example. She taught me that working hard is important and honing your skills on something you are passionate about is crucial, though it doesn't hold anywhere near the significance of helping others and having a legacy of kindness and integrity.

Every Thanksgiving, my mom's side of the family gathers for a huge celebration. She was always the one who cooked, spending hours getting everything just right. All she cared about was making the holiday perfect for everyone else.

One Thanksgiving, she decided to go all out and slow-cook a beef bourguignon. This took more than two days to complete, and when she served the dish on Thanksgiving eve prior to making a turkey the next day, everyone was ecstatic. She never even blinked when one of my younger cousins politely requested some ketchup (which, to be fair, he added to everything he ate). Some may have taken this as a slight, but my mom, along with the rest of the family, burst into laughter at the absurdity of his request. In this way, my mom taught me that life does not need to be serious all the time and that, as long as you have a loving family, you can endure any hardship.

Holding Out Hope

Watching the woman who raised me deteriorate physically with each visit was demoralizing. What kept me going was I knew she wanted me to persevere and get my degree so I would become the man she knew I could be.

Although my mom was the smartest woman I knew, there were circumstances around her final months that still puzzle me. She was getting sick rapidly, yet she refused to go to the doctor or divulge information about her health to the rest of my family. She never wanted anyone to worry.

Eventually her condition progressed to the point where she could no longer ignore it, so she finally sought help by going to see several doctors. She was diagnosed with a long list of illnesses, including respiratory syncytial virus (RSV), pneumonia, and severe issues with both her liver and her kidneys. The prognosis did not look good, but the doctors were hopeful that with a liver transplant she would make a full recovery.

I never lost sight of the goal of her getting better. Even when she was put on a ventilator, I never lost hope. I wonder if that was something she instilled in me from a young age, or if I simply refused to believe the worst was possible.

Either way, I remained hopeful. Juggling a rigorous MBA schedule with traveling into New York City whenever possible was difficult. Knowing that my mom would be furious if I delayed getting my degree was what helped me graduate on time and not miss any assignments.

Last Moments

Although she didn't know it at the time, when she checked into the hospital in December 2023, she would remain there until her death in March. Through all of those horrible months, my mom remained her strong and witty self. The lesson of remaining true to yourself and staying strong in the face of adversity is one that I will always carry.

I was the last person to have a conversation with her before she was unable to respond coherently. It was the day before my birthday, March 29. We talked for hours, and I was able to stay well into the night. Then I left to go visit my friends in Manhattan. I left with the promise of a birthday celebration the following day at the hospital.

"I love you. See you tomorrow," I said. My mom said, "I love you too." Later that night, she was put on a ventilator and we were told she would not wake up. I spent my twenty-third birthday saying goodbye to her. She died on March 31, 2024.

Having that last moment with her gives me some comfort. Knowing my mom, all she would want is for my brother and me to continue to live our lives fully. Staying true to who I am and to her teachings is calming for me. Knowing that she was seen as a leader at work and in her day-to-day life inspires me to find my passion and live every day to the fullest.

My mom continues to inspire me every day. Although I miss her constantly, the lessons she taught me and her impact on my life and others will never be forgotten.

> **Three Things I Learned About Life and Leadership**
>
> 1. Kindness
> 2. Integrity
> 3. Determination

***

Finding Dad: A Story of Love and Transformation

by Carol Gausz, Founder and President,
Blue Heron Associates Inc.

My dad, John A. Gausz, was a bright, generous, mischievous, and challenging man. He was 33 and an electrical engineer with RCA when I was born, the fourth of five children.

He had many interests and a strong sense of responsibility that contributed to a rich life and wonderful legacy. These same qualities also seemed to burden him and contribute to a curmudgeonly manner for part of his life. He was generous in welcoming strangers, supportive of family and friends, and volunteered for causes he believed in.

Dad also had a playful side, which has provided me with many fond memories early in my life and later in his life. He could be challenging though, with his high expectations for us in school and work. I strove to meet them and have had a good life as a result.

What Had an Impact on Me

Dad had a strong sense of commitment and responsibility—to his family, job, community, and the Earth. He earned a degree in electrical engineering from Rutgers University and landed a job with RCA. His job provided a strong foundation for raising a family but also led to significant stress since he was the sole breadwinner with five kids.

I recall him being easily angered from when I was about 10 until I was in my late forties. Our relationship was strained when I was in college and for several years after that, but this motivated me to learn other ways to deal with stress and anger—his and my own.

Dad was an avid organic gardener. It was a way for him to feed the family and to create beautiful surroundings. We had a huge garden that supplied us with vegetables year-round.

He was also active in the community—as a volunteer firefighter, on the conservation board, and with various school alumni activities.

When he was 82, Dad was diagnosed with a large brain tumor that his doctors believed had been growing for years. Due to his love and commitment to my mom, he was unwilling to have surgery unless my siblings and I promised to support her (she had become quite dependent on Dad due to her own health challenges). The process of moving in with Mom for periods of time during his surgery and recovery—on a rotating schedule with my siblings—while sometimes difficult, was a special opportunity to see each parent in new ways and deepen my relationship with each of them.

Dad found joy in many things—family, chocolate, road trips, nature, music, and welcoming and getting to know others. He loved road trips to historical places, beautiful back roads, camping near Chesapeake Bay, and hiking in the Endless Mountains of Pennsylvania.

He sparked joy in us when we were young by reading Dr. Seuss in silly ways, bringing out his 78 records so we could dance, and making French fries from scratch when Mom was sick.

He loved meeting people from all walks of life—his World's Fair pen pal from England, exchange students from Europe, neighbors, and people he met in his volunteer activities—in addition to maintaining relationships over the decades with his college buddies and keeping his Scotch Plains School class connected well into his eighties.

Circumstances Around His Life

Dad liked to say, "I was born on a kitchen table in Spanish Harlem, New York." His parents emigrated from Hungary in the 1920s and Dad was raised in Scotch Plains, New Jersey. We were raised in Watchung, New Jersey, which was out in the country but close enough so that Dad could take a train to New York for work.

He was strict and had a strong sense of what he wanted for his family. We were expected to help around the house and could play once the chores were done. Unfortunately, there were always more chores to do.

We were expected to work hard and excel in school. Even though we often had the newest television in the neighborhood because my dad worked for RCA, we were not allowed to watch "the idiot box" very often. If he walked into the living room and saw us watching, he would ask if we had finished our homework—then he'd ask whether we checked it, and again whether we'd checked it twice.

As an adult, I'd kid him at times about how strict he was. One of his recurring fatherly messages was, "Don't come home unless you have an A." In his later years, he would say, "I wasn't that bad, was I?" The evidence came when he was cleaning out his study and sent me all my report cards. On a second or third grade report card of mine, I had received A's for academics, O's and S's for behavior, plus one B+. In his distinctive printing, Dad had written in the comments section of the report card, "Carol's mother and I have discussed her slippage, and she assures us she will improve." Seeing this, I giggled to myself, called, and read it aloud to him. We had a lot of fun laughing about it. In retrospect, it was clear that my dad had the best intentions for us, even if he didn't always express them well.

Dad had a generous spirit. There was always room for one more at the dinner table. When anyone in the family had trouble, my dad was always there to help, opening our home and (I imagine) his wallet. When school friends would come over to play, they often stayed for dinner, and we had three international friends stay with us over the years through pen pal and exchange programs. It created a warm and interesting vibe in the house.

I learned the value of hard work and the pride of significant accomplishment from my dad being upfront with me about college. He said, "You will go to college, but I can't pay for it." I babysat and delivered papers until I was old enough to work as a server, which was much more lucrative. I worked all through college at a few jobs and am proud that I paid my way through a bachelor's degree and two graduate degrees.

His Death

On February 9, 2018, at around 5:00 a.m., I saw a text from my sister, Ann. "Are you up?" it read. She was in Michigan, and I was on the north shore of Oahu, Hawaii visiting my daughter and son-in-law for a few weeks. I sensed then what she was texting about, so I went outside with coffee, sat watching the ocean, and called her.

She explained that Dad had been unusually cheerful that morning at breakfast, after which he went back to his room to take a nap. When his aide went to check on him some time later, she found him lying peacefully on the bed. He was gone.

Ann and I shared a few stories, tears, and laughs. After we ended our call, I sat for quite some time and thought of Dad—his playfulness when I was young, those challenging times with him in my teens through my forties when the stress of life took its toll on him, and then the return of his mischievous joy later in life after his "lobotomy" (as I would kid him after they removed his brain tumor).

As I sat there, I felt grateful to have some time to be with this news in such a nature-filled space. I felt a sense of sadness, but also a sense of peace. For part of his life, Dad was tormented by a strong sense of responsibility to his family and to being a part of creating a better world. He was uneasy, quick to anger, and often not satisfied.

He found joy in my siblings and me, although he didn't express it directly to any of us until he was much older. When I talked to him about something good in my life, his response was often limited. Only later would I learn that he had shared his pride in me when talking to one of my siblings. He was like that with each of us. His eight grandchildren were another clear joy for him, and I'm glad my daughters remember his playfulness.

A clear memory of Dad sparking joy was late on the day we had Mom's celebration of life. A large group of family members stayed to visit long after the scheduled end time of the event. The security officer on duty in the retirement community where my dad lived called out of concern. I assured him that one of us would take my dad to his room soon. When I got off the phone and told Dad, he got a huge grin on his face. "I'm AWOL. Haha!" he said, with a hint of mischief. He drew so much joy out of "getting away with something," and that day he made sure everyone at the celebration knew the story as he was saying goodbye.

As we planned his celebration of life, I asked my family to share three words that came to mind as they thought of him. The top three were "Family," "Mischievous," and "Nature." The next on the list included "Intelligent," "Honest," "Dedicated," and "Stubborn." Among the other 15 to 20 words were "Elmer Fudd" and "Dr. Seuss!"

Lasting Impressions

Dad clearly had strong love for his family and cared deeply for many others. Yet, what he expressed most in the middle of my life with him was his disappointment or anger. I was motivated by his high expectations. As a result, I have a good life. Yet, I think of the missed opportunity during that stretch of time when he seemed so burdened and angry.

I can only imagine the possibilities had he been able to express more love and shine a light more on what was working. I have come to understand that expressing care and appreciation fosters growth much more effectively than anger and criticism. The former can create connection and understanding, while the latter can create distance and hinder understanding.

I'm not sure if it is the wisdom that many of us gain with age, the physiological impact of removing his brain tumor, or the psychological impact of spending many weeks in bed as he learned to walk and talk again post-surgery. Whatever the reason, I'm glad I got the dad back I felt such love with early in life and that my daughters, nieces, and nephews got to know him in that way.

Dad could find joy in many ways—in chocolate, sharing a good meal and great conversation, exploring on road trips, being out in nature, or taking care of the Earth, just to name a few. He sparked joy in his playfulness early and later in my life. Even during his middle years when he seemed angrier, there were glimpses of this that were very precious to all who knew him.

> ## Three Things I Learned About Life and Leadership
>
> 1. Express care and appreciation (heart), more than anger and disappointment (head) to foster understanding, connection, and growth.
> 2. See beyond yourself and find a way to contribute to making things better.
> 3. Find and spark joy.

✱✱✱

The Art of Unseen Leadership

by MaryAnne McCormick Hyland, Ph.D., Dean of the Robert B. Willumstad School of Business at Adelphi University

While many of the authors in this book have chosen to write about family members they have lost, I am fortunate to be at a point in my life where the family members who have most influenced me are still with me on this journey. However, one special person who was a part of my career for 18 years is a perfect fit for this essay. Let me introduce you to my colleague, mentor, advocate, and department chairperson, Dr. Allan S. Ashley.

Allan, also known as Dr. Ashley or A^2 ("A-squared"), connected with his colleagues through caring. He cared about their careers and their personal lives. He had an outgoing personality and enjoyed walking the hallways of our building to check in on colleagues.

What impressed me most about his caring was that he did not just support a few colleagues, but rather almost all of the 40 or so faculty members of our business school. Allan also was a consummate family man. He and his wife, Jean, were together for more than 50 years, and he was a caring father to his two daughters, Heather and Allison.

Allan began his career as a faculty member in the business school at Adelphi University in Garden City, New York in 1967. He had a Bachelor of Science degree in Electrical Engineering from Rensselaer Polytechnic Institute, and both a Master of Science in Industrial Engineering and a Ph.D. in Operations Research and Management from the Polytechnic Institute of Brooklyn. Allan was promoted from assistant professor to associate professor to full professor, and then became chairperson of the Management, Marketing, and Decision Sciences Department in 2004.

Creating a Culture of Belonging

Allan was a champion for inclusiveness and belonging. While these terms were not common parlance at the end of the twentieth century, and Allan did not use them, he demonstrated what it means to foster an inclusive workplace.

What I remember most about Allan making everyone feel welcome was his daily ritual of walking the halls and asking everybody—and I mean everybody—if they would like to join him for lunch. Our building had one long faculty hallway, so he would start at one end, and by the time he got to the other, he usually had a small group with him. Some colleagues would meet him in the cafeteria after wrapping up their work, while others respectfully declined. Whether someone joined him for lunch every day, once in a while, or not at all, Allan always invited everyone.

I remember when I first joined him for lunch, I felt a bit uncomfortable because the lunch group that day consisted of faculty more senior than me and the discussion was about the stock market, which was not a subject I was comfortable discussing. I don't remember exactly what he said, but Allan found a way to bring me into the conversation by talking about something other than stock prices.

Lunch discussions were not just small talk. They were an opportunity to "talk shop" as well. Some of my colleagues even kidded him by calling the cafeteria his "office."

Allan also spent a lot of his time in the hallways talking with colleagues about work. He exemplified "management by walking around (MBWA)," which was popularized by Tom Peters and Robert Waterman Jr. in their 1982 book, *In Search of Excellence: Lessons from America's Best-Run Companies.*[1] Colleagues have shared with me that at least once a week, Allan would stop by their offices to ask about their work and their families. Several told me that in these drop-in meetings, he often provided invaluable career guidance, ranging from how to focus their research plans to the importance of making friends at work.

Enthusiasm and Support: A Winning Combination

Allan was a likeable colleague. He was outgoing, quirky, and fun, and he almost always had a smile on his face. He was interested in robotics and liked to talk about remote control and automated vehicles. He was the first person I knew to purchase a robotic vacuum cleaner. He was so excited about it that he brought it to work and let it loose in the faculty hallway so that all of his colleagues could see this marvelous new invention.

Some of Allan's adventures attained near folklore status, such as the time when the building lost power and he brought in a generator from his van so he didn't have to cancel class! He and a colleague from Canada shared an ongoing joke that lasted for years about what Allan liked to call Long Island's "temperate climate," which sometimes can be less-than "temperate."

He also was unfailingly supportive of his junior faculty. He would offer his support, connect colleagues with each other, and stand up to anyone who put down one of the faculty members in his department.

Allan made sure that his colleagues, junior and otherwise, got the recognition they deserved. When a faculty member had a strong publication record, he shared the news like a proud parent would for a child. Allan's "superpower" was supporting others. I learned from Allan the importance of not only recognizing others' achievements within our unit but promoting others' achievements throughout the organization. The idea of promoting our department and school within the larger organizational structure was something I hadn't thought much about earlier in my career.

Subtle Yet Impactful Influence

While I always thought of Allan as an amazing colleague and department chair, I must admit that for many years I didn't really think of him when I thought of "leadership." Allan was informal in his approach to creating an inclusive culture. He was often behind the scenes making the case for new initiatives or advocating for his faculty, so I didn't see all that he was doing. His leadership was subtle.

It wasn't until he got sick that I realized just how much of a leader he was. Colleagues missed his daily lunch rounds and jolly nature, and there were multiple times when someone said, "Allan would know what to do" or "Allan would know who to talk to to get this done."

He was a master at getting people on board for a new initiative before it went up for a vote (in academia most curricula and other initiatives are voted upon before they can be implemented). Allan would often go for coffee or a soda with the dean. I thought he was being social and perhaps offering support to the dean on a stressful day, but I later realized that in addition to doing both of those things, he also was building strong relationships and advocating for his department and his faculty.

Only after I took on a leadership role did I think about how Allan intentionally sought formal and informal leaders in the school to promote his faculty and drive ideas forward. He worked to get colleagues to support a proposal before the committee or faculty meeting where the proposal was presented. He taught me the importance of seeking input from colleagues and adjusting proposals before bringing them to the table. I had heard of the concept of "a meeting before the meeting," and Allan helped me understand just how to execute such pre-meeting meetings.

One More Class

Allan continued as chairperson until he became ill with cancer in 2016. I believe he was 76 years old. You might think, given his age, that Allan should have retired. After all, some people that age don't work as hard as they used to, don't care as much as they used to, or have become hardened or even bitter. But not Allan. He worked hard, cared tremendously about his colleagues and the organization, and had an amazingly positive attitude.

Although Allan had advanced cancer, he desperately wanted to come back to Adelphi to teach again. I didn't go to visit Allan when he was sick, but I spoke with him on the phone. He never wanted to talk about his illness. He only wanted to hear about what was going on at Adelphi.

As time passed, it was increasingly apparent that he would not be able to come back to teach a course. That didn't stop Allan from hoping, though. He continued to insist he could come back to teach, even if just for one day. Allan never did get to, and I sometimes wonder what he would have done if he had. Would he have used the same approach he used for years to teach "Math for Managers," or would he do something very different, such as what terminally-ill Randy Pausch, a professor of computer science at Carnegie Mellon University, did with his well-known "last lecture," where he delivered heartfelt messages on living fully despite his illness?[2]

After Allan passed, I learned that he had suffered terribly with pain during his illness. His wife shared with me that even during my phone calls with him he was often in pain. I was shocked to hear this since Allan was always upbeat during our calls and never mentioned any pain. His focus was on Adelphi, my work at the school, and my home life. I know from others that his conversations with them were similar.

Allan was still acting as a leader from his hospital bed—thinking of others rather than himself. He was supportive of his team until the very end. During his last few weeks, Allan did not talk on the phone very much. At his memorial service, his wife Jean lovingly shared that they held hands a lot in his final days. While I know that Allan suffered terribly, his family said that he fought his illness and ultimately accepted his impending death with grace, showing unending love for those closest to him.

> **Three Things I Learned About Life and Leadership**
>
> 1. Be inclusive—invite others to join you for coffee or lunch.
> 2. Advocate for your people—don't be shy about publicly praising your team.
> 3. Look for and support the leaders around you.

***

Finding Light in Darkness: Reflecting on My Father's Legacy

by Jonathan "Jake" Jacobs, Partner, Rose, Snyder & Jacobs LLP

February 4, 1963. 7:00 a.m. Long Beach, New York.

I was a typical 14-year-old getting ready to go to the bus stop for school. My mother stopped me in the hallway. She said my father was not in bed and asked if I could go look for him.

I felt a sense of urgency, but didn't fully understand why. So, I just went outside to start looking.

At the time, my father's parents lived 10 feet away from us in a house identical to ours. Both homes were brick two-stories with sunken basements. My grandparents were in Florida for the winter and their house was dark.

I must have heard noise coming from their garage (I don't recall) because I ran down the driveway and opened their garage door. Inside was thick with smoke and the car engine was running. I opened the driver's door. There was my father, David Sherman Jacobs, aged 45. He had taken his own life.

Seeking the Positive

How could my father be the subject of an essay for *Lives Lost and Leadership Found: Lessons from Special Somebodies*? Certainly, at the time, there was nothing positive to be gleaned from what happened.

My father taking his own life was unthinkable. How could he do this to us? What was going to happen to us? How was I suddenly the man of the house at age 14, unable to cry because it was considered unmanly?

Writing this essay has given me the opportunity to reflect on my father's life and appreciate the profound lessons I have learned from him.

Sowing the Seeds

David Sherman Jacobs grew up in the Bronx, New York, the son of Jacob (Jack) Jacobs and Anna Sherman (Jacobs). They were "Grandpa" and "Nana" to me.

Anna was the consummate mother and grandmother, always baking and otherwise taking care of the family. Jack was in the apparel business and also a very religious man, helping build a temple in his community. Jack was also a tough son of a bitch, and made it seem that nothing anyone could do was good enough. I rarely saw him smile, but I do remember him telling me, "Chew, chew, chew," when eating. I also remember my grandmother telling him numerous times in Yiddish to "leave him (me) alone." He didn't have much use for me and basically told me that I would not amount to much. (I can only imagine what it was like for my father growing up.)

Courage Under Fire: World War II

David graduated DeWitt Clinton High School in the Bronx, graduated New York University with Honors, and got his law degree from Harvard University. He was working as an estate lawyer during World War II and was offered a desk job in Washington D.C. Instead, he joined the Air Force as a second lieutenant navigator/bombardier, flying in a B-24 Liberator, also known as "the flying coffin."

He flew 50 missions over Germany in 1944. On his last mission, his plane was shot down. As he was trying to bail from the plane, he got stuck in the door. Only a roll of the plane to its side allowed him to get out, where his parachute got caught in a tree, thereby saving his life. He was in the middle of Germany, so the first thing he did was throw away his dog-tags, as they showed his Jewish religion. He wound up spending 11 months in a German POW camp with members of his flight crew who did not perish when the plane crashed. He was rescued at the end of the war.

For his service, he was awarded numerous medals, including the Distinguished Flying Cross with oak leaf clusters, and he was also promoted to captain. Interestingly, he never talked about any of this with me. I only knew because one day I opened an innocuous desk drawer and found all of his medals there, lumped together.

Unseen Battles at Home

Unfortunately, David came home with what is now known as severe PTSD. There was no cure back then except for shock therapy, so every year he would go away for a time for "treatment." The illness caused him to endure extreme highs and lows on a regular basis.

When he was in a positive state, he was loved by the people that knew him. He was smart, funny, a leader in the community and in our temple, an excellent bridge player, and a superior athlete. He was an exceptional estate lawyer.

In the depressed state, he could not concentrate on anything, which had to be extraordinarily frustrating to him. He also suffered from physical pain (gout) and had recurring nightmares reliving his wartime experiences.

His wife, my mother, had lost her mother when she was nine. She spent the rest of her childhood taking care of her father and brother. When she got to the point of marrying my father, she had limited emotional energy as a caregiver. I don't think she was aware of my father's condition when they married, and it took its toll. Ultimately, she was having an emotional affair with a person who became my stepfather soon after my father's passing.

Snapshots of Togetherness

I never got to know my father as an adult, but I do remember my experiences growing up. When I was six, we went to the Nevelle resort in the Catskills for a "vacation." It was really a place David's doctors thought he could go to experience some joy. The way I learned how to swim was when my father picked me up and threw me into the middle of the giant pool. He also let me "drive" our car on a winding mountain road with no guardrails. To say the least, in both instances, I was terrified. Only later did I realize he was helping me grow up.

He took me to a variety of activities, but we rarely directly interacted. We went to an amusement park, where I would ride the carousel and try to grab the brass ring. We went to the real ponies, rode around the track, and then enjoyed a Nathan's hot dog.

When I was 13, I spent my only summer in a sleep-away camp. There was a father/son baseball game. They had me in left field when my father came up to bat. He was an imposing right-handed batter, and they moved a "better player" to left field and me to right. That's when my father switched to batting lefty so he could crush one way over my head. I made the most spectacular over the head catch of my life—Willie Mays had nothing on me!

Secrets and Revelations

I grew up on a street where there were no secrets. One day, we heard that a neighbor down the street was physically abusing his wife. I remember my father leaving and walking toward that house. He came back a short time later and never said a word. To my knowledge, the man never physically abused his wife again.

As a kid, I remember him "grooming me" by taking blackheads off my nose. I didn't understand what was going on, but today I realize it was a primitive way of showing affection.

When I was eight, my aunt took me to the Statue of Liberty. When I came home, I had a baby sister. I didn't even know my mother was pregnant! My father called her his "happiness," and I felt relegated to something "lesser" because he never called me something similar.

I lived for the next 60 years with those feelings, then my mother passed away, and in her papers, there was a letter to me from my father. He had written it when I was about nine, and I believe in retrospect he was contemplating suicide at that time. In the letter, he had written how I was his "precious" and how he wanted us to be brothers for all time. He told me what he was hoping for me in my lifetime and the ways he hoped I could live my life. Interestingly, the letter had been opened, presumably by my mother, but never shared with me.

Lessons Learned, Leadership Found

The first lesson I'm able to take away from how my father lived and died is don't judge someone until you fully understand them. As leaders, we judge people all of the time and don't necessarily try to understand why they behave the way they do. How often do we lead people without understanding what makes them act the way they do? How often do we try to resolve conflict without getting to the root cause of the disagreement? How many people judged my father without understanding why he chose to take his own life?

The second lesson is that people love you the best way they can. I never really understood how much my father loved me, because it wasn't necessarily obvious ... and we never had the chance to get around to those kinds of discussions.

The third lesson is that sharing my pain helps others heal. Each year, my wife Karon and I host 25 "wounded veterans" at the Reagan Library as part of a crash course in entrepreneurship at the UCLA Entrepreneurship program. As part of the evening, I share my father's journey and my journey. Invariably, many attendees approach me afterwards in tears, sharing that either they or someone close to them has been affected by suicide. Those who have attempted suicide often tell me that, after hearing my story, they feel compelled to open up about their experiences and help others heal.

My father was an amazing man. I hope that he would be as proud of me as a person and a man as I am of him, and that I am now finally able to cry.

Three Things I Learned About Life and Leadership

1. Don't judge others until you fully understand them.
2. People love you the best way they can.
3. Sharing your pain can help others heal.

***

Sometimes a Rose Only Blooms Once

by Katie Lopez, CHRO, Panavision Inc.

If someone said to you, "There is a job that might be the hardest leadership job you will ever do. You will not be paid for doing it, and once you start, you can never quit. If you make the commitment, you stand a chance of it becoming the most rewarding thing you will ever do," would you take it?

I am speaking about the role of stay-at-home parents. I have the deepest respect for parents who are leaders and who have a calling to make this their primary life's work. For the first twenty-plus years in this job, expectations change frequently as children grow into what parents hope will be empathetic, responsible, adaptable adults. It is a role that can bring the most joy, the most worry, and the deepest love—sometimes all in the same day!

Meet My Grandmother

My maternal grandmother, Inez May Swanborough, dedicated her life to serving others, including her children, Heather and Michael, and husband, Leslie. Pronounced "E-nes," which, to my grandmother's dismay, she spent a lifetime explaining, I lovingly called her "Nanny." (Heather, her daughter, is my mother and also an amazing stay-at-home mother.)

My grandmother, Inez May Yardley-Dudney, was born on May 7, 1925, in Brighton, Sussex, England. At 31 and 29, respectively, her parents, Bernard and Eleanor (May Mead), were relatively old by the standards of the time when they had Inez. Inez's father, born Herbert Bernard, served in the medical corps in World War I, having started training as a chemist before the war broke out. He returned to finish his training around the time he met and later married Eleanor.

Their ages and a late start to his career were perhaps why Bernard and Eleanor had only one child, but no one in the family—including my grandmother—knows for sure. Nanny used to say her mother always told her, "Sometimes a rose only blooms once."

Learning on the Job

Being an only child always bothered my grandmother. Coming from a family of 13 children, her mother, Eleanor, sensed her daughter's loneliness and would make a point to play with her and teach her things. She would also take Inez to spend time with her grandmother and grandfather in Brighton, where she would get to see her cousins.

Brighton is home to the Brighton Royal Pavilion, a former royal residence next to the seaside. Inez's grandfather was an auctioneer and owned a warehouse there, which she loved to visit. Some of her favorite memories were of walking around the showroom with her cousins. Her grandfather had many exciting pieces, which is where I imagine Inez developed her interest in antiques. It is also where she got an insider's view of running a business. It must have been quite exciting to see her grandfather moving furniture from Buckingham Palace to the Brighton Pavilion for the Regency Exhibition.

Inez's father, whom she described as a clever man, was not used to children and didn't like a lot of noise. The only chemist in their village, Bernard spent most of his time in the shop he owned next door to their home in Staplehurst, Kent. This was another place where Inez likely learned about running a business. She would help her father after hours and he would teach her how to measure and weigh ingredients because most things back then did not come pre-portioned. (Some of my fondest memories are of playing in Nanny's kitchen with the same set of scales she used with her father!)

By the time World War II broke out, Inez was 14. Life in 1930s England was simple. Her father built a wireless set for entertainment, and they would listen to programs during the evening and on weekends. My grandmother used to say, "Nobody had a TV set back then!" If you owned a car, you couldn't go far because petrol was rationed and everyone had to stay within their local area due to the war.

By war standards, at age 14, Inez was not considered a child who needed looking after, so her mother worked as the "post lady" in the next village to supplement the depleted labor force. Bernard was also called upon to work an additional night shift to support war efforts. As a result, Inez had to get herself ready for school and make her father's breakfast. In summers, she had to work various jobs while soldiers were overseas. Later, but still during the war, Inez went to Ashford College at night to learn shorthand and bookkeeping—skills that eventually led her to working for Lloyd's Bank.

Foundational Lessons

My grandmother could learn anything she put her mind to, was observant of the businesses she grew up around, and was naturally independent. She was frugal, precise, and practical. She would always say, "Watch the pennies and the pounds will take care of themselves." She was raised to embody a strong sense of duty and loyalty to family and The Crown, and she enjoyed helping her parents and grandparents.

After passing her school certificate exams, Inez started her early career as a shorthand typist at the Kent War Agricultural Committee. Though an obsolete skill now, I remember being fascinated when she patiently taught me how to write shorthand as a child. She did not talk about this phase of her career much, but she likely ended up working for the agricultural committee because she did not like working at Lloyd's Bank. She described the bank as having "poor accommodations," talked about "working under the road with artificial light," and that "making up people's accounts was boring."

Inez met her husband, Leslie Swanborough, at a local village dance in June of 1946. They married soon thereafter and, by 1950, had started a family. There was likely never any question that my grandmother would stay home to raise their children.

Inez loved to make clothes and, as was the norm back then, she was great at knitting and needlework. She was also a master list maker and always organized. She was fond of saying, "Never put off until tomorrow what you can do today." The family considered her a brilliant packer with a knack for getting as many things as possible into a small bag—like a master Tetris player before there was such a game.

She never lost her sense of self as a stay-at-home mother. Instead, she discovered that her passions could co-exist alongside raising the children. The lessons of self-reliance and self-care her experiences taught me have provided a foundation for my leadership. I consider these qualities a prerequisite because leaders must first know how to care for themselves.

Bringing People Together

By all accounts, Inez was a great cook. She always made sure the family had something delicious to eat, which taught me about the power food has to bring people together. We made many visits to my grandparents' house for meals she prepared. This was one of her key roles as homemaker—to bring people together, feed them, and create memories.

During one particularly memorable meal, I learned that my grandmother had immovable standards and boundaries. My grandfather, who had a rather cheeky sense of humor, tried to tell a joke about the difference between a lady in a bubble bath and a parrot. My grandmother rapidly shut it down saying, "Leslie Bill! not in front of the children." (We didn't get to hear the full joke for another decade!) I had never heard my grandfather called by his full name, and in that moment, my grandmother was the true guardian of our family values.

I loved to help Nanny prepare meals, especially baked goodies. As she taught me how to weigh ingredients and make batter, I also got to learn more about her life. She talked about Blackie, her cat, friends or clubs she belonged to, and conversations she would have with her neighbors, the "two Stephanies," as they set her hair in rollers. To my grandmother, friendship meant you were interested in other people's problems, let them confide in you, and offered a shoulder to lean on. This taught me that creating safe spaces for people to work through their thoughts and being a good listener are the hallmarks of good leadership.

While I have yet to bring knitting and needlepoint to work, the experience of cooking a meal together is one of my favorite team-building activities. It's a fantastic way to create memories and gain insights about other people.

Able to Do Anything

Inez returned to office work later in life as a secretary in the mental health department of Queen Mary's Hospital in Carshalton Beeches, Surrey. She worked for quite some time after my grandfather retired early due to a heart attack induced by a prescription medication. True to form, the doctors and other staff soon came to rely on her. The department served children, and Inez enjoyed supporting other parents.

At the time, I didn't think anything of my grandmother working and my grandfather being retired. Looking back, I can see how her being in charge of the household and having a job influenced the choices I have since made in my career as a working parent. Her example as a capable, strong, able-to-do-anything woman was inspiring.

I don't think I ever deeply knew Nanny until after Grandpa passed away. She had always lived dutifully to support him, care for her mother—who lived to be 99—and serve the rest of our family. She kept track of everything for my grandfather, reminding him of what he needed to remember, planning and organizing, and never saying "I told you so" when his handyman skills failed him—like the time he blew up the boiler, covering the kitchen with black soot after she suggested they call a plumber!

Over time, as I brought my daughters to spend summers with their great-grandmother, I began to realize that she had always been a natural leader, the one really in charge. She created the conditions for everyone around her to be happy and to achieve their goals.

Her capabilities became very clear to me in the last few years of her life. She would read the newspaper, ask me to help her learn new technology—although the iPad for FaceTime proved a little challenging—manage her finances and paperwork, and protect her money so she could pass it along to her children. (A few years before she passed, she read in the *Financial Times* that a new tax law would negatively impact her estate, so she contacted her solicitor to change her will!)

Capturing Memories

My Grandmother wrote many of her memories in a notebook I gave her called "Memories for My Grandchildren." We spent evenings chatting about what she wrote, all while enjoying glasses of wine or cups of tea. In her memoirs, she shared that losing her husband of 61 years was the hardest thing she had to overcome, second to that of both of her children moving far away to America.

"You have to be strong to overcome first being alone and then continuing to live with it," she wrote. Near the end of her life, Inez's mother—we called her "Nana" to differentiate her from Nanny—often told me she had lived too long. This stuck with me, so I would share with Nanny that I wanted her to decide when it was her time to go and that I would be at peace if she got to choose.

I always expected to be there at the end with her, taking care of her so that she would not die alone. In September of 2020, at age 95, my grandmother fell in her home and broke her femur. This was during the COVID-19 pandemic. She made it through surgery and even into a nursing home. I can only imagine the road to recovery seemed insurmountable to her. I know she never wanted to be confined to a wheelchair.

Sadly, the pandemic meant I could not keep my promise to be by her side. Because of a neighbor's kindness, though, we were able to see her on video and tell her we loved her. She had a rally of energy that day, one of her last, and I remember her smiling at us. I like to believe she chose her time to go, and sharing her story helps me replace my unfulfilled promise with something I think she would have liked … a story about her family and her legacy.

Inez Swanborough never called herself a leader, yet there is no doubt she was one. She was the purest definition of a servant leader—someone who enables others and puts their needs first. To be this kind of leader, you must draw on inner strength, have a clear sense of purpose, be a good listener, be supportive, unite people, and be the guardian of the values. She embodied all of that and more.

Three Things I Learned About Life and Leadership

1. Family comes first.
2. Humility is important.
3. Leadership doesn't "happen" within the leader; it occurs in the act of serving others.

***

The Illuminator: In Memory of Fortuna Samuel, My Mom

by Orly Maravankin, Ph.D., PCC, President and Founder, Edge Consulting

"She already got her medicine," I heard my sister, Becky, say to someone who entered my mother's hospital room. I was calling overseas from the U.S., monitoring the care for my mother, Fortuna, after she fell and broke her hip.

"No, you are wrong. These meds are for her," a heavily accented male voice replied. "I need to make sure she takes them."

"Actually, you are wrong," Becky shot back. "I have been here by her side the whole time. She already took them."

I heard the man speak again, now louder and more agitated. The argument escalated for another 15 minutes as I listened. Finally, a different voice cut through. This time female. "This isn't Fortuna's medication," the voice said. "It's for the patient next door."

I heard Becky exhale, relieved. So was I. The man, a nurse, apologized profusely, explaining how he was sleep-deprived from back-to-back night shifts.

We later learned the errant medication could have endangered my mother's life. Becky's vigilance averted a human error, saving our mom. Adding to the drama were the heightened tensions and deep mistrust simmering in the country between different ethnic groups, the fact that the male nurse belonged to one of those factions, and that the date was October 7, 2023.

Managing Distance and Disease

Miraculously, my mom made it through hip surgery. Released from the hospital, she moved in with my older sister, Hedi. A few months later, she contracted COVID-19 for the first time after three years of careful shielding. My sisters became her tireless angels, tending to her physical, emotional, and spiritual needs.

The distance between us was difficult. My mom often asked to see me, so I flew in for an extended stay. Despite her frailty, she was visibly excited to see me and her face would light up. For the two weeks, we shared stories, hugs, and precious moments that now felt like treasures.

Before I left, I gently stroked her hand and whispered, "I love you, Mom." In her kind, gentle voice, she replied, "It was so good to see you. You made me very happy. I hope to see you again." I smiled and said, "Of course, you will."

Mom survived hip surgery and the ordeal of COVID-19 only to face another cruel twist: a severe case of shingles. She experienced relentless pain that defied the limited relief medications could offer, and her doctors cautioned that stronger treatments might jeopardize her life. As the days wore on, though, the spark of her will to live seemed to dim.

My husband Gabriel and I flew back to see her. We were shocked to find she was a shadow of her former physical self, weak and fragile. She barely spoke. Over the next two weeks, she would occasionally glance at me and say, "Come back home," repeating it like a mantra. She had never questioned my decision to stay in the U.S. before. Yet, in the last month of her life, she returned to those words again and again, revealing the pain that me living far away must have caused her—a pain that she had long hidden, perhaps even from herself.

After two weeks together, the time for me and Gabriel to leave arrived. Mom, despite her exhaustion, summoned every ounce of strength to stay awake for 90 precious minutes, just to be with us. As we said our goodbyes, the weight of the moment was almost unbearable—it felt so hard to walk away.

Final Moments, Lasting Impressions

Over the next several months, my mom's condition continued to worsen, and she seemed to shift into varying levels of consciousness. A beloved matriarch of a large tribe, my mother received many messages from family and friends, some of them recorded. My sisters would play these messages for her, and she would nod faintly as family members shared stories and expressed their love. When messages from her grandchildren played, she would lift a hand gently to her lips, as if to blow them kisses.

My mom passed away at home—as she wished—on July 3, 2024, surrounded by my sisters. In her final moments, a baby-naming ceremony for her great-grandson was taking place. My sister, Hedi, connected via Zoom to the event, turned up the volume so Mom could hear the ceremony in real-time. Unaware of my mom's imminent passing, my niece Maia named her baby boy after his great-grandmother, at the exact moment my mom took her last breath. Mom was gone.

In keeping with her faith, Mom was buried just a few hours after her passing. Living overseas, we couldn't arrive in time and had to join the funeral service virtually. Despite the short notice, many people from across the country came to honor this extraordinary woman, my mom.

Mom's Life

Fortuna Samuel grew up in the 1940s, an era defined by the upheaval of war, uncertainty, and resource scarcity. As the eldest daughter in her family, she faced tremendous responsibility at a young age. When her father passed away unexpectedly, she was just 15 years old. Suddenly, she found herself stepping into the role of caregiver for her ailing mother and five younger siblings.

Determined to provide for her family, Fortuna learned to sew and took on various odd jobs while attending school. She later became a nurse, a role she continued after marrying my father, and dedicated herself to both her patients and her family—until the birth of her second daughter, me.

Though gentle and soft-spoken, my mother possessed an incredible inner strength that carried her through hard times. Her quiet determination and resilience were the foundation of our home, where she nurtured us and created beauty as an exceptional cook and talented dressmaker, among other things. She could transform simple ingredients into delicious meals and vibrant fabrics into stunning clothes. Our home was routinely alive with the sounds of uncles, aunts, cousins, and friends. You could often hear multiple languages spoken—a reflection of our diverse heritage.

I have vivid memories of her weekly sewing gatherings with my aunt Allegra. I would come home from school to the warmth of her embrace, the inviting aroma of their cooking, and a dining table covered with colorful fabrics. Together, my mom and aunt would pore over fashion magazines, sketching designs that would later come to life as beautiful garments for themselves and their daughters.

A Way with Words

My mom's nurturing nature was not just limited to us. Even as a child I could sense that she was what I'd call today "an illuminator." Through her way of being in the world, she made people feel seen, valued, and cared for. She had a

way with idioms, using them to teach lessons and inspire us to live meaningful lives. She lived her life by those idioms and set examples for us. After her
passing, I developed a fuller appreciation for how deeply these idioms (three of
which I share here) shaped my life and leadership.

> *"If I am not for myself, who will be for me? And being for my own self, what
> am I?"*
>
> (Hillel, BCE)[3]

My mom exemplified resilience and self-reliance, continuously learning and
adapting. In the face of challenges, she drew on her skills and utilized external
resources. When life tested her—such as when she became a young widow—
she made astute financial decisions and emerged stronger.

Her strength was rooted in:

- **A deep sense of purpose**—a spiritual person, she was guided by a purpose
  greater than herself and a strong commitment to make a difference in the
  lives of others.
- **Perspective**—in both success and failure, she'd say, "Honey day, lemon
  day," reminding us of life's impermanence and the importance of staying
  grounded through life's highs and lows.

> "Who is rich? Those who are happy with what they have."
>
> (Pirkei Avot 4:1)[4]

My mom embraced this philosophy with a fantastic attitude: "I will be happy
now." Modest by nature, she found joy in life's blessings. Her deep sense of
gratitude allowed her to turn her focus outward, always seeking ways to help
others. Whether offering warm hugs, caring for those in need, preparing meals,
or crafting beautiful garments for special occasions, she was a constant giver.
She believed in sharing what little she had with others. She often said, "You
never know who you are going to touch."

> "Life and death are in the power of the tongue."
>
> (Proverbs 18:21)[5]

My mom understood the weight of words—their power to uplift or harm.
She rejected gossip, spoke sparingly, and chose her words with care, often to
encourage and support. "The most important words we say are those we say
to ourselves," she'd remind us, intuitively sensing that our self-talk shapes our
identity and how we engage with the world. She urged us to be both honest
and gentle with ourselves.

Additional Lessons

My mom also taught me much about gratitude, resilience, and the transformative power of words.

Gratitude. Inspired by my mom's profound sense of gratitude, I've built a daily gratitude practice that anchors me through life's ups and downs. When faced with setbacks, this ritual shifts my focus from what's going wrong to what's still going right. This practice not only keeps me grounded but also reminds me of the positive impact I can make.

Resilience. When I was 23, my husband and I moved to the U.S. to pursue our doctoral studies, a challenging journey that took us far from family and familiar support. Soon after, we welcomed our first child, Micah, and I was determined to create a thriving environment for our growing family. Following my mom's resilient path, I built a support network to help me balance part-time work, demanding studies, and parenting. Today, as an executive coach, I help leaders build resilience as a core quality that distinguishes thriving people from those who languish.

Power of Words. My mom taught me that words are a powerful weapon, capable of shaping reality and influencing those we speak to. She emphasized that when we speak, we breathe life into our thoughts, so we must choose our words carefully and listen deeply. Guided by her wisdom, I now coach leaders to use language that builds trust, fosters connection, and resolves conflicts while avoiding triggering words. I've seen firsthand how the right words can transform relationships and enhance leadership effectiveness.

In her passing, Mom imparted one final, profound lesson: the importance of processing emotions as they arise.

Emotional Awareness. I have long known that unresolved issues can linger in the subconscious, but I have gained a deeper understanding of how they can surge unexpectedly in moments of vulnerability. For my mom, the pain of having me so far away was a burden she quietly carried, never sharing it. Through this, I've come to realize the value of facing intense emotions and embracing difficult conversations—no matter how uncomfortable they may be.

My mom, Fortuna, embodied the fortune her name evokes to those fortunate enough to be around her. She named me Orly, meaning "light," and taught me that light isn't meant to be kept—it's meant to be shared. In life and in her passing, she remains my guiding light.

> ## Three Things I Learned About Life and Leadership
>
> 1. Count your blessings—celebrate your blessings and give generously to others.
> 2. Live with resilience—face challenges head-on, maintain perspective, and move forward stronger than before.
> 3. Choose your words wisely—speak with kindness to uplift, and balance honesty with empathy when engaging in hard conversations.

✳✳✳

Las Tres Ranas (The Three Frogs)

by Sade Salazar, MBA Student, Binghamton University School of Management

Blanca Arrona Sanchez was my loving grandmother, my friend, and my inspiration for much of my early years. She was known as "Meche" by her five children, "Killos" by her two sisters, and "Doña Blanquita" by those who respected her.

During my younger years, she often took on a maternal role while my mother worked grueling overtime shifts. We became nearly inseparable.

Her impact on my life is unforgettable. Not a day goes by when I don't think of her warmth and her smile—and not a day goes by when I don't dwell on the what-ifs and circumstances surrounding her passing.

This essay is dedicated to the lessons she taught me during my turbulent youth, where she served as a beacon of stability in uncertain times.

Wisdom and Wonder

My grandmother was known for being compassionate, empathetic, and wise. She started her career by studying Mathematical Physics at the Meritorious Autonomous University of Puebla (BUAP). In her early years, she taught life skills and crafts to physically impaired individuals between the ages of 18 and 60. During her free time, she would often work on oil paintings or attend metaphysics discussion groups in secret to further develop her philosophical ideas.

My grandmother was also a spiritual person. Living her college years in Mexico during the chaotic and repressive 1970s exposed her to numerous old and new age theologies. She would read dense tomes—ranging from thick novels to metaphysical explorations spanning thousands of pages—in between cooking, sewing, or looking after me. She was also an avid alien enthusiast. Often, in my adult years, I would wake up to a bizarre link in my email to a photoshopped UFO only hours after a deep and thought-provoking conversation with her about the nature of the universe.

When I was around six, I began to ask more intricate questions about life. They were the kinds of questions that have no right or wrong answers. One day I asked her, "Why are there bad people in the world?" Instead of answering, she simply told me, "You'll be able to answer those questions yourself one day."

While I wasn't able to understand the wisdom behind her words at the time, I understand now. Everyone has different perspectives and beliefs, and as I get older, I realize that not everyone truly understands this. Some are more eager to cast everything as black and white, leading to preconceived notions, often to their detriment.

My grandmother was most passionate about truly listening to people, a skill that I've tried to harness the older I get. In our workplaces and even in our personal lives, we tend to make quick assumptions based on surface level information. We don't truly listen. Biases cloud our judgments; rumors influence our actions—but they never swayed my grandmother. Now, as I delve deeper into the world of leadership, I want to influence others to remain clear-minded and open.

Speak No, Hear No, See No

A strong memory I have is of my grandmother sewing a dress at home. I am sitting next to her as I pull out my own crafts. She is surrounded by things that matter most to her, such as her sewing box, books, glasses, and pictures of family. Although material items, these are her outlets for conversation and seeing others clearly. She also has three little green frogs on her bookshelf. One is covering its eyes, one its mouth, and the other covering its ears.

I recall how, on more than one occasion, she pointed to these frogs and asked me, "Do you know what the frogs represent?" Of course, when I was very young, I had no idea, so I told her as much. "The frogs represent 'speak no evil, hear no evil, and see no evil,'" she would explain, adding that they were from a Japanese proverb and that they have been the focus of many interpretations throughout history.

My grandmother explained how some interpret the "see no evil" frog as turning a blind eye to anything bad. However, she believed its meaning was more metaphorical, emphasizing the importance of not perceiving negativity when encountering something we don't understand or agree with.

Similarly, she saw the "hear no evil" frog as a reminder to be mindful of the environments we place ourselves in regarding negativity. For example, you might be in a setting where you have to listen, but that doesn't mean the message is meant for you or should be taken to heart. Ultimately, you get to decide what you hear and what you let others hear about you.

To her, the "speak no evil" frog represented the control we have over what we say. It can affect others who don't follow the philosophy of the frogs and can cast you in a negative light. She would advise me that when listening to others, it's best to stay open-minded but not easily influenced or reactive.

The Unexpected

My grandmother passed away unexpectedly on June 20, 2024. I received the news via text after not answering my phone. With my family being scattered all over the world, our most effective means to connect is often through text message, when prescheduled phone calls and video chats aren't possible.

Being miles away from any family, I sat alone in a dimly lit room to process the moment. As I called my uncles and aunts to check on them, I noticed their emotions and reactions varied. Some felt deep anguish, while others sprang into action by organizing funeral arrangements, travel, and flowers. Others cried when reliving fond memories or contemplating unresolved conflicts or grudges they may have had with her.

Like me, my mother didn't cry until she saw my grandmother's casket. In that moment, I realized that her passing reinforced her teachings—that everyone has their reasons for viewing life (and death) a certain way, which ultimately influences their behaviors and attitudes toward themselves and others.

What She Left Behind

The day after my grandmother passed, I met with Ian Ziskin, lead author of this book and a mentor who has consistently reminded me of my potential and the possibilities I can create. Meeting so soon after my grandmother's passing—mapping and discussing my goals and plans for the future with his guidance—was a poignant reminder that life has to be lived, even when a pillar of its foundation is suddenly gone. At the time, I wondered if I should let my foundation crumble or rebuild it with careful reflection?

After someone's death, if we let our emotions overshadow us, we can forget how instrumental they have been in structuring our pillars. My grandmother left me with bright, hopeful eyes for the future. She left me with a curiosity to learn more about the world and others. During our last interaction, she told me she couldn't wait to see my vision for the future come to fruition. She wouldn't have wanted me to reschedule my time with Ian. She would've wanted her departure to help me remember my purpose.

I returned to my internship after only two days, still in shock and disbelief. I hadn't yet processed her passing fully. As I sat at my desk, I saw a reminder from her on my phone. I couldn't help but think, "So that's it? Am I really meant to go on filling out spreadsheets as though nothing happened?"

An irreplaceable person in my life was gone, leaving a void that made such tasks feel mundane and hollow. Who would I now call on a random Tuesday night when I wanted family recipes or to hear family stories? Part of me felt lost. Tasks I didn't particularly enjoy, briefly, felt unimportant.

In the first days after she passed, I was distraught. My recent conversations were too fresh and her presence too ingrained in my mind to comprehend that she was really gone. As the weeks passed, though, I began to reflect on what she left behind. I also began to adopt her thought processes almost subconsciously—at work, at school, and even with strangers on the bus. We all have people who were once part of our lives who left one way or another, either through death or on their own terms. They shape or mold us as we grow, but we don't always realize—or we forget—that this applies to everyone else around us, too.

One day, soon after she passed, I took a break from my studies to look out the window of the seventeenth floor, realizing more than ever that I wanted a more interactive experience of the world. I wanted to expand my horizons and let risks and opportunities build my life. I wanted to delve into my emotions but channel them toward my education and passion to drive change—something she had always wished she had devoted more time to doing.

Shortly after her funeral, my uncle sent me a journal she had written about me. I was only three years old when she started writing it. In the journal, she described me and my idiosyncrasies in detail, reminding me of where I started. Some of these traits are still accurate today. My grandmother's serene awareness of others and the world around her afforded me a profound sense of safety as she raised me—another instrumental part of the pillars she built.

Embracing Selflessness

In life and death, my grandmother taught me new ideas to apply to leadership. Some were more obvious, while others were more subtle.

Her generous nature inclined her to prioritize the needs of others before her own. While she was in college, the suspension of a car her father was repairing collapsed, crushing his leg and resulting in amputation. As the eldest of three sisters, she became head of the household. Unable to afford the cost of tuition and supplies, she dropped out of school.

By trying to care for others, my grandmother had to let go of many of her own dreams and aspirations. And as her life grew more complicated, her goals seemed to become increasingly humanitarian. She would advise others to look inwards, while at the same time she took on everyone else's burdens—something that was not sustainable as she aged and health problems ensued.

It's not uncommon for people to shoulder too much, often to their own detriment. Even those who are well-liked can inadvertently leave negative imprints. As a child, I often overheard my aunts and uncles speak of the lingering pain left behind because my grandmother's selflessness meant she sometimes set aside their needs for comfort and care as children. Perhaps the lesson to be learned is that we sometimes need to trust that a lighter touch can nurture growth and bring greater harmony for all.

Through her keen, bright green eyes my grandmother could see people for who they truly are. This gift endeared her to many. Those who met her felt seen, heard, and understood. In a world filled with clashing views and opinions, few possessed my grandmother's ability to step back, set aside differences, and see through the eyes of others.

At times, some in my family viewed her as a "black sheep" because she opened her heart to others they felt were undeserving. I believe she did this right up until her last days because she felt every soul was worthy of kindness and forgiveness—that we all carry our own wounds while, at our most fundamental, we remain human.

Enduring Lessons

The first lesson I took away from my grandmother's passing was to reflect on emotions. Sometimes fewer spoken words or actions can convey messages or accomplish goals more effectively. With self-reflection, we can consider consequences without angst or impulsivity. A lack of emotional reflection can have negative effects in the long run.

The second lesson is that presence—the ability to inspire confidence, trust, and respect in others—always matters. Everybody brings a unique role, personality, and energy to a relationship. It's this energy, whether positive or negative, that has the power to create change. We must be cognizant of who people truly are. Humans are pattern seeking creatures. We like to make quick categorizations, so we're swift to judge. However, with practice we can learn self-restraint. After all, in leadership, we must communicate, listen to, and consider all feedback to create change. Being present is essential for making others feel they can come to you no matter what the situation.

The third lesson is to remember yourself. Helping others is a noble and selfless pursuit, but you can't pour from an empty cup. Seek support when you need it. Cultivate relationships with people who can remind you of your essence. This synergy will fuel you and may help others in your support network. Know that one day, we will look back at our lives and either wonder where our dreams went or be satisfied with the outcomes we've achieved. The choice of which path we take lies within ourselves.

Three Things I Learned About Life and Leadership

1. Reflect daily.
2. Practice presence—it matters.
3. Remember yourself.

***

Lead with Heart, Discernment, and Compassion

by Michele Stowe, Executive Coach, Speaker, and Founder, SkyRocket Coaching

Sister Lillian Murphy never smoked a day in her life, yet it was lung cancer that was killing her. She lived in San Francisco and I resided in Colorado. During phone conversations, I noticed her voice getting softer, but never shaky. I was certain she'd beat this—and so was she.

While Sister Lillian was in treatment, my mother passed away suddenly. Not realizing how frail Sister Lillian was, I asked her to come to Colorado to offer a prayer at my mother's memorial service.

"Of course, Michele. It would be my honor," she replied, her voice never wavering.

With the support of our friends and colleagues, Sister Lillian pulled together her reserves to travel from San Francisco to Denver.

With Strength and Faith

Sister Lillian had always struck an imposing figure. She was tall, strong, confident, and beautiful. She literally took charge of every room she entered.

While the woman who walked into my mother's memorial service was still every bit the confident Sister Lillian I knew, cancer had clearly gained the upper hand. There she stood, my mentor, friend, boss, and leadership icon, comforting me and my family as she faced the inevitable next chapter of her own story with strength and faith intertwined.

With strength and faith is precisely how Sister Lillian led Mercy Housing, the nation's largest affordable housing nonprofit, as its CEO for nearly 25 years. I worked with Sister Lillian for 10 years as her COO, and every day I knew how fortunate I was to be part of her team and learn from her. She was fierce, had a dry wit, and was supremely quotable. As an introvert, she chose her words and her delivery of them very carefully.

Sister Lillian passed away just a few weeks after my mother's service. These two women left an indelible mark on my heart, and it was heartbreaking to lose them both in the same year.

In the five years since Sister Lillian's passing, I have noticed how many colleagues, friends, and associates still quote her, mention her name, and speak about her way of leading as an example they continue to aspire to. It has only been since her passing that I have realized the scope and extent of her impact on three generations of leaders in affordable housing.

Assume Positive Intent

More than 200 people attended Sister Lillian's memorial service. Every attendee received a memorial card and a button imprinted with the words "Assume Positive Intent."

These three words captured Sister Lillian's approach to the complexity of relationships embedded in the work we did. Building affordable housing required bringing together partners with different motivations, goals, and personalities.

Sister Lillian built Mercy Housing from its origins as a handful of affordable housing properties scattered across Nebraska and Idaho into the nation's largest affordable housing developer, owner, and manager.

To have any success at all, she knew that we had to start from an earnest place of listening and understanding, to assume positive intent, and to give others the grace and dignity not to be perfect. Whether we were talking to community members, bankers, auditors, donors, investors, or employees, assuming positive intent could only help us understand one another better so that we could get down to the hard work of building the housing our communities so desperately needed.

Within my first month on the job, I witnessed first-hand the power of "Assume Positive Intent." Developing affordable housing required strong partnerships with investors and banks in order to have enough capital to buy the land, build the building, and pay the staff. In 2009, big banks were making the news for receiving "too big to fail" bailout money and I was struggling to identify any positive intent in their partnership interests with Mercy Housing. I shared this concern with Sister Lillian as we entered a meeting with one of the big banks Mercy Housing had worked with for years. Sister Lillian smiled wryly at me and said, "I have an idea that may help you see the positive intent in the room."

After welcoming our guests, Sister Lillian asked each of us to introduce ourselves and share one reflection on why we were in this meeting to help support the development of affordable housing for American families. One by one, our banking partners told stories of their personal experiences with poverty, hunger, and homelessness. With this simple exercise, Sister Lillian shifted the energy in the room, not just for me, but also for the banking partners. They had worked with each other for years, and many of them did not know these personal stories. It grounded us that day in the work we were doing and certainly opened my eyes and heart to the possibilities of working with banking partners going forward.

Make Hard Decisions and Stay True to Your Core Values

By 2005, Mercy Housing was a $2 billion organization. It had operations in 45 distinct markets with a loose affiliation of leaders and little infrastructure. Mercy Housing was big, getting bigger, and it was messy. We were at an inflection point all too common with fast-growing organizations. The value of our size was lost within our disorganization, and we struggled to realize the benefit of our scale. Sister Lillian knew something had to change, so she engaged the support of two experts who could support her in exploring what to do next.

Sister Lillian involved the entire leadership team in the discernment process. She ultimately concluded that Mercy Housing would need to be restructured into five core markets. This was a heavy lift. It meant hiring executive talent from for-profit real estate organizations—something that made many in the organization question if Mercy Housing had lost its moral compass. One of the experts Sister Lillian had hired advised that the recommended changes could be implemented in about six months.

Once committed to this course of action, this change initiative was named, "The Transformation." Sister Lillian personally communicated the long-term vision and value of the changes with leaders and their teams. She reflected on how these changes would support the future growth of Mercy Housing. Speaking with many employees about how the changes would take place, she ensured the plan was consistent with the core values of respect, justice, and mercy.

Little by little, the changes envisioned began to take hold. Sister Lillian was there every step of the way—at town halls, communicating via all-employee newsletters, and meeting one-on-one with impacted employees to ease their concerns and help them settle into the many organizational changes.

With every new leader hired, Sister Lillian would embark on a road show, introducing them personally to staff and partners. In 2009, some four years after The Transformation began, an exhausted Sister Lillian shared the enormity of this journey with me when I was hired. In a candid moment, as she recalled the conversations she had when The Transformation was conceived, Sister Lillian shared that she had asked the consultant why he hadn't told her the changes would take much longer than six months. "Well, Sister Lillian," he replied, "if I had told you it would take five years, I am afraid you would have never done it."

Sister Lillian could have made the decision for The Transformation all by herself. She could have led the change from a corner office far away from employees. She could have saved herself a great deal of travel, time, and heartache by taking the easier and less personal route of sending written communications out to her team. She could have … but she didn't.

Her dedication to discernment, careful consideration of her plans, and willingness to walk side-by-side with affected employees through all the changes were exactly what made The Transformation a success. Now, 20 years later, Sister Lillian's legacy lives on. Mercy Housing is a $3 billion non-profit organization with 2,000+ employees and more than 47,000 individuals housed. The organizational structure that she introduced, with such care and discernment, is still intact and driving the organization into the foreseeable future.

Demonstrate Compassion by Taking Care of Ourselves and Each Other

The work of affordable housing is hard. At the property level, it means working with individuals at times when they are most vulnerable. Sister Lillian ensured that the organization concentrated its efforts on people in every way—through a fair compensation philosophy, generous benefits plan, in-house training, and leadership development.

While many leaders and organizations check these boxes and think their work is done, what set Sister Lillian apart is that she connected personally about this message of self-care with the board, staff, and community partners.

In every conversation, she would say, "This work is hard. Please remember to take care of yourselves and take care of each other." This repetition worked. Leaders within Mercy Housing began saying these same words and employees would say them to each other. Sister Lillian created the expectation of a culture of caring simply by repeating her expectations and hopes for each of us.

Sister Lillian modeled this behavior by taking two weeks every year to go on retreat with her Sisters of Mercy community. During that time, she was fully out of contact—recharging and reconnecting with her community and faith while stepping outside the crushing pressure of her CEO position. As leaders, actions speak louder than words, and Sister Lillian showed us all the power of role modeling this self-care for our teams. Years later, those of us who worked with Sister Lillian still reach out with these words of compassion.

A Lasting Impression

Sister Lillian left an indelible mark on the world of affordable housing. Many years after her passing, leaders still quote her. They bring Sister Lillian's compassion into the room with the request to take care of each other. They bring her focus on core values into their decision-making processes. And they bring her positive intent into conversations that benefit a whole community by finding common ground and giving grace.

In comforting my father when my mother died, Sister Lillian encouraged him to move through his grief and remain grounded in the here and now. She told my father that, "Life is for the living." Indeed. By inspiring many of us to lead with heart, discernment, and compassion, Sister Lillian continues to live on in our hearts and in the hearts of those we lead.

Three Things I Learned About Life and Leadership

1. Assume positive intent.
2. Make hard decisions and stay true to your core values.
3. Demonstrate compassion by taking care of ourselves and each other.

The Love in Leadership

by Shannon Wallis, President, Cascade Leadership

How can she even be alive?

My mother, Patricia Gray, lay in the hospital bed, pale and unmoving. Her blood pressure was dangerously low. We were at Evergreen Hospital outside of Seattle. The nurse asked me to step aside so she could tilt my mother's head down lower than her heart in an effort to try and raise her blood pressure.

As I stepped aside to let the nurse work, my mother's doctor hurried into the room. "We are moving her to ICU," he said. "And we need to go over her plan for resuscitation one more time."

My heart sank. Less than an hour before, I had spoken to my brother-in-law who managed facilities for two large hospitals. "Well, at least she isn't in ICU," he had reassured me. "Most people don't come out of there." Devastated, I began to wonder, is this it?

Always the Survivor

My mother has always been a survivor. "Against all odds" could be her middle name. Born Patricia Gray on April 1, 1940, she was truly a miracle baby, entering the world after her mother endured eight miscarriages.

A precocious, charismatic child, life never seemed to give my mother a break. At seven, suffering from terrible asthma, she developed pneumonia and nearly died. She was hospitalized for more than a month and given life-saving penicillin, the first antibiotic of its kind. Unfortunately, she developed a terrible allergy to penicillin and nearly died again when she was nine years old from the very same life-saving drug.

Obviously, she survived, growing to become a mother of four children. I am her oldest. Our life was intensely challenging. My father, a serious alcoholic, didn't help make things any easier.

"Life is tricky," my mother liked to say. Eventually, she found the courage to divorce him, but his absence left our family in a precarious position. As a single parent without a college education, she could only find minimum-wage jobs, which meant she raised all of us under the poverty line. Her income covered the mortgage on our modest home, but very little else.

We received government assistance for food, healthcare, and heat. Still, she kept the thermostat at 58 degrees Fahrenheit during the brutal South Dakota winters because that was what she could afford. When her station wagon finally died, she walked or rode her bike to work. When my siblings and I complained or cried one Christmas because we didn't get real presents, she still gave us hand-drawings she created for each of us.

Elusive Dreams

My mother was an amazing artist and illustrator who specialized in drawing children and characters. She routinely made drawings for friends and created her own cards. Often, she talked about launching a line of cards, and this diamond of an idea kept hope alive in our family. One day, she would "hit it big" and our problems would be over. She had beautiful plans for what we would do with the money. Beyond taking care of our needs, she'd create a company called God's Shop, where people just like us could shop without paying for the household items they would need.

She thought beyond us. She thought big. She thought of making a difference.

Unfortunately, the line of cards and God's Shop never came to pass. Like many women before her, my mother was riddled with fear, self-doubt, and a belief that her ideas—and therefore she—just weren't good enough. She couldn't see a step-by-step way out. She didn't know how to start, so she'd quit before beginning.

It's hard to self-actualize when you are fighting for basic survival needs like food, clothing, and shelter. As a teenager, I was painfully disappointed, embarrassed, and even ashamed that my mother never realized her dreams. I lost my patience with her and her inability to follow through on her line of cards.

Ironically, this disappointment would fuel my desire to make a difference later. As an adult, I have compassion for her younger self. She did her absolute best just to keep us together with very little support and no one to mentor her or nurture her ideas. Her challenges have informed my work and how I support my clients. I focus on not only inspiring others never to give up but also on giving them a roadmap to achieve their dreams.

Belief in Others

While my mother didn't believe in herself, she believed in others. She not only believed each of us was uniquely gifted but also seemed to think everyone else was too. Even when their flaws emerged, she'd say "That is their behavior; it isn't who they are. When someone acts like that, ask yourself, 'What happened to them that caused them to behave that way?'"

Even when her friend's son went to prison, she continually told us, "That was his behavior, it isn't who he is." She had a term for her perspective, "underlooking." She prayed for him and wrote to him and celebrated with him when he was finally released and turned his life around.

Today I call her perspective, "Everyone has a story," but when I was a teenager, I hated it. I would want to be justifiably angry at someone I thought had wronged me, only to be humbled when she'd say, "You need to underlook them Shannon." Now, as a leadership consultant, I tell my clients and own teenage children virtually the same thing: "You have to look deeper and with compassion for what is truly driving their behavior."

Believing in others was also a reflection of her faith. One thing that was constant throughout her life was prayer. She would tell you that she didn't think much of the Catholic Church she was raised in, but she loves Jesus a lot, and in the midst of her many challenges, she always prayed the rosary. She didn't just pray for herself. Mostly, she prayed for others. Over time, I came to believe that her prayers could work miracles and asked her to pray the rosary for my friends who were in need. It seemed like she had a direct line to God.

Fighting the Odds

After my siblings and I completed college, she moved back to her hometown of Seattle. One September afternoon at a Mariner's game, she was hit by a foul ball that detached her retina. "It was truly a miracle," she told me later. "Neither my 80-year-old friend on my right nor the two-year-old toddler to my left had been hit. That would have been a travesty; I don't see how they could have survived."

When she was in her sixties, she was diagnosed with Stage 4 uterine cancer that had spread to her lymph glands and ribcage. With a 5% probability of surviving five years, she fought the odds and won.

The years went by—15 to be exact. Then, in October 2016, she had a major stroke, collapsing in her home just as she was starting to dress for the day. Naked, she lay on the cold tile floor for 12 hours until I found her. She survived that as well.

Next came pneumonia in March of 2017, which led to a four-week hospital stay and the news of a new heart condition that was so challenging her doctor told me to call my siblings and urge them to fly to Seattle. I will never forget the moment he looked me in the eyes and, with compassion, said, "This could be a very hard day." It was a Friday in April.

Miraculously, my mother defied the odds once more, escaping the death grip of the ICU. Nearly eight years later, she is still with us—but her life is a shadow of what it once was. The stroke and ICU visit left a devastating mark. She has never regained her vitality, and her cognition is slowly slipping away.

On her better days, her gifts still shine. She'll trace a piece of prior artwork to create a birthday card for a grandchild; she'll marvel at how special and unique each of her children, their spouses, and her grandchildren are, certain that each is about to change the world. She still spends every morning in prayer telling me that we must also pray for those we don't like because we just don't know what happened to them.

My mother may have never opened a brick-and-mortar store called God's Shop, but to this day, even in her more difficult moments, she is still offering gifts to everyone around her. Much of what I have learned about leadership and put into practice with my own teams and clients over the years started at home with her.

Three Things I Learned About Life and Leadership

1. Leadership is about love and service to others.
2. Find, spotlight, and amplify the special gifts in everyone.
3. Always bring compassion to look more deeply for what drives people's behavior.

***

Sparkle, Brilliance, and Fire

by Samantha Wasserman, MA, President, Growth Curve Consulting and Coaching

Seeing the familiar Dr. Pepper bottling site from my backseat window, I could feel my excitement climb. This was the landmark that told me we were close. We then saw the stately campus of Southern Methodist University and heard the familiar hum of cicadas resonating through the muggy Dallas air.

The combination of sensations coming through the car window enveloped me like a protective blanket. Soon we would arrive at the home of my grandparents, Frank Henry and Elizabeth Dadik Thomas. Best of all, we would get to see what was new in my grandfather's workshop.

Human Sparkle

My grandparents met in Akron, Ohio, married there, and had twin girls, one of whom would become my mother decades later. Frank moved to Dallas in December 1941. His wife and girls followed as soon as he had saved enough money for a down payment on a little white house.

Like many salesmen in his field at that time, my grandfather needed alternative work when his employer, Seiberling Tire company, repurposed their products to support the war effort. Having risen to the top of Seiberling's sales organization due to his naturally affable personality, my grandfather applied his ability to recognize and bring out a special sparkle in others to future roles.

Everyone who encountered my grandfather sensed something unique about him. He felt that everyone he met was worth beholding and worthy of his complete attention—like a fine jewel prized for its rarity. His enormous blue eyes seemed to amplify his pure absorption in the person in front of him. His interactions seemed reserved for them only, so it's no wonder he was a top salesperson in his company.

Frank's focus on others showed up in many ways: his strong relationships with customers, his generosity creating objects of beauty for his family, and his availability to his church community to problem solve when needed. He offered his time to his church so generously that his wife, Betty, often wondered when he would be available to fix things around their own home!

My grandfather loved juicy problems as much as he enjoyed helping the people he cared for to solve them in innovative ways. He did this just by being himself: a man genuinely interested in his neighbors while sharing enthusiastically in their common interests.

How he nurtured his relationships, at work and elsewhere, helped him to expand his customer base while simultaneously allowing him to be more present at home. He understood the need to deliver a quality product as well as to optimize time for everyone involved in the sales process. Long before the advent of e-commerce, upon receiving each order in person (all sales back then were done on site), he would call Betty with the information to expedite the completion of order forms. Betty would then mail the orders in as quickly as possible. This meant customers got their tires without any lag time and Frank was able to return home to focus on his beloved wife and twins.

He also brought his curiosity and creativity to his hobby of photography. He had a knack for capturing the special "somethingness" of people through the camera lens and the ability to teach others to do the same, which came as no surprise. In my work, I find that leaders rarely possess the ability to experience others deeply enough to see what is uniquely brilliant about them. The curiosity that enabled Frank to explore these deeper dimensions of others required observation, presence, and patience—skills that are hard to find in a society harried by time pressures.

A Curious Learner Strives Toward Mastery

After his tire sales job temporarily disappeared, Frank put his "superpower" of truly seeing others to work. He became the head of the camera department at Thermond Randels, a retailer in downtown Dallas. My grandfather's special lens through which he saw others was just one of the ways he applied his natural gifts to this new position. It also made him a perfect fit for the job.

Frank's curiosity and interest in others expanded during his time at Thermond Randels. His eye for photography was just one way in which his creative abilities surfaced. My grandfather quickly built relationships with the managers of adjacent stores. In particular, he developed a special friendship with the owner of a fine jewelry store nearby. As that friendship blossomed, Frank became an apprentice, learning everything there was to know about jewelry making.

What I remember most about my grandfather was his love for and knowledge of gemstones. He knew their types, sizes, shapes, depths, and color. Each stone had its own special sparkle. He would share how certain jewels possess "fire," a vibrancy and richness in their colors when stones capture the light. This fire could be drawn out of a stone based on its characteristics, cuts, and polish. He passed on his love of stones to me through my mother, and I am grateful that I have pieces to remind me of him.

Frank quickly learned an innovative molding technique where a designer could place molten metal in a centrifuge and spin the metal fast into a tube, molding the jewelry into whatever shape would position the stones most beautifully for maximum sparkle, brilliance, and fire. This method could shape rings, broaches, bracelets—nearly any setting for a gem.

Frank spent precious time with his daughters teaching them how to make jewelry. He would take them to his friend's jewelry workshop, which was filled with equipment and tools. There, my mother learned to use the tumbler to polish her chosen rocks and a special casting machine to mold gold and silver into objects that would serve as settings for the brilliant, sparkling, newly polished stones. A generation later, I remember my grandfather explaining to me how to make the colors in a stone dance.

Not only did jewelry making become one of Frank's most beloved hobbies, but he was also generous with what he created. He gave me signet and sapphire rings. He was always purchasing beautiful gifts for his wife whenever he traveled.

He was also generous with his knowledge and time. Since he taught his twins the art of jewelry making, my mother passed on to me the ability to spot finer antique cuts in gemstones. From my grandfather and mother, I have always learned new things about gemstones and the craft of jewelry making because of his curiosity and the passion he passed on to her.

Throughout his retirement, I remember him in his workshop, which he built right beside the little white house. Every time we visited, we would listen with excitement as he explained his plans for various new creations. The setting was rapturous to my sister and me: a workshop full of tools and gems, a small, white, southern house with a swinging porch bench on a massive lot, covered in thick green grass, old and weathered pecan trees, and more lightning bugs than a young girl could catch.

A Thirst for Innovation

Once Frank was on a tear with one of his hobbies, he would go full tilt toward innovation. That fire to learn, create, and innovate didn't end with nurturing relationships, capturing the best in people through a lens, or spinning gold and refining gemstones. Frank was a tireless student of others who were masters of their craft so that he could put his own talents to work creating and innovating. This craving for learning and innovation made him who he was.

Lawnmowers were an innovation in the 1950s. Having a massive plot of grassy land, these new inventions intrigued my grandfather. Having the curiosity to create things himself, he visited the local Sears & Roebuck to study the mechanics of the first lawnmower of its kind, promptly returning home to the same well-equipped workshop that held so much magic in spinning gold into jewelry. There he constructed his very own version of a lawnmower based on his notes, his memory, and his conversations with the salesperson at Sears.

Passing On

Spending time with my grandfather was one of my greatest joys. I had no idea those experiences would mean so much to me after his passing.

I will never forget attending school the day after I learned of his unexpected death. Inflammation in his lungs led to his heart failing. The person that gave me so much confidence in my own specialness was suddenly gone.

When my mother left for Dallas, I spent most of that cold October day in the girl's middle school restroom, hiding from the reality of a world without him in it. He was the first person close to me I had lost, and one of the most significant. Frank Henry Thomas died on October 25, 1983. I was 13 years old.

The image of my grandfather that remains is what most drew me to him: he took time to nurture relationships, and he saw beauty in the things he was most curious about. He loved to help people and solve complex problems. His gift was to perceive the unique sparkle, brilliance, and fire deep in the hearts of the people he met.

When he worked with others, he used his craft to mold, shape, and polish so they could shine like every piece of jewelry he made. This ability aligns with what a great leader does, no matter their role in life.

We all have an opportunity to see the brilliance, sparkle, and fire in others. This is an important facet of leadership. We can take every opportunity to be present, to see others through a lens that has the potential to bring out their dimensionality and colors, to shape how they shine, and to leave them better off by bringing out their sparkle.

Three Things I Learned About Life and Leadership

1. Use your lens to see the possibilities in each person you encounter.
2. Bring sparkle to your relationships; people remember how you make them feel, so be a gem.
3. Lead with fire in your belly and curiosity in your soul: master your craft and be generous in sharing it.

***

Notes

1. Tom Peters and Robert Waterman Jr., *In Search of Excellence: Lessons from America's Best-Run Companies* (New York: Harper & Row, 1982).
2. Randy Pausch and Jeffrey Zaslow, *The Last Lecture* (New York: Hyperion, 2008).
3. Hillel the Elder, "If I am not for myself, who will be for me? And being for my own self, what am I?" *Pirkei Avot* 1:14, in *The Talmud of the Land of Israel: A Preliminary Translation and Explanation*, trans. Heinrich Guggenheimer (Berlin: Walter de Gruyter, 2000).
4. Ben Zoma, "Who is rich? Those who are happy with what they have," *Pirkei Avot* 4:1, in *The Talmud of the Land of Israel: A Preliminary Translation and Explanation*, trans. Heinrich Guggenheimer (Berlin: Walter de Gruyter, 2000).
5. King Solomon, "Life and death are in the power of the tongue," Proverbs 18:21, in *Tanakh: The Holy Scriptures*, trans. Jewish Publication Society (Philadelphia: Jewish Publication Society, 1985).

Chapter 7

Curiosity (and Purpose)

Chapter 7 includes 10 essays that integrate the passions of lifelong curiosity and living with purpose. You will read stories that highlight themes such as live life to the fullest, find and pursue passions, keep learning, have a clear vision and values, be intentional about priorities and actions, be authentic, maintain a sense of humor, embrace each moment and experience, and live a life of no regrets.

The Giant: Anthony Andora, My Father

by Elizabeth Andora, Former SVP & CHRO, Maxar Technologies

"Tony Andora was a giant," a friend once said, describing my late father. He was the child of Italian immigrants who arrived in America in the early twentieth century. For those who knew him, he stood small in stature but was larger than life in every other way.

Facing Hardship Head-On

My dad had a simple childhood. He grew up in a modest home during the Great Depression where making ends meet was a challenge. His parents, my "Pop Pop" (grandfather) and my "Nonni" (grandmother), faced widespread discrimination as Italian immigrants, encountering frequent prejudice and hostility. Throughout their lives, they held various jobs, primarily working in factories in Paterson, New Jersey.

I recall my dad telling me stories about how Italian immigrants, even in his time, were considered the lowest form of immigrants. My mother—a child of Irish immigrants—shared that when she chose to marry my dad her family expressed concern about how society would treat them as a mixed ethnic couple.

DOI: 10.4324/9781003585633-11

Despite such challenges, my dad was surrounded and supported by a strong community of family and friends who genuinely believed the United States would provide them opportunities the old world could not. As a product of this environment, Dad believed in possibilities and never took them for granted. He held a strong ethos of giving back to the community and aimed to have a positive impact on the world.

Finding a Sense of Mission

Tony was born on November 20, 1930, in Paterson, New Jersey. He was an adventurous hard-working little boy, the pride and joy of his mother. He had a younger sister, Joan, who idolized him.

Dad loved school and seeking challenges. He was passionate about the Boy Scouts and earned his Eagle Scout at 15. As a youngster, he held jobs typical of his age, such as newspaper boy. As he got older, though, he assumed jobs that demonstrated resourcefulness. This included being a door-to-door salesman, first selling vacuum cleaners and later women's makeup. (The notion of my dad selling makeup makes me laugh, even to this day. If you knew my dad, makeup or anything about women's hygiene was not on the top of his list. I like to think that maybe the experience primed him to become the father of four daughters!)

Becoming the first in his family to graduate from Rutgers University and later earning a law degree from New York University made his parents proud.

After graduating, he served as an attorney in the U.S. Army Judge Advocate General's Office in Germany. He often told my mom—and she would share with us—that he was instantly drawn to the Army and the work he did in Germany. He loved the structure, discipline, and sense of mission that the Army embodied. Perhaps, for the first time, he felt he could do his best work without the burden of being judged by his ethnicity.

Travel was not a privilege he experienced as a child, so the Army also exposed him to new cultures and languages in ways he hadn't experienced growing up. In Germany, he embraced the people, learned their language and customs, and developed a deep appreciation for cultural differences. He remained close to his German friends for the rest of his life.

A Lifetime Pursuit

My dad's sense of duty and purpose continued after returning home from Germany, serving as a county prosecutor and later as Deputy Attorney General for the State of New Jersey. While he found the work fulfilling, it wasn't exactly what he had envisioned for his life, so he transitioned into private practice. From there, his journey expanded. He entered politics, became an entrepreneur by founding several businesses, and actively engaged with various nonprofits, from hospitals to educational institutions.

I could list many more of my dad's professional accomplishments, but I think you're getting a sense of who he was. Tony was a man who truly lived life. He continued to pursue his passions until the very end, when it seems like he simply ran out of time. Just before he died, he was racing to complete the Appalachian trail, learning how to play guitar, and was attending Columbia University, where he was pursuing his third postgraduate degree—this time in American History.

The Side of Dad I Saw

While others outside my family may remember the "serious, hardworking Tony," I knew a different side of him. He was often silly and playful. He loved to be outdoors exploring nature or competing on the tennis court.

He spent many weekends teaching us how to swim, play tennis, and ski on the East Coast. In the fall, he'd take us hiking on the Appalachian Trail. He was determined to complete the section from Maine to New Jersey.

We spent our summers traveling across the country in a paneled station wagon, towing a tent trailer so we could visit all the national parks. With five kids, we each had a role in setting up camp, and Dad—with his Army-trained precision—made sure we did it efficiently. Our winters were spent skiing, often in the Catskill Mountains in New York or the Green Mountains in Vermont. For a man who was inordinately busy, he was always present for us and gave us the gift of his time.

Dad could also be incredibly stubborn, non-communicative, and difficult. There were times when I felt I was in the Army with him, and he was our Lieutenant General. (Perhaps it comes with the territory.)

I felt the push to succeed; it was expected. But I knew he cherished us. He taught us the value of hard work, determination, self-reliance, and, most importantly, the profound meaning of family. Though he wasn't outwardly expressive, his love was obvious.

The Last Journey

During the winter of 2009, I was visiting my parents in New Jersey, making my frequent trips—often two to three times a year—from Colorado. While in his home office, Dad asked if my sisters, brother, and I were up for exploring Machu Picchu. By this time, most of us were married with children, but Dad wanted this excursion to be just for his children. Mom opted out.

In June 2009, we went with an outfitter that could accommodate our various needs. By this time, Dad's health had already started to decline, though we didn't yet fully understand the extent of it. What we hoped would be a fulfilling adventure turned out to be quite challenging. The high altitudes of the Peruvian cities took a toll on him, as he unknowingly battled a heart condition.

As we hiked through the ruins and explored the sites, it became clear that he was struggling. He grew agitated and wasn't his usual adventurous self. My sister expressed concern, but Dad pushed through, determined to complete the trip.

Still, it was hard for us to ignore that he was no longer the "go-getter" dad we all knew. Rife with moments of tension due to his declining health, the trip was bittersweet.

I remember saying goodbye to him at the airport. My sisters and Dad flew back to New Jersey, while my brother and I returned to Colorado. I left for Colorado with a mix of emotions: frustration over some disagreements, worry about his health, concern for our time together, and an overall sadness about how the trip had gone. Over time, I've come to appreciate the trip more. It turned out to be the last time we all had together where he was still mentally and physically present—and I cherish that we shared the experience.

When Dad returned to New Jersey, his health took a more serious turn. He began experiencing transient ischemic attacks (TIAs), or mini strokes. In August, while kayaking at the local lake, he had another TIA, this time with significant memory loss. Alarmed, my mother insisted he see a cardiologist immediately. The diagnosis was severe: he had a faulty aortic valve that allowed only a small amount of oxygen to reach his brain. The doctors recommended immediate heart surgery.

True to my parents' nature, they didn't share the gravity of the situation with us. In fact, my sister and I weren't even in town during the surgery because they downplayed the risks, assuring us all would be fine.

The surgery proved to be successful, so we were relieved. But five days later, everything changed. Dad suffered a massive stroke. For the next six weeks, nothing went as we hoped. While he regained some ability to recognize us, his communication and cognitive abilities were severely impaired. We started him in rehabilitation, but it quickly became apparent that recovery wasn't going well. His health continued to deteriorate as his heart issues and the stroke led to complications with his kidneys.

I never truly got a chance to say goodbye. I flew back after his massive stroke, but not before the surgery. During the long yet fleeting six-week period that followed, my brother and I returned to New Jersey three or four times to be with him. Each time, we experienced a rollercoaster of emotions—hope that he would pull through rehab, followed by the crushing realization that he was declining. After each glimmer of hope, we'd return to Colorado, only to find ourselves back on a plane as his condition grew worse, joining my sisters and Mom to support them. After three rounds of hopeful moments dashed by despair, we made our final trip.

Two weeks later, with Dad intubated and on dialysis, the six of us made the painful decision to remove him from life support. Surrounded by love, he slipped away peacefully.

Dad passed away at 78, which was far too soon for me.

Lessons Beyond Life

After his passing, as I approached milestones in my life, assumed larger career roles, and while my girls were still very young, I found myself wishing for his counsel. Of course, he'd already given me everything I needed. To this day, his voice echoes in my head with each new challenge, reminding me to learn, explore, and trust my instincts. Even in his absence, he continues to be my greatest teacher.

Dad taught me so much that he did not even know. I learned the value of being a lifelong learner. I learned that I can be resilient and deal with whatever comes my way. I learned how to have passion and follow what I love. I learned about adventure and the importance of seizing the moment. I learned about service and giving to others and the community. I learned about family and bonds that can never be broken. These are the special gifts from Dad. He really was a giant.

Three Things I Learned About Life and Leadership

1. Follow your passion and all else will fall into place. Life is short and there is no time to do things you don't love.
2. Create and give back to the community.
3. Family, family, family—there is no greater gift than family and friends.

***

Not Nobility, Just Noble

by Alysia A. Bullock, HR Consultant, Leadership Coach

My grandfather, George Seward Daves Sr., was born on February 20, 1920, in Mellette, South Dakota —the son of Seward Adlai Daves and Elsie (née Buttner). His younger brother, Robert, was born three years later.

Shortly after the birth of his brother, his mother left the family home in South Dakota with both young boys and returned to New York City to be closer to her sister and cousins. Soon after the move to New York, she placed both boys in the Christian Home for Children, an orphanage in Fort Lee, New Jersey, due to financial hardships associated with the Great Depression and being newly divorced. Within a year's time, she returned to the orphanage but only to collect her youngest son, Robert, leaving my grandfather in the home where he remained through high school.

After graduating high school in 1939, at the age of 19, he picked up work in the street department, maintaining meters and pipes for the Public Service Electric & Gas (PSE&G) utilities company. In January 1942, one month after the bombing of Pearl Harbor, he enlisted in the U.S. Navy. He served as a "tin can sailor"—a term used to describe sailors on destroyers due to their lighter construction compared to battleships—in the Pacific during World War II.

During one of his ship's ports, he met my grandmother, Ann Matejik, an immigrant from Czechoslovakia living in Astoria (Queens), New York. Ann was the divorced mother of a young girl, Naomi.

Coming from divorced parents and marrying a divorced woman with a child were quite unconventional for the early 1900s. Yet, as both he and Gramma told their story over the years, it was truly love at first sight. Described in his discharge papers as 6'6" with a ruddy complexion, my grandmother thought he was the "cat's meow." He married her in 1944 and raised the little girl as his own.

PSE&G made good on its guarantee to continue his employment when the war ended, and Grampa used the GI bill to return to school in the evenings. He began his college journey with New York University, pursuing a degree in electrical engineering.

My father was born in 1951. My grandfather graduated in 1953. He later retired from PSE&G after 40 years of service. My dad was truly the apple of his eye, and quite the spitting image of him. Not just in height and looks, but also demeanor. It is no wonder that my father truly followed in his father's footsteps, also retiring from PSE&G as an electrical engineer.

All in a Name

My grandfather's grandfather's full name was Noah Noble Daves. I was always intrigued by his middle name. After all, "noble" is defined by Merriam-Webster as "having or showing fine personal qualities or high moral principles and ideals; characteristics such as wisdom, generosity, patience, and integrity."[1]

My grandfather embodied all of the characteristics his grandfather's name implied. To me, my grandfather was noble.

Wisdom and Patience

"Tell me and I forget, teach me and I may remember, involve me and I learn."
(Benjamin Franklin)[2]

When we are told something, the information is fleeting. Being taught something may make it more memorable, but learning something makes it unforgettable. My grandfather was the consummate educator and one of the smartest men I've ever known.

My sisters and I spent many summer mornings at his farm in upstate New York. He greeted each day with the same routine. He'd wake up, kiss Gramma, grab coffee, and settle into the undersized white wicker chair on the sun porch.

The *New York Times* crossword was no match for him, and I thought he knew every word in the dictionary and almost all the answers to *Jeopardy*, a staple in his nightly TV ritual. He was also a fountain of random information such as New York Mets baseball stats, gardening and canning tricks, and he could recall every detail of his Lionel trains in his meticulously crafted train room in the attic.

As a young child in awe, I believed he knew everything about everything, yet he would share his wisdom in a way that kept me inspired to learn from him even more. His approach was calm and accepting, never authoritative or overbearing. Despite knowing and experiencing more than my young mind could conceive, he would speak in a gentle manner that would draw me into conversations as an equal. He'd tell his story while encouraging my ideas and thoughts, creating a dialogue instead of a one-way sermon.

This approach held true for most, but not all occasions, such as when anyone under 20 tried to use a steak knife at the dinner table—a practice he considered off limits. For him, this was a one-way discussion. There was no negotiation. (I suspect that having a truncated, bulbous thumb with no fingernail due to a woodworking incident with a rogue hammer made him a bit overprotective of his granddaughters and their fingers and thumbs!)

Aside from the steak knife moratorium and all his infinite wisdom, he had the patience of a saint. He was a towering man who could slowly lower himself to the Earth, leveraging every inch of support from his compression socks, to explain even the smallest, remedial task—leaving you feeling like you could have done it yourself all along but just needed a dash of encouragement that he was never short on offering.

I recall climbing into his lap or sitting on the floor near his gigantic knees on the sun porch and pouring out all my questions and thoughts while he tried to complete his crossword puzzle with a cheap Bic pen. He would peer over his bifocals, sip his Sanka coffee, and make me feel like the most important person in the room, aside from Gramma. He would entertain my spirited interrogation despite the constant interruption, and he would do it with the greatest patience.

I can picture him at his workbench carefully placing each roofing shingle and gluing the delicate wallpaper in the tiny rooms of the custom Victorian doll houses he built for each of his granddaughters. To this day, I can see his oversized, calloused hands with a bum thumb patiently arranging every detail until the grand reveal. My dollhouse even had my parents' wedding picture framed above a miniature fireplace—it's a detail I will always remember.

The Greatest Gift: Patience

I always thought I had the most talented grandfather who taught me essential life skills: how to throw a ball, play a mean game of Uno, pick pole beans, and cheer at a demolition derby (as long as I didn't play near the well, of course).

However, I've since discovered that Grampa's unwavering patience was his greatest gift.

As I get older, I find myself relying more on patience—with myself, my young adult son, my aging parents, and also in the workplace as I mentor and support others. Patience has allowed me to release the stress of going fast and accurately and replace it with creating space with and for others as they learn skills for themselves.

Patience can also play a key role in innovation as it allows employees the space to feel comfortable when learning new skills, testing assumptions, and possibly failing without fearing the ramifications of a leader with no patience. As my grandfather demonstrated, a willingness to listen and support creates a level of trust where others are willing to try and fail—a key component in the innovation cycle.

Penny Wise

My grandfather stressed the importance of family and community. He was a giver of his wisdom, time, and teachings—and a model of kindness. In his later years, he and my grandmother would collect toiletries from hotel travels and make care packages for homeless or displaced families in their community.

He was an active member of their church and offered a pair of hands to anyone he saw in need, even if they were too proud to ask. His generosity was so genuine that I imagine he was almost impossible to turn away.

"See a penny, pick it up. All day long you'll have good luck."[3]

During one of our walks when I was still a child, I noticed a penny on the ground and started to bend to pick it up. My grandfather's giant hand gently grabbed my wrist before I reached the coin. He said, "See a penny leave it be, someone needs it more than me."

While his words stuck, it wasn't until many years later that I truly understood and appreciated the lesson. I loved him deeply for his patience, kindness, and sense of gratitude, despite the many hardships he endured.

Unlike many men of his generation, Grampa was an unlimited source of hugs, a kind word, and fountain of encouragement. He did the right thing because to him it was the right thing to do. His internal compass was so steadfast, he did things out of fulfillment, not out of obligation.

To this day, I see a penny on the ground and smile in remembrance.

New Meaning to Nobility

Grampa claimed he would live to be 80 years old, often shaking a fist in the air as he made the declaration. It was a running joke with us for many years. I guess this was his way of declaring his "vision."

Grampa suffered from Parkinson's and Alzheimer's for several years before his passing. He and my grandmother were living in Florida at the time, so my parents would make recurring trips from New Jersey to Florida, trading off to provide in-home care and support during his final weeks.

I remember watching them brave comforting smiles as they spared my sisters and me a few details about his declining health. I couldn't imagine him being so weak considering the bear hugs he used to give that would almost crush my ribs. How could that mountain of a man crumble when I always thought him invincible?

Grampa was buried in the family plot in the southern New Jersey town where my sisters and I were raised. He was honored with a military rifle salute and the playing of "Taps." Gramma joined him there many years later.

True to his vision, Grampa passed on his 80th birthday, February 20, 2000. This gentle giant of a man was laid to rest, honored as a decorated soldier, a devoted husband, and dedicated father and grandfather.

In 1977, my mother named her first born, baby girl, "Alysia" (me). She told me my name is derived from the Old English word "ele" (meaning noble) and "eynn" (meaning kin or family). In other words, my birth name means "born of noble birth."

By definition, no one in our family would use the word "noble" to describe our clan or any of the legacy of the Daves name. However, my grandfather lived a life anchored in family, community, generosity, patience, and integrity. I believe his early experiences shaped his values and allowed him to embody a life that truly was noble. In his own way, he was noble, and so was his only son. I am proud to be of such noble birth.

Three Things I Learned About Life and Leadership

1. Wisdom is the power of teaching what you know while inspiring others to learn.
2. Patience with and for others develops a deep sense of trust and connection.
3. Integrity is doing the right thing for the right reason.

***

Fully Embrace Each Day

by Barbara Frankel, Founder and President, Coaching Initiatives LLC, and Adjunct Faculty Member at Quinnipiac University School of Business

On June 5, at 5:00 a.m., I woke up wondering why my mother was laughing so loudly. It turns out she wasn't laughing. No one else was up. I went downstairs and saw my mother administering CPR to my 41-year-old father, Almon Frankel. She yelled, "Get out. Go call your uncle!"

I was only 12. On the phone with my uncle, I could barely speak. "Daddy can't breathe. Mommy said to call you." I was in shock.

My Father's Death through the Lens of a 12-Year-Old

When the ambulance arrived, my mother asked me to wake up my 14- and 10-year-old brothers, leaving my five-year-old brother asleep. We gathered in my eldest brother's bedroom, and my mother told us we could not go into the master bedroom.

I was concerned because I had not kissed my father goodnight at bedtime the night before, which was unusual for me. My 10-year-old brother and I had a silly fight and we'd asked my father to referee. He had raised his voice to both of us, which was very unusual for him, as he was a gentle soul who rarely expressed anger. So, being upset, I hadn't kissed him goodnight.

Now I felt compelled to see him and either kiss him goodnight or goodbye, depending on the situation. So, under the guise of needing to go to the bathroom, I snuck into my parents' dark bedroom. Only my father was in there, lying still on his side of the bed. I kissed him goodbye and told him I loved him. I remember thinking that my brother and I making him angry was responsible for his sudden death—a thought I held for many years, along with feelings of guilt.

In hindsight, I am so glad that I listened to my inner voice and was able to express my final goodbye. Life is change. Nothing stays the same. At age 12, in one moment my entire world transformed from one of feeling loved and secure within a close-knit family, to being "at sea," "alone," and part of a family that was no longer whole.

My father was the one who united us. I adored him. He was my favorite person. He created family "gymnastic nights" where we tumbled with pillows and made blanket tents. When he died, I felt like an orphan and was fearful that my mother would also die.

My father passed away due to a damaged heart caused by rheumatic heart disease, which he contracted as a child from an untreated strep infection. Years later, I learned that he chose not to have open-heart surgery to replace his mitral valve because the surgical procedure was not fully developed at the time and was risky. As a result, my father knew his life would be short.

Thankfully, my parents made the wise decision to protect my siblings and me by not letting us know how sick our father was. It spared us all from daily fear and anxiety.

At the time of his death, my mother was 38, devastated, and unequipped to care for four young children. In this new reality, I had to learn how to be responsible, resilient, and responsive.

Learning About My Father through the Lens of Others

I was always told by anyone who knew my father that he "loved people and life," which confirmed what I, as a child, saw and knew about him. Al—as he was called by his friends—was "warm and joyful," they would say.

- "He was easy-going, playful, and always wore a smile."
- "Making others laugh fulfilled him."
- "He had a positive outlook and appreciated every moment."
- "He never had a negative thing to say about anyone."
- "You could sense the joy in everything he did, including his vegetable garden, fishing, and neighborhood walks."

I learned that he was devastated over losing his mother in his twenties, which reinforced for him the preciousness of life and the importance of making the most of each day.

As children, my siblings and I never knew he had any physical limitations. Remarkably, despite his tenuous health status, he and my mother enjoyed downhill skiing, dancing, partying with friends, traveling, and playing ball with us.

While others with a compromised heart might not have traveled on transatlantic flights, my father did. He loved traveling for business and pleasure. He was once featured in *The New York Times* in an article entitled "Wrong Way Frankel," which detailed how he fell asleep after boarding a plane, expecting to see snow in Amsterdam upon arrival, and woke up instead to palm trees in Puerto Rico. Plan A became Plan B! Nothing was a major impediment to my father. I imagine he probably laughed and saw such potentially unnerving events like this as challenges to be solved!

They say when one has limited time, there is greater clarity and focus. Family, friends, community, faith, making a difference for others, and building a business with his father and brothers all took on great significance as my father's raison d'être (his purpose in life).

Both my paternal grandfather, Fred Frankel, and father shared a love of Judaism. Fred was a wonderful role model who had been the co-founder of Young Israel of Flatbush Synagogue and Yeshiva of Flatbush in Brooklyn. So, when my family moved to Long Island from Brooklyn, and my father discovered there wasn't an Orthodox synagogue in town, he joined five others to build one—a first for the community. Later, he became the first president of the synagogue's Men's Club.

My father was the kind of leader who could rally people forward and bring them together to serve the greater good. He both inspired and supported his community, embodying the values of teamwork, authentic connection, service, creativity, and resilience.

Without any fanfare, my father and grandfather quietly left legacies of helping others who were sick or less fortunate, serving as exemplars for others to do the same.

Through the Lens of an Adult Daughter

My father laid the foundation for who I am and how I live my life, acting as my primary role model and guide. He taught me that every day is a gift and precious. Because of him, I am a "yes" to life—and when presented with opportunities, I lead with "yes."

I tend to fill each day with as much as possible … and then some. I took a large course load in college and graduated early. I was involved in campus activities and clubs and studied abroad for a semester. I worked two paid campus jobs, and I volunteered with the crisis center as well as a developmental program on weekends. I was recruited to lead all the group facilitators in the first "Death and Dying" university course in the United States. Later, I led three professional organizations in my field.

Over time, I have learned to set limits. I no longer need to "do it all." Thankfully, I now live with greater ease about the choices and decisions I make, which allows me the freedom to savor each experience.

My father also taught me at an early age that differences are not disqualifying and how important it is to live my life with integrity, consistent with my core beliefs. As a typical nine-year-old, I wanted to be like other children. I remember a friend's birthday party where I couldn't have the same lunch as the other children. I was raised in a kosher home, so eating kosher food was important to my father and he set clear expectations. I was upset after the birthday party and told my father I did not want to be kosher any longer. He immediately understood, showed compassion, and transformed the conversation away from being "different" into a lesson about being my own person and following my own beliefs or practices. He explained and reassured me that others would respect me for following my beliefs. As we discussed a plan for me and my alternative "lunches" at birthday parties, he shared what he did when dining at other people's homes. He did not make a show of keeping kosher. Instead, he simply ate whatever was kosher and moved the other food around his plate. In his own special way, he did things in a quiet fashion … and he showed me how I could do the same.

My father cherished the core principles of Judaism. He believed in and took actions consistent with the Tikkun Olam, a central concept in Judaism that means "repairing the world." It's about taking action to improve society, the environment, and the greater good for future generations.

In this vein, my father's death inspired me professionally as an executive coach and faculty member to help organizations and individuals succeed and thrive. It also motivated me to use my capabilities to save lives by setting a goal to eradicate rheumatic heart disease (RHD) worldwide through prevention and awareness. Some 250,000 children and young adults around the world die needlessly every year of RHD. As a volunteer with Team Heart, I helped to write, produce, and distribute a coloring book and crayons to children and their families in Rwanda. The purpose of the coloring book is to educate and encourage families so they can properly evaluate and treat sore throats. So far, the coloring book has been distributed to more than 10,000 children and their families.

I am a firm believer that knowledge is power. Lifespans can be extended. Medicine can be efficacious in reducing and even eradicating preventable diseases. No one should lose a loved one from an undiagnosed case of strep throat!

Through the Lens of a Leadership Coach

Quiet Leadership: My father exemplified quiet leadership. His warm and inclusive nature brought people together. As a community and team builder, his actions were directed for the greater good. He showed that what you do, not just what you say, is an important measure of authenticity. Quiet leadership is ideal where goals are delineated in "bite-sized" portions and successes can become exponential over time.

Communication: My father listened carefully, gathered other viewpoints, and communicated with authenticity. This allowed him to be more aligned with the people he led in his business and community activities.

Relationships: My father was a man of his word. As a result, he built strong relationships with team members and other stakeholders. Rapport and trust are the essential ingredients that empower one's working group.

Team Leadership: People knew they were valued by my father. People around him felt supported, valued, and engaged, so they were inspired to do their best. Leaders must acknowledge the efforts of others along the way, showing members of a team that their efforts matter. It's a self-perpetuating loop where much can be accomplished.

Resilience: Because of his health issues, my father knew his life would be short. As a father and community leader, he knew he had to adapt by being proactive to changing circumstances. Having a plan B and C demonstrated flexibility, courageousness, and openness to new ideas.

Three Things I Learned About Life and Leadership

1. Life is a gift. Cherish each moment and the people in your life.
2. Use your unique capabilities to make a difference for others.
3. Go for it! Be proactive. Find the courage to go beyond who you know yourself to be.

***

Finding Purpose in the Sangre De Cristo Mountains

by Stephen Frenkel, Founder and Lead Consultant,
Voyager Executive Consulting, LLC

Jean Mayer (pronounced Djohn Ma-yay) was an unassuming hero. By the time I met him, he was in his seventies, standing proud at about five feet three inches with leathered skin from his years skiing in the northern New Mexico sun. Yet, anyone could see he had a way about him—a joie de vivre, a twinkle in his eye—that showed you how much he had lived and how much he was still enjoying it.

The TSV

Jean was the founder and proprietor of the Hotel St. Bernard, a small hotel at the foot of Taos Ski Valley (TSV). He built this hotel by hand in 1960 after being gifted the land by TSV's founder, Ernie Blake, on request that he host the ski valley's guests. To Jean, hosting was a most sacred honor.

By design, guests would stay for an entire week—Saturday to Saturday—returning year after year with the same groups, reconnecting like long lost family. Jean greeted all guests as they arrived, bid adieu to them as they departed, and served almost every meal to them by hand—three exquisite daily meals of French cuisine, family-style. He would write the menu on the board by hand, and as he served, he would sing French songs and ring the old shepherd's bells scattered around the dining room. When it snowed, he would bring in platters of fresh snow, throwing it around by the handfuls gleefully during dinner, never one to take himself too seriously.

It became clear to me upon arrival in TSV that a job at the "St. B" (as it was affectionately called) was the most coveted job in the ski valley—even though Jean preferred to start new hires as dishwashers, regardless of their experience. I couldn't help but wonder how washing dishes for this guy was somehow more glorious than being a ski instructor in one of the top ski schools in the world. I'm glad to say I didn't have to wait too long to find out. After a few persistent phone calls and brief conversations, I was thrilled to hear that Jean found a spot for me on the dish line.

I quickly learned how unique working for Jean and the St. B would be. To start, there was no stated hourly wage, nor any discussion about what you would be paid. There were no job descriptions, no performance reviews, no tasks to track, and certainly no management structure or supervision. Everyone was expected to come to work, learn from those who came before them, find their way, and put the guest experience first. There was only one requirement—to look Jean in the eye and shake his hand on payday, proud of your contributions.

Did it feel odd to start a job in this way? Of course. And yet, somehow, we all knew that Jean would take care of us. There was no question. We knew we were a part of Jean's greater passion for skiing and his vision for the ski valley, the hotel itself, and the quality of the guest experience. Jean somehow knew that the key to his guests "getting it" was to ignite the passion in his staff, enabling us to serve as his megaphones and great "brand" champions (yes, even at 5:30 a.m. with a mop in my hand!).

Watching Jean fulfill his life's mission and how he led his staff and his team with focus changed my life, my work ethic, and my understanding of effective leadership. Jean's leadership enabled me to unlock something in myself that I didn't know was there. His trust in me, and the whole staff, inspired me to perform at my best when no one was looking, to define for myself what my best was, and to bring that to the St. B every single day. Because what mattered most was that I was proud of myself when I shook his hand. It was as a dishwasher for a small hotel in the Sangre de Cristo mountains of New Mexico that I found my own standards and my own work ethic. And what I discovered was that my standards were high, and that my best was darn good.

Living the Vision

Of course, Jean's style of leadership bit him in the butt from time to time. People took advantage of his generosity. They mistook his warmth and kindness for softness. But this risk never seemed to stop him. He operated from a mindset of abundance. He let the moochers mooch and the haters hate—and he still led a very successful business and a fulfilling life until the very end.

I also watched Jean grind. For four to five months a year, he served almost every meal to his guests by hand, and taught lessons as Technical Director of TSV's ski school. Yet, he seemed not only to enjoy it, but to thrive in it. I had never seen anything like it. He lived and breathed the St. B. It was an extension of him. Jean wasn't looking to take the easy way out. His commitment came with sacrifice and dedication.

Sharing His Legacy

Unfortunately, Jean passed in 2020 from cancer. I was heartbroken. In my grief, I remember quite vividly declaring that I would live my life inspired by Jean's leadership and that I would share his story, the lessons I learned in his shadow, and the impact he had on me. It's these lessons that I look to share with you here.

First, I want to call out the impact of leading with passion and commitment to one's cause or vision. Jean's dedication to his hotel, his guests, his staff, and the ski valley itself was inspiring. His reputation as the employer of choice was well known in the ski valley, and it attracted the best of the best to want to work for him—even if it meant starting in the back of the kitchen.

One of my favorite quotes comes from Kouzes and Posner's *The Leadership Challenge*: "Leadership is the art of mobilizing others to want to struggle for shared aspirations."[4] Jean did just that. He created an environment where we wanted to "do right" even when no one was looking or giving credit for a job well done.

Second, Jean led with trust and empowerment. With his vision clear, he left us to our own devices to figure out how to do and be our best. With the help of our colleagues and our internal barometers, he led us to find our way, find our value, and ultimately to find our place in his vision without ever really telling us how.

Third, delightful customer service can only be provided by delighted staff. Focusing on one's customers without focusing on one's employees leaves a gap that can't be filled with slogans, mantras, or values. We offered great customer service from wherever we stood in the hotel. We were thrilled to be there ourselves and we were clear and committed to Jean's vision. The result was a book of business that was almost completely sold out a year in advance. Our patrons enjoyed their experiences so much that they couldn't bear the thought of missing out on their spot the following year. It truly was amazing to witness and be a part of.

Fourth, nothing comes for free. Leadership has a price—especially if you're doing it right. Jean's commitment to his vision had him sacrificing elsewhere in his life. He had very little down time in the winter, yet Jean seemed to float from task to task with ease and joy. The work and the play were one and the same to him, leaving it to others to figure out which was which.

Finally, as my friend Alan likes to say, the person with the "bigger context" wins. Of course, there were people who would take advantage of his approach and try to ride Jean's coattails. But he was playing too big to let their smallness bring him down. Those who did try to exploit his generosity found themselves on the outs—not just in the job, but in the St. B community. Jean's leadership and generosity fostered a loyalty unlike anything I have ever seen. And with that loyalty came a fierce army of defense against anyone that might hurt our leader or his vision and our mission.

I can still hear Jean's voice as I go about my day, encouraging me to keep going and to "en voie"—to "send it!"—whatever "it" was at the time (the soup, the skiing, the fun). Now that I think about it, maybe Jean started the "Send It!" craze? Would he want the credit? I doubt it. It's likely enough for him, from wherever he is, to hear my children shout "en voie!" as we head down the ski slope.

Here's where I will give him credit, though. My own leadership and the style of leadership that I teach started from my experience with Jean Mayer at the St. B almost 25 years ago. My time working with him helped shape who I am, how I lead, and what I teach to others.

I firmly believe that leaders who inspire people to rise to their own expectations and discover their own standards and capabilities stand above the rest. Leaders who lead in this way have a way of letting go, untapping what was latent and unseen, and discovering it together with their team, without prescription. They simply create space for possibility to emerge. I'd like to think that the people I've led and supported in my career have benefited from Jean's style, even if they didn't know him personally. And I'd like to think they pass it on in some way, even if they're not sure why.

Three Things I Learned About Life and Leadership

1. Lead with vision and passion—no one can create that but you.
2. Trust and empower your people—let go of control and reap the rewards.
3. Delightful customer service is provided by delighted employees, there's just no other way to get there.

***

A Life Imprinted with Love and Leadership: In Memory of Auntie Nancy

by Anna-Sophia Kristjansson, MSc Neuroscience, Founder and CEO, Lexicon Lens

There are moments in life when the words, actions, and deeds of a single individual can impact one's life beyond measure. Nancy Madge (Ally) Milan imprinted messages of love and leadership deeply into me throughout her life. She knew me from birth. She was my godmother, and I called her Auntie Nancy.

Auntie Nancy was born in Tacoma, Washington, on November 30, 1941; she passed in Seattle, Washington, on October 23, 2023. She was born into a middle-class American family.

At the age of four her father was fatally shot while hunting, leaving her mom, Bernice, to raise two girls. Bernice remarried and Auntie Nancy later recounted for me how she was an "invisible" child at home. There were no expectations she would amount to anything, and her mom and stepdad rarely inquired about her whereabouts.

By all accounts (and the pictures I've seen), she was an adorable girl: petite, with blond curls, big brown eyes, and a warm grin. She was outgoing, a cheerleader in high school, socially focused, and wise beyond her years.

Sowing the Seeds of a Lifelong Friendship

At the age of seven she met my mom, Tina, and the two of them bonded, becoming best friends for life. They loved ice-cream sundaes, playing games, and riding bikes. They were also sneaky. One time, they took Tina's stepdad

Peter's car for a spin, dressed in his suits. They were 14. Nancy would giggle whenever speaking of this adventure. My mom drove while Auntie Nancy tried to stuff her own blond curls into Peter's hat, all the while praying they wouldn't get caught. Although Peter was suspicious, he never confronted them. He let them have their moment.

Both met the loves of their lives in middle school—Nancy her husband (my Uncle Paul) and my dad (John)—and the four shared all of life's big experiences until the end. Both husbands preceded their wives in death. Auntie Nancy and my mom's deep friendship lasted their entire lives.

College and Teaching

My Mom applied to the University of Washington on Auntie Nancy's behalf. Auntie Nancy never thought about college (after all, nothing was expected of her). Both were accepted and pledged sororities, an experience which Auntie Nancy loved. She counted her sorority sisters as good friends throughout life.

Auntie Nancy earned her bachelor's degree and became a lifelong teacher of the deaf. She went on to earn her master's degree in teaching from Seattle University. She ardently supported students and their families' needs. She loved teaching, pioneered inclusiveness for her students, and developed a team-based approach to teaching. She volunteered on a regular basis, most recently at her daughter Carla's school.

Flourishing Family Times

Auntie Nancy and my mom both had two girls, close in age. My sister, Naomi, and I became close friends with Auntie Nancy's children, Carla and Kate. We shared holidays, birthdays, and vacationed annually at Black Butte Ranch—growing and experiencing the rollercoaster of life as two bonded families.

We four girls experienced relative freedom during our times at the ranch, and my mom and Auntie Nancy would plan elaborate dinner menus, including items such as Swedish meatballs, potato chip chicken, spaghetti, and lots of pies and treats that Auntie Nancy excelled at making. At the end of a typical, full Black Butte day, Auntie Nancy would make her rounds to say goodnight. She liked to help us relax with gentle strokes on our cheeks.

Nancy was authentic, kind, and truthful. She made me feel safe and loved.

Our Last Meal Together (Though We Didn't Know It)

The last time I broke bread with Auntie Nancy was at her home on September 15, 2023, a warm, sunny day in Seattle. We sat on the back patio to enjoy grilled salmon, asparagus, and potatoes. Memories of my childhood flooded my mind as I walked through her house. There were so many smells reminiscent of growing up, and I felt as though the walls could talk. We chatted about the neighborhood, my son, people who had passed, and my mom's health condition. She brought out photos and we talked about all the fun times we had together. It was a precious evening. Nothing had changed in her personality, although I could see her frailty.

Life Will Never Be the Same

On October 23, 2023, I drove from Boulder, Colorado, to Lincoln, Nebraska to be with my mom who had been admitted to the hospital in septic shock. Her prognosis was not good. The day before, I talked with Auntie Nancy and explained the situation. She cried about her best friend and asked that I call when I knew more. I didn't hear from her during my drive to Lincoln, which was unusual, so I thought I'd update her once I saw Mom in the ICU.

After the harried trip, which involved driving through a corn field to avoid an accident on the highway, I arrived at the hospital 10 minutes before visiting hours ended. I saw my mom and realized the severity of her situation. Nurses worked to keep her comfortable, but she wasn't responding as they hoped. I thought about calling Auntie Nancy.

I checked into the hotel exhausted and feeling a little lost knowing my mom was seriously ill. I had just sat down when my phone buzzed. It was Auntie Nancy's daughter, Kate. I answered with a tired "hello" and Kate delivered a message I was not expecting. Auntie Nancy had died in her sleep in the early hours of that day.

I was numb. Devastated. Lost. My heart was pumping hard. The air had been knocked out of me. I honestly didn't know what to do because the shock was almost too much to handle.

I called my sister to relay the message. We let the news sink in. We couldn't tell Mom. It would be too much for her in her current state. Our lives were now permanently changed. My husband (Orn) and son (John-Thor) arrived. I gave them the news and watched them get knocked off balance, just as I did. It was the first moment of the seven days to follow that rocked our world to its core. Mom passed on October 30, 2023, seven days after her best friend.

Auntie Nancy's Life Lessons Began Early in My Life

I was always an active child ready for any fun opportunity. Kate's sister, Carla, is two years my junior. When she was three, I convinced her to sit in a rotating chair that I twirled as fast as possible. This made her scream with delight (and probably some fear). Auntie Nancy rescued a very dizzy Carla from the chair and took me aside. She gently and lovingly explained that Carla was younger and smaller and not as strong as me. She needed me to be aware of my strength and how I played with Carla. I paid attention.

In second grade, Auntie Nancy passed on another important lesson. At the time, I felt kids were being mean on the playground, so I refused to play outside at recess. She explained to me how the real lessons of life would happen on the playground. Classroom learning was important, of course, but it was experience on the playground with all kinds of kids and situations that would help me grow into a strong, confident woman. She gave me some tools to communicate with the other kids and winked. She innately knew how to give me a path forward.

Integrity Is a Blend of Purpose, Passion, and Values

Auntie Nancy's ongoing lessons of awareness and communication were coupled with a map for life. She often asked about my purpose, passion, and values. She wanted me not only to articulate them but to live by them. I didn't always want to. Sometimes I rolled my eyes. Many times, I shied away from speaking up or advocating for myself. She would watch and redirect me.

When I told her I was starting a business, she said, "You know what I'm going to ask you?" I did and I was ready. She inquired about the purpose, passion, and values driving my organization, eager to understand my "why" for founding it. I shared each with clarity and conviction. I swear I could sense her smiling through the phone.

For her, life was not only about advancing herself; it was also about commitment. This meant lifelong commitments she made to contribute to her family, school, colleagues, friends, and community. She led by example and admitted her own mistakes. While she admitted mistakes, she knew they weren't meant to take her down. She'd use them as teaching moments so that I would remember to follow my own path of service and become the best version of myself.

As I look back, I realize that her life lessons were cumulative, grounding me in a foundation that will never shake. She became my life advisor.

Even today, I still hear her say, "Oh good. Now what do you want from this situation and how do the people working with you feel about it?" or "You can lead through influence but to do that, you need to live with integrity" or "Remember your values, Sophia, and think about the kind of person you are. I believe in you. Believe in yourself."

Over the years, I stumbled plenty of times. Sometimes, I felt her wanting to say, "I told you so," but she never did. Her honesty could sting, but I knew I could trust her advice.

Auntie Nancy and I always ended our conversations with, "I love you." She would then say, "I love you more." The shock of her death has passed, but I will never get over the fact that I won't hear her voice again or her words, which felt like a warm, cozy blanket enveloping me with feelings of deep love and safety.

Auntie Nancy had a profound effect on how I shaped myself as an adult by teaching me to observe, thoughtfully interact, and lead with integrity. She also taught me that love means encouragement, honesty, leading by example, and integrity.

> **Three Things I Learned About Life and Leadership**
>
> 1. Act from your purpose, your passions, and your values as they will never lead you in the wrong direction.
> 2. To lead, start with yourself and have a clear sense of the contribution you want to make for others.
> 3. Love everyone equally and without judgment that isn't parsed out but given freely.

✳✳✳

Lessons on Belonging and Leading from My Friend, Rosalind "Roz" Wyman

by Mitch Lippman, Executive Coach, Facilitator, and Leadership Trainer, The Mitch Lippman Group, Inc.

I've worked with many leaders, but no relationship has come close to the friendship and mentorship I enjoyed with Los Angeles legend Rosalind "Roz" Wyman. Although Roz and my father were born in the same year, Roz was much more a friend than surrogate parent. I'm truly lucky to have been able to spend time with and learn from her—and I'm grateful for the profound impact she had on my life and my approach to leadership.

Pioneering Spirit

In 1953—at the age of 22—Roz ran for Los Angeles City Council and won. She was the youngest person ever elected to the City Council and only the second woman to serve (the first woman having served some 40 years earlier). The headline of one Los Angeles newspaper the day after the election read, "It's A Girl!"[5] and one of the burning questions post-election centered around where Roz would use the bathroom,[6] since there was only a men's room available for Council members. Roz was entering a space reserved for men and had to earn her stripes. She did this by working hard and delivering results.

Roz's passion and vision to make Los Angeles a world-class city included attracting arts and professional sports there. She was instrumental in bringing the Dodgers to Los Angeles and had a hand in bringing the Giants to San Francisco and the Lakers to Los Angeles. She also advocated for building The Music Center in downtown LA. Not only did the Center become reality, but it also became the permanent home for the LA Philharmonic, the LA Opera, various dance and theater projects, and it features world-class venues for touring and resident productions and programs.

Roz's work in Democratic politics—especially in California—was unrivaled. A valued advisor to candidates and elected officials, she was close friends with Speaker Emerita Nancy Pelosi, the late Senator Dianne Feinstein, and many other prominent leaders. Her advice and fundraising prowess were much sought-after. She had, after all, helped organize and fundraise for then-Senator John F. Kennedy's 1960 Presidential Campaign,[7] and was the impetus behind his historic outdoor nomination-acceptance speech.[8]

Not the Girl Who Types

I met Roz through my husband, Michael, who had worked closely with Senator Feinstein from 1990 to 2000, and with whom we enjoyed a friendship ended only by her death in 2023. A few months after Michael and I relocated to Los Angeles from New York City in 2004, Roz was hosting a small event in Dianne's honor at a suite at Dodger Stadium. Upon learning from Dianne that Michael and I were in town, Roz extended an invitation.

Having worked with famous and powerful people, I wasn't star-struck—but I was a fan. Following the event, Roz asked Michael for help with an upcoming political fundraiser for Nancy Pelosi and other candidates. As things began to take shape for the fundraiser, I was asked to help where I could. I wrote speeches, tracked donations and RSVPs, and handled other logistics.

After that event, Roz asked me to help her with some technology and correspondence. She had recently gotten a Blackberry and a Yahoo.com email address. (A few years later, she would upgrade to an iPhone.) Roz embracing technology was big news to all who knew her … and she needed some assistance.

Unlike most working women of the 1950s, Roz did not type, so she needed help responding to and crafting emails. She wanted someone discreet and capable who knew how the technology worked and how to write. Impeccable communication was a hallmark of Roz's personal brand. There could be no misspellings and no typos—only crisp, clean prose that furthered the impression (and reality) that she was serious, well-informed, and infinitely credible. While a few of us wrote for Roz between 2006 and 2014, it was mostly my job. She didn't pay a salary, but the perks were phenomenal: Michael and I were Roz's guests at many Dodgers games, plays, musicals, concerts, lunches, dinners, and events. It was a priceless experience that I will always treasure.

"Not typing" was a very conscious choice for Roz. As a result, Roz never became the "secretary" for any group, thus maintaining her personal brand as a leader, not the "girl who types." (Over the years, I've observed many smart, capable women in positions of power being asked to type or take notes by their male peers, suggesting their contributions were somehow less important.)

Roz easily learned how to find and read her emails and texts. She would call or invite me over to her house to dictate her responses, which I typed and copyedited. There were also letters, invitations, research, and much more. Over time, we would work together crafting a message. And later still, Roz would tell me her strategy, position, or opinion, and I would write and submit it for her approval and edits.

When I met Roz, I was already an established executive coach, facilitator, and corporate trainer. I was also sought-after for both my logistical/management skills and my writing and editing skills. But this was something new to me. Writing to Speaker Pelosi, to senators and House members, state and local officials, members of the press, and crafting messages to presidential candidates was all thrilling and, at first, nerve-wracking. Our style difference was substantial: where I was deferential in my approach, Roz was confident. Bold. Brave.

In Search of Authenticity

As a gay man who had entered the workforce in the early 1980s and faced no small amount of discrimination, I had developed a very specific work persona. I used humor a great deal, much of it self-mocking. I was deferential and diplomatic, anticipating and fulfilling the needs of those around me. Not only did I avoid conflict, but I actively sought to reduce it whenever it occurred. I figured out how things worked and could solve problems as well as anticipate and prevent them. If someone asked me a question, I was there with an observation, my own questions, or a suggestion that added value.

My self-deprecating humor mostly centered around being gay—lots of jokes about how my "real" skills lie in areas such as interior decorating, flower-arranging, and providing fashion advice. In fact, I'm not very good at any of these things, but I felt—and still feel—that those jokes paved a path for me; they were my membership card into the workforce.

It would be years before I fully let go of my deferential persona to own my authentic self in the world. Roz's example helped me realize it was something I didn't need any longer. She had fought many of her own very tough and very public "you don't belong here" struggles and won. She was also unapologetic about owning her power, and unafraid to wield it.

I remember once, early on in our working relationship, we were crafting an email to someone—I can't remember who—but Roz wasn't happy with something that person had done. I stopped and asked her, "Are you sure you want to say that? That's rather abrupt." She replied—without any malice—"This is me writing to them, not you." Of course she was right! My deference wasn't appropriate for her message.

At the January 2007 swearing-in celebration for Nancy Pelosi's first stint as Speaker of the House, actor Amy Brenneman made a speech. She began with, "Hi. I don't know exactly why I'm here, but Roz Wyman told me to be here, so I am." The line got a big laugh, and her words undoubtedly echoed the sentiments of many: Roz was tough, perhaps even a little scary, and incredibly compelling as a leader.

What I came to learn was that while this persona was truly authentic to Roz, there was more that she didn't share publicly, particularly her vulnerability and fears. These attributes weren't helpful to her, so she forged on with strength and hard work.

Respect, Reverence, and Fun

Roz lived according to her values, which included a very strong moral/ethical center and a solid sense of altruism. She believed it was our responsibility as a society to help those who needed help. She also had no desire to suffer fools or incompetence. Roz could accomplish a huge amount of work, and while she was dedicated to helping others and truly loved humanity, she didn't want to be hindered by people who didn't know what they were doing, played games, or otherwise slowed things down.

She worked with a unique blend of respect and reverence for history and institutions, and an impish, childlike spirit that liked to shake things up. For example, at the time of this writing, Roz Wyman is still the only woman in U.S. history to have chaired a national convention for a major political party: the 1984 Democratic National Convention in San Francisco. While she navigated the metaphorical minefield that is a national political event and honored the history and solemnity of the occasion, she also fought hard to feature indoor fireworks and chose an "official ice cream." Why? Because Roz loved fun and she believed ice cream and fireworks would ensure people enjoyed themselves and remembered a great time.

Seeing Roz be so authentic and so deliberate with her image and her brand inspired me. I no longer made self-deprecating jokes about being gay. I no longer felt the need to earn the right to be in the room or apologize for being there. Her impact was life changing. I started to be bolder, to ask questions, to challenge authority and the *status quo*. That came from Roz.

Preserving Her Image for Posterity

As she grew older, Roz withdrew from most socializing and events. Eventually, she would only speak to me by phone, and I learned this was true for all but her immediate family. I realized that outside her family, no one was going to see Roz Wyman in anything less than impeccable shape. I've never discussed or explored details with the family, but I'm certain this withdrawal was done to maintain her public image.

Later, she stopped calling or taking calls from me. I will not speculate on what kind of decline any individual goes through as they approach death. I only know that if Roz couldn't put her best foot forward, she wouldn't take a step.

The fact that I didn't see Roz in the months leading up to her death saddens me. I loved her as a friend and mentor, and I missed our chats and visits, her humor, and her strong opinions and point of view. At the same time, I'm also very grateful to her for ensuring that I never saw her at less than 100%.

Reflections and Key Learnings

As I look back on my relationship with Roz Wyman with a sense of loss, grief, and gratitude, I have wonderful memories of hard work, tough conversations, and much fun. I see that I'm a different person and a different leader as a result of having had her in my life.

I no longer make fun of myself—although I have never lost my sense of humor about myself.

I own my power without apology, realizing that my voice counts, and I certainly don't have to apologize for being in a room, nor ask permission.

I learned to pay more attention to image and persona—and to what I share publicly. Roz had a knack for being completely authentic while still crafting an image that helped her lead. She would admit when she didn't know something or was unsure about what to do next, but I never saw her share her frustrations, her sadness, or her disappointment. Those were private and personal.

Saying goodbye was hard, but my life and my work are forever changed for the better by having worked with Roz and by witnessing her approach to death with dignity and her thoughtfulness regarding her image and legacy.

I've always encouraged authenticity in my coaching clients, as well as the importance of image and personal brand in leadership. But working with Roz, I had taken a journey in my own authenticity and personal brand that helps me help others to this day.

In the fall of 2023, Michael and I gathered with many others at The Music Center for a memorial to Roz Wyman. Surrounded by Roz's family, friends, and colleagues, we experienced the event—impeccably planned and executed to Roz's exacting standards. There were tearful moments, hearty laughs, and wonderful tributes. There were stories from politics, sports, the arts, and much more. And then we all went outside to Grand Park to continue the celebration with hot dogs, popcorn, music from a marching band, and ice cream. It was exactly as Roz would have wanted: some business, some fun, some music, and, of course, ice cream.

So long, Roz. I miss you, and I hold the memories and the lessons in my heart.

Three Things I Learned About Life and Leadership

1. Own your own power without apology—your voice counts.
2. Pay attention to image and persona—and to what you share publicly.
3. Maintain a sense of humor—have fun.

***

Gifts from My Dad and Scout

*by Sally Breyley Parker, Founder, TimeZero Enterprises,
Entrepreneur, Daughter, and Mom*

My life has been shaped by many influences. Two in particular stand out as having had the most profound impact on who I am today: my dad, Robert (Bob) Breyley, and my Carolina Dog, Scout (Scouty) Parker. My dad was my champion and Scouty was my best friend and confidant. While my experience with each was quite different, the life and leadership lessons they taught me have marked similarities.

My Dad

Dad loved life and taught me to live fully. He worked and played hard and knew how to balance the two. A perfect example of this was a beautiful Monday morning in the spring of my ninth grade. As my sister, brother, and I sat down for breakfast, silently preparing for (and dreading) the week, Dad came in and asked, "How about we play hooky today and go boating?" With that, our three heads jerked up in delighted surprise. We knew this was a big deal because he placed high value on our education, often reminding us that education was both a privilege and a responsibility. Dad's invitation to go boating and skip school demonstrated his gift for balancing the "both/ands" of life and leadership. While he knew how important high school was for our futures, he was also able to seize the moment and make memories with his family.

As I've aged, this lesson has taken on even more importance. It is so easy to get caught up in preparing for the future that we fail to live fully in the now, missing so much of what life has to offer. While I do not remember what I missed that day at school, I will never forget how special he made me feel that one particular Monday.

As part of living fully, Dad emphasized the importance of intention, purpose, and vision. He always said, "If you don't know where you are going, any road will get you there."

He encouraged me to know and live my purpose and to make a difference with my life. This guidance has given me the courage I've needed to stay the course during some of my darkest hours. His lessons also taught me to reflect before I dive into action … to slow down in order to speed up. It is why I try to start every meeting with a clear intention and every engagement with a clear purpose.

Dad was an executive who led with his head, heart, gut, and spirit. He was also a marketing genius. He was creative, innovative, and always open to new ideas from anyone, anywhere. He was real. He visibly cared about people.

When I was cleaning out his home office after he passed, I found letters from colleagues. They talked about how much he shared of himself, what an incredible boss and mentor he was, what a great teammate, collaborator, and friend.

The way he led his life taught me that our greatest strength often lies in our ability and willingness to be vulnerable.

Dad repeatedly told me, "You can do anything to which you put your mind and heart." He trusted me, and from the time I was small, I felt that trust.

I was recently at a conference focused on building a culture of trust. As the speaker invited attendees to reflect on their professional lives, she posed a question. "Who trusted you?" That question stopped me in my tracks. I was transported back to times in my life when people, such as my dad, trusted me, and how their trust enabled me to trust myself. I also realized that this lesson about trust has long been a cornerstone for who I am as a parent, colleague, mentor, and leader.

Dad was inherently curious and loved to learn. Though he had strong opinions and convictions, he was fluid with what was emerging, quickly taking in and integrating new information. I remember his knack for seamlessly switching sides in the middle of a debate, often bewildering his "opponent." (You could say that one of his superpowers was having soft eyes, holding things lightly, and never taking himself too seriously.)

Perhaps most importantly, Dad taught me to accept and work with what is, rather than losing energy fretting over what could or should have been. "Play the hand you're dealt with everything you've got!" Remembering this has helped me get unstuck and see a way forward many times. It's also allowed me to support others to do the same.

Dad passed away on October 22, 2015. Bedridden for two years, his legs were paralyzed and his hands were clubs. He couldn't do anything for himself … even hang up the telephone when I would call. I never heard him complain about the pain he felt, he was never resentful about his situation, and he was always incredibly gracious to the people who took care of him—who fed him, changed him, tended his bed sores, shaved him, got him into his wheelchair, and repositioned him in bed.

My life has been deeply imprinted by my dad … by who he was and how he chose to live his life. It has also been deeply affected by who he chose to be toward the end. At a time when no one would have blamed him for being resentful, angry, impatient, or for closing down, he chose to be gracious and appreciative. He lit up at the small things which in turn gave joy to those who were with him. He continued to joke and see the bright side. And while he may not have been in charge of his body anymore, he remained in charge of his intentions, of how he showed up, of how he used himself, and of how he made a difference with his presence.

My Dog Scouty

In late April of 2005, Scout Parker came into this world—a more adorable pup there never was! She joined our family in July, complete with cone and immense energy. For the next (almost) 13 years, she was my walking buddy, travel mate, confidant, and best friend.

Scout was a Carolina Dog, the most indigenous dog to the North American continent, an angel with an ancient bloodline. She was basically a natural or wild dog without centuries of human intervention, and I soon realized that trying to "train" her would be futile, not to mention painful for us both.

I didn't think that because I'm a human, I'm smarter. I didn't try to assert my will over hers. Instead, I became curious about who she was. As I did, I witnessed her deep connection with life in the NOW, as it unfolded. I became more aware of and attentive to her cues and in turn, my own inner wisdom. As our relationship deepened, she taught me a great deal about my own nature and together we "trained" each other.

From the moment she joined us, Scout knitted our family together with love. Like my dad, she loved life and lived it fully. She "sang" as only dogs can when we came home and at various squirrels and rabbits that dared enter our yard. She loved to be outside in nature. She ran and slept hard and was so fast and agile—leaping over fallen trees, running figure eights, and sometimes even twirling in circles on her back legs. She loved her family, her rides in the car, her breakfast and dinner, her goodies, and snuggling on the sofa.

She left us on February 23, 2018, after a long battle with cancer. I spent the last two months of her life angry as I watched her waste away. Our days often centered on whether she ate or not. She lost muscle mass. Her skeleton became more and more visible, and her back legs weakened and were no longer reliable for getting her up and down the stairs. For a time, I was paralyzed in indecision, not knowing what to do. We knew she wouldn't get better, and we didn't want her to suffer.

As I grieved, I became less angry and afraid. I learned to stay present with her and as I did, I noticed that while she didn't have the energy she used to, she didn't feel sorry for herself. She wasn't angry, and she didn't sulk. She wasn't wasting energy over something that shouldn't have been. She wasn't repelled by how her body was changing. She just accepted it. She was present to what was happening.

She just loved to stand out in the front yard and take in this incredible planet—to breathe in the air, sniff all the smells, feel the grass at her feet. It was like she was saying "I'm going to miss this place." She never failed to wag her tail when she saw me or give me kisses. She never stopped loving. She never wasted a single moment by not being present.

Being present with her helped me be present to myself. I found I was less upset over how skinny she was and was even seeing the beauty of her skeletal form. I was able to let go of my angst and just be with what was happening, trusting that she would tell me when it was time. She did.

I learned from her about how to live fully from a place of love and how to live fully in the final stages. She taught me to accept what is happening with grace and presence. Through these lessons, my heart grew stronger, my capacity to love expanded, and my appreciation of life deepened.

Gifts to Me

Both my dad and Scouty taught me to love life and to live it fully. They taught me to trust my inner wisdom and to be me, warts and all—to demonstrate the power of vulnerability and to show up as a whole being. Most importantly, they taught me to be present with what is and to play the hand I'm dealt with everything I've got, standing in grace and love.

Both were and continue to be gifts, teachers, friends, confidants, and makers of memories that I will carry with me and continue to share until it's my turn to leave this planet.

> ### Three Things I Learned About Life and Leadership
>
> 1. Be present with what is—play the hand you're dealt with everything you've got!
> 2. Live life fully, with love, intention, and purpose.
> 3. Be real—live and lead with head, heart, gut, and spirit.

✳✳✳

The Last Lesson: How My Father Taught Me to Live Fully

by Pallavi Ridout, Executive Leadership Coach,
Keynote Speaker, High Stakes Conversations Facilitator,
and World Traveler

The inevitable was happening. But how? He was always so full of life, the life of the party, and always ready with a smile to entertain us.

On August 5, 2016, I received news I had been dreading. My brother, Abhi, who had flown from Dallas, Texas to India, was calling with news about our ailing father. Within a day, I arranged care for my six-year-old son and bought a ticket. The journey from Los Angeles to Belgaum, where my father was hospitalized, took 28 grueling hours—21 by air to Mumbai, followed by a seven-hour car ride.

We called him "Baba," the Marathi (my mother tongue) word for father. The rest of the world knew him as Dr. Prabhakar Kashinath Jadhav, though to most of his friends and family, he was simply Dr. Jadhav.

My Baba was the most gregarious person I knew. He was social, outgoing, witty, and a natural host. Well-read and cultured, he was knowledgeable about countless topics and loved to travel. His progressive outlook and generosity in providing opportunities to underprivileged individuals made him remarkable. While highly accomplished, his endearing quirks and shortcomings made him even more interesting. Even now, years after his passing, memories of his amusing antics bring smiles to our faces.

As the oldest and only daughter, with two younger brothers, Abhi and Charu, losing both parents within 13 months left us suddenly orphaned in August 2016. I found myself unexpectedly lost. The people who had shaped me were no longer there to ask about my childhood or to ask for advice about parenting and life.

While 2015–2016 brought deep sadness to our family, thinking about those years allows me to reflect on my parents' legacies of strong morals and values. I hope to pass these same values on to my son, who was just six when his grandparents passed.

My father had an amazing life, and I want to share snippets of it, as well as the leadership and life lessons I picked up from him along the way.

Perseverance and Hard Work Pay Off!

At age six, my father walked two hours round-trip on unpaved village roads to attend school. It was a journey that would deter most children. This early determination led him to eventually earn a Ph.D. in Agricultural Economics, though he'd initially dreamed of becoming a medical doctor.

Orphaned young—losing his mother at five and his father at 13—he and his brother grew up poor in a village called Viheergaon (which means "village with a well") in Maharashtra's Vidarbha district. His older brother recognized my father's potential and sacrificed much to support his education. My father funded his studies through small scholarships and tutoring, proudly buying his first bicycle and wristwatch with his own earnings. His was a remarkable rags to riches story!

Glass Ceilings Are Meant to Be Shattered

In 1970s India, when I was born, my father surprised everyone by distributing "pedhas" (round Indian sweets), a celebration traditionally reserved for sons. He never treated me as lesser than my brothers or pushed me toward traditional roles.

His dream was that I should either become an IAS officer (a prestigious position in Indian Government) or pursue higher studies abroad, which I was able to fulfill by pursuing a master's degree in the United States. His big dreams for me, coupled with his encouragement to achieve anything I could put my mind to, shaped me into the confident, successful professional I am today.

Pursue Your Passion Not Money

We led a comfortable life with great perks through my father's corporate job. He was content with what he made and while it was never a rat race for him to make more, through his hard work, passion, and ambition he went from being a poor orphaned kid from a village in India to retiring as a CEO in corporate India. We learned that money does not bring happiness. Instead, pursue your passion, do what you believe in, be a good human being, and you will find success and happiness.

Value People Not Things

Though we enjoyed a comfortable life, my father taught us that success or money does not supersede treating people with respect and valuing them as individuals. He demonstrated this through his interactions. He treated everyone, from household help to VIPs, with equal respect. Once, he surprised a painting contractor by inviting him into our living room, breaking with Indian social norms (India is a highly segmented society with wide disparities within classes and the caste system). Even in his final days in the ICU, he insisted that we find the barber who shaved him and tip him well.

Do Good in This World: Have a Purpose

My parents built deep connections wherever they went, always ready to help those in need. My father's impact was particularly profound. He helped four underprivileged individuals secure jobs, setting them and their families on paths to success. Their eternal gratitude speaks to his legacy of creating life-changing opportunities.

Broaden Your Perspectives

As a voracious reader in multiple languages, my father developed perspectives far ahead of his generation and traditional Indian culture. His knowledge spanned politics, geography, religion, and poetry. Our extensive family travels across India taught us to respect and embrace differences in thought, food, religion, and customs.

Be a Good Sport: Laugh at Yourself

We often teased my father about his quirks. His good-natured responses fostered an open, honest relationship. Years later, we still laugh about his predictable party behavior of having a few drinks and oversharing personal details, which earned my mother's morning-after reproaches at the breakfast table. His tendency to overindulge was legendary, whether it was with crisp tailored clothing, endless cups of chai (loose leaf Indian milk tea), mutton curry, or pithla (a simple chickpea flour dish). Despite regular promises of moderation, he'd inevitably repeat these indulgences, met with knowing smiles from the family.

Be Content Every Day of Your Life: Lead a Life of No Regrets

When my mother passed, I finally understood their 43-year partnership and how they made marriage and parenting look effortless. After her death, my father, diagnosed with prostate cancer, chose not to fight—he was ready to join her. A few months before he passed away, he uttered these words that I will always remember: "I have no regrets. I am happy. I am content, and I am ready."

Seeing this level of contentment within someone raised without parents, in poverty, and without basic comforts, allowed me to start my own journey toward "leading a life of no regrets." For years, I had postponed my dreams, telling myself, "One day I will pursue my passion and start my own business, reduce stress, and NOT be the last parent at after-school pickup." For years, that day never came as I juggled early morning calls, deadlines, and endless to-do lists. Evenings found me exhausted when my child needed me most— my patience depleted just when teaching and guiding him required it most.

My father's final words about contentment and living without regrets became my catalyst for change. Looking back at his remarkable journey—from a barefoot village boy to a respected leader who touched hundreds of lives—I realized that his greatest legacy wasn't in his achievements, but in how he lived: with purpose, joy, and genuine care for others. Today, as I make choices about my own life and raise my son, I find myself asking, "Would this make Baba proud?" and, more importantly, "Am I living a life I won't regret?" His lessons continue to guide me, reminding me that true success lies not in what we accumulate, but in the lives we touch and the love we share along the way.

I am truly honored to have my father's influence in my life. Everything I am today and will be tomorrow is owed not only to him but also to my mother. My advice to anyone reading this essay is to cherish not only your parents but all loved ones near and dear. Treat every day like your last day and live life to the fullest. Be content and be at peace. Be a responsible citizen of this world and leave a legacy to be proud of.

Three Things I Learned About Life and Leadership

1. Lead a life of no regrets.
2. Be a good sport—laugh at yourself.
3. Perseverance and hard work pay off!

***

Strength to Teach, Lead, and Persevere: The Inspiring Life of "Ms. Sage"

by Eva Sage-Gavin, Board Director, Former CHRO, and C-Suite Executive

The person who had the greatest impact on my life and leadership style is my late mother, Theresa Veronica Bufalo Sage. She was fearless, full of life, and a trailblazing pioneer.

She instilled the belief in our family that we could be anything we wanted to be and achieve anything we set out to do. While these may seem like the kind of words most parents would tell their children, they became particularly meaningful to me as I researched my mother's life for this essay. She was a lifelong teacher, special education tutor, Marine, coach, scout leader, and single parent.

An Inspiring Presence

As a teacher, "Ms. Sage" inspired in us a passion for learning, often as an incredible adventure. She took us on camping trips every summer, drove us from Boston to Washington, D.C., to visit the Smithsonian Museum, and spent weekends at the Boston Museum of Science or Plymouth Plantation.

Some weekends we went to her first-grade classroom to help decorate the walls and cork boards with homemade seasonal stories and lessons. I learned so much about visual storytelling, the power of color and imagery, and, in particular, how she featured positive recognition for her students.

One of our favorite family memories was attending the World's Fair in New York City in 1964. My mother was determined for us to see what the future might hold and brought four young children, ages two to six, and my older cousin Michael, age 12. My favorite exhibit was "Futurama II," which portrayed the world of 2064. All things considered, it was pretty accurate about what was to come (thus far) and cemented my passion and interest in the power of technology.

A Legacy of Creativity, Optimism, and Good Humor

Despite very tough life circumstances, my mother had an amazing spirit of optimism and good humor. Her favorite saying was that "she never graduated from first grade" because she taught that level for 38 years—right up until a few months before she passed away due to breast cancer at age 58.

She would do home repairs by herself, sometimes not very well, and laugh when the wallpaper peeled off the wall because she used the wrong paste. She was creative and loved fun and celebration.

While leading our family, Ms. Sage also always seemed to find time for others. Some of my earliest memories were of us traveling to the homes of children with special needs for tutoring and individual lessons. She was patient, infinitely kind, and could make everyone smile.

My mom was proud, courageous, and strong in her life, which—now that I am an adult with a grown child—I can only begin to completely understand. She broke boundaries to fiercely protect and lead her family through trying circumstances in a society that generally did not support women who broke gender stereotypes.

Energy for Career, Volunteer Interests, and More

My mother attended Emmanuel College in Boston, Massachusetts, where she showed wide-ranging interests ahead of her time. The school's 1952 yearbook featured her participation as "dramatic editor" of the college paper, as well as being on the debate and field hockey teams. Though she graduated near the top of her class, she faced the reality of limited job opportunities for women at the time—largely in teaching, nursing, or administrative roles.

She volunteered to join the U.S. Marines in 1954 shortly after the Korean conflict. She served in Parris Island, South Carolina, in a new field called "Personnel" (now known as Human Resources)—a career path where I've been able to apply many of her leadership lessons.

She married in 1957 and became known as "Terry Sage" for the rest of her life.

She became a teacher in her hometown of Cohasset, Massachusetts. She never left first grade, although she was qualified to teach higher levels. She felt it was the most pivotal grade where she could launch students on a great lifetime path. She did that for me: I entered first grade reading at a third-grade level, thanks to her tutoring. I'm sure that helped me later with the 1,000 pages I had to read each week for my labor law classes at Cornell.

Her energetic leadership had no boundaries. Ms. Sage coached the women's field hockey team when there was no funding, their equipment was second-hand, and team bus trips were paid for with bake sale funds. She served as my Girl Scout troop leader when she had already spent a long day teaching and had papers to grade at night. This was in addition to her weekly tutoring.

When she passed away, I was overwhelmed by how many of her former students came to her wake. It touched my heart in a way that I know she would have loved (if only it had been her retirement or birthday party instead of her wake).

A Lifetime of Strength and Resilience

My mother was the seventh and youngest child of immigrant parents from Ireland and Italy. Born during the Great Depression in the winter of 1930, she persevered to become one of two siblings to graduate from college, near the top of her class.

When I was a child, she shared that she had served in the Marines. Being so young, I did not appreciate how unique that must have been for her, particularly in the 1950s—what a fearless and bold role model! I believe it helps explain why, when I applied to an Ivy League school with no money and slim chances of being accepted, my mom gave me the courage to "just try." She was the embodiment of, "Why not? If not you, who? If not now, when?"

Later, as a single parent raising three children in the 1960s and 1970s, my mother faced many hard-to-imagine obstacles. She often stood up for herself and her family through medical and emotional trauma, frequently challenging the "norms" of marriage, religion, and gender. She took a late-night job at a coffee shop to help pay for my college tuition at Cornell, hoping that none of her students' parents would see that we were struggling to make ends meet.

Looking back at my own life and career, I seem to have replicated her leadership in so many ways: always doing more, having difficulty saying "no" when there's a need to be met, and a desire to help others to ensure they rise.

And now I see the same passion for service and leadership in my daughter.

Taking Care of Self

Seemingly without warning—at least to the rest of the family—my mother's health declined drastically and dramatically. Being such a strong woman, always focused on others, meant her own health often took a back seat.

She was 51 years old when diagnosed with Stage 4 breast cancer and was rushed into surgery on Thanksgiving Day. While she lived for another seven years, doctors said if caught earlier, she would not have died so young at the age of 58.

Throughout her life, my mom was fiercely proud and the last to ask for help. I believe it was this singular focus on caring for everyone else that took her from us much too soon. That was the hardest lesson I learned from her life: tomorrow is not a promise. Live "all out" now because you may not get a second chance.

A second hard lesson was to trust my intuition if something feels not quite right. Advocate for yourself and your family … and get a second opinion. My mother had physical exams every year, yet her doctor missed her cancer in its advancing stages. We later learned that more than a dozen other women in this same doctor's care also suffered from advanced breast cancer. This lesson was the most difficult but became essential later in life when two family members faced critical and life-threatening illnesses. They got the care they needed by standing up for themselves, learning about their medical conditions, and collaborating with multiple medical experts.

Lifelong curiosity and learning, self-care, and a willingness to "put the oxygen mask on yourself first so you can help others" are enduring lessons.

Life Experiences Are the Greatest Teacher

Living life with a "no obstacles that can't be overcome" upbringing enabled me to be bold in my career, lead through big, difficult challenges, and leave what I hope is a legacy that will continue to lift others—while prioritizing personal and family health.

My mother's emphasis on education, helping others, and breaking barriers became themes for my career and leadership style. I co-led an Aspen Institute initiative to create job training and career opportunities for community college students; worked with Cornell University to create programs that prepare and support hundreds of future Chief HR Officers for the leap to leadership; and became the first female board member in multiple technology companies.

I'm perhaps most proud of helping to improve the safety and livelihoods of garment workers in Southeast Asia, particularly women, by using my influence as a corporate HR leader to create international coalitions across the retail industry, governments, and non-governmental organizations to address wellbeing collectively.

I'm sure my mother's example of strength and caring provided the foundation to tackle this work.

Of all the lessons learned, the most important is to take care of your family, starting with yourself, your health, and your ability to be there. Every possible resource that can keep you well, give you insights for change, and create rest stops in a busy life and career is key to living a vibrant 100-year life. That is why, like my mother, I have taken on more. I serve on the Advisory Council of the Stanford Center on Longevity to share my passion about "healthspan" vs. lifespan, and how we can collaborate on new ways to maximize every decade of a 100-year life.

There is another lesson that I have spent decades trying to understand. My mother's nickname for me was "PNP," which stood for "Pretty Nearly Perfect." I loved it when I was younger because it motivated me to strive for my best. But as I got older and had to make tough choices about paths to take or skip, I often was paralyzed with concern about making the less-than-perfect choice, leading to second-guessing, procrastination, and self-judgment. Imagine my delight in marrying a partner of 35 years who was the opposite and could find that balance with the right level of effort for the most effective outcome. And our daughter learned from him that sometimes good enough is just right!

Three Things I Learned About Life and Leadership

1. Be proud, courageous, strong, and lead with integrity. Know who you are; your strengths and weaknesses.
2. Be compassionate to others. Help those who need it; build a community and bring others along with you.
3. Learn with a beginner's mind and the fresh and open eyes of a first grader.

***

He Came to Change the World

by Sonya Sepahban, CEO, OurOffice, Inc.

My early memories of my dad, Amir Hassan Sepahban, are anything but typical. Instead of bedtime stories and playing games with me, Daddy often talked about the world economic balance, price of oil, advancements in computing, and other far-ranging topics with the five-year-old version of me! He had a mind like a steel trap and a curiosity that knew no bounds.

He lived by a strong moral compass, guided by a constant drive to learn, explore, and grow. Born in Iran, he had excelled in his studies, especially in math, but he had other talents, too. He played the violin beautifully, loved ballroom dancing, and had a sense of adventure that took him from his homeland to the United States in his early twenties.

Driven by Curiosity and Purpose

My dad's journey to America was driven by his thirst for learning and innovation. He wanted to be part of an exciting world full of possibilities. As he often told me, he didn't come such a long way just to play it safe; he came to change the world. He threw himself into learning, working, and challenging himself in ways that I didn't fully appreciate until I was a grown up and navigating my own career path.

After graduating from Harvard, Dad worked with some of the most innovative companies of the 1960s, such as Philco and Martin Marietta, where he helped develop advanced systems for guiding and controlling space vehicles. Decades later, I would work at NASA on similar systems—a coincidence that makes me feel close to him to this day.

Dad's curiosity was boundless, and his drive to master new fields of knowledge was awe-inspiring. He didn't just focus on one area; he transitioned from electronics to the oil business and even to complex economic theories. I remember him studying my high school chemistry books, working through organic chemistry problems with me so he could better understand the science of oil production and its impacts on pricing. He wanted to figure out how oil could bring about macroeconomic good to the world. Eventually, this passion took him to organizations such as OPEC and the United Nations, where he advocated for "win-win" pricing policies that would help oil-exporting countries prosper while encouraging consumer countries to conserve non-renewable resources.

I remember one proud moment when he visited me at Cornell University in my sophomore year. He was heading to New York City to give a talk at the United Nations, and he invited me to join him. I felt so proud helping him prepare his flip charts and walking up those steps with him. I felt I was part of something much bigger, something that affected a lot of people—and it impressed upon me the desire to look beyond myself as I considered career options.

Nobody's Perfect

We all have our flaws and my dad's was managing time effectively. He often lost track of time and was always late. My mom used to shake her head and mutter, "Your dad is always running on his own schedule."

Of course, from his perspective, he was working on big, world-changing ideas which made it hard for him to keep track of everyday things. He would throw himself into his work with an energy that was inspiring but exhausting to watch.

His life was his work, and his work was his life, which sometimes left little room for family. Growing up, my mom did a great job creating a rich and fulfilling life for us with sports, trips, and adventures. As I look back, though, I've become quite aware of areas where one parent simply can't fill the void left by another.

Despite the distance, my dad's influence on my career is undeniable. He always spoke about my future as if it were a foregone conclusion—that I'd go to college, study something meaningful, and make a real impact. He believed in the power of creating, building, innovating, and giving back. From a young age, he planted the seed of purpose in me that has guided me through my life.

Not Without Sacrifice

Dad's commitment to his values often came with sacrifices, especially when he was working in the Middle East. He refused to get involved in any "gray areas," as he called them. This wasn't always easy, and it probably made his life more difficult. But ultimately it kept him alive, especially during the tumultuous years of the Iranian revolution when many people were executed or jailed. He wasn't interested in cutting corners or making deals that didn't align with his principles. This steadfastness became one of the most valuable lessons he taught me—never compromise on what you believe in, even if it comes at a cost.

Toward the end of his life, Dad was diagnosed with Alzheimer's, a cruel disease that took away some aspects of the brilliant mind that had defined him. Watching his memory slip away was heartbreaking, especially knowing how much he loved his work. As time went on, he started to forget familiar faces, although—somehow—he could always recognize me to the last day, even when he couldn't remember my brothers or my mom.

His reasoning remained mostly intact to the end. At his eulogy, my youngest brother read from a diary Dad kept in his final years. It revealed his ongoing efforts through those years to create a framework in his mind to make sense of the world, even as his memories of how it worked were slipping away.

The Depths of Loss

In his final years, my work and family life kept me busy, and I regret not spending more time with him. But the night before he passed away, I had a strong feeling that I needed to see him. I brought him to my mom's house for dinner. He didn't remember her, but he was still polite, thanking "the beautiful hostess" for the meal. The next morning, I got the call that he was gone. I was hit with a strong wave of sadness and profound loss, well beyond anything I had ever experienced or frankly expected.

After his passing, I was surprised by how deeply I grieved. I had always thought of our relationship as somewhat distant—he was often working, and I had my own responsibilities. But in that moment of loss, I realized our connection had been stronger and deeper than I had ever known. Even now, I sometimes feel his presence. I see him in my dreams, standing by my side, offering silent support and encouragement. And over the years, I've come to understand that the impact he had on my life goes beyond the time we shared. In many ways, as I often think of him when I reflect on my values and key choices, he has taught me more after his death.

Looking back, three main lessons stand out to me—lessons that have shaped these values and choices and guided my life and my career in profound ways.

1. Be Curious About the People Around You

Dad was endlessly curious about the world, about science, and about big ideas. He loved to explore new fields and master new skills. But sometimes I wish he had shown that same curiosity toward the people around him.

Once we were on a train ride from London to Margate, a seaside town on England's southeast coast. I was going to spend the summer at a boarding school there before enrolling in a British high school that Fall. He surprised me on the train ride by sharing how much he loved my brothers and me, even if he couldn't always be around. It was a rare moment of openness that I've carried with me ever since.

Now, as I have my own family and lead my own team and work with people from all walks of life, I try to be as curious about their experiences and stories as Dad was about his work. Everyone has a story, and showing interest and caring about those stories is the stuff of real relationships and a rich life.

2. Keep Learning, No Matter What

Dad's love for learning never faded, no matter how old he got or how much he'd already accomplished. From electronics to oil and economics, he kept pushing himself to understand more, to dig deeper, and to innovate. He never let himself get comfortable, and he was humble and eager to learn from everyone.

That's something I've tried to emulate in my own career. As a leader, I know there's always something new to learn, and I make a point of challenging myself to grow and learn from our team members. Life is full of discoveries. Keeping an open mind and seeking new experiences and awareness make all the difference. Dad's curiosity was his superpower, and I try to carry a piece of that with me every day.

3. Don't Compromise Your Values

One of Dad's strongest qualities was his integrity. He believed in doing the right thing, even when it was difficult, even when it might have been easier to look the other way. He worked in regions of the world where corruption and shortcuts were common, but he never gave in, not even an inch. He held himself to a high standard, and that example has been a guiding light for me in my own journey.

As a leader, I've made it a priority to build a company that stands by its values, even in a challenging business landscape. Leadership, as Dad taught me, is about more than success; it's about staying true to what you believe in.

Enduring Lessons

In the end, Daddy may not have been there every day, but he left me with something far more valuable than time—he left me with a sense of purpose, a moral compass, and a lifelong love for learning. He taught me to be curious, not just about the world, but (albeit in an indirect way) about the people around me. He showed me that learning is a journey that never ends, and that true leadership is rooted in integrity.

His presence is still with me in the quiet moments when I'm facing a tough decision or a new challenge. I know he'd be proud of the path I've chosen and the lessons I carry with me. And for that, I am deeply, profoundly grateful.

Dad's life was a testament to the power of curiosity, resilience, and unyielding integrity. He left a legacy not just in the fields he worked in, but in the lives of the people who were touched by his innovative ideas and accomplishments.

Three Things I Learned About Life and Leadership

1. Be curious about the people around you.
2. Keep learning, no matter what.
3. Don't compromise your values.

✳✳✳

Notes

1. "Noble," *Merriam-Webster.com Dictionary*, accessed October 2024, https://www.merriam-webster.com/dictionary/noble
2. Benjamin Franklin, "Tell me and I forget, teach me and I may remember, involve me and I learn," *Goodreads*, accessed October 2024, https://www.goodreads.com/author/quotes/289513.Benjamin_Franklin
3. "See a penny, pick it up. All day long you'll have good luck." *The Quotations Page*, accessed October 2024, http://www.quotationspage.com/qoid
4. James M. Kouzes and Barry Z. Posner, *The Leadership Challenge* (San Francisco: Jossey-Bass, 2007).
5. "Roz Wyman: L.A.'s First City Councilwoman of the Modern Era," *Update*, University of California, Berkeley Library, June 5, 2018, accessed November 2024, https://update.lib.berkeley.edu/2018/06/05/wiener-wyman
6. Richard E. Meyer, "The Political Insider", *Los Angeles Magazine*, July 1, 2020.
7. Richard E. Meyer, "Postscript: Roz Wyman," *Los Angeles Magazine*, June 17, 2010.
8. Richard E. Meyer, "The Political Insider", *Los Angeles Magazine*, July 1, 2020.

Part III

What ... Life and Leadership Actions Will *You* Take?

Chapter 8

Tensions of Intentionality

Now that we have examined the neuroscience of loss and leadership, extracted lessons from famous celebrities and a wide variety of survey respondents, and most importantly experienced "growth and improvement" via 35 essays about special somebodies, the time has come to process and summarize some common threads about life and leadership.

The Paradox of Contradictions

Giselle Ibarra, a 28-year-old Mexican painter, entrepreneur, and influencer, beautifully captured the essence of this chapter when on January 11, 2024, she posted on X, "…life is a paradox. In order to heal you must hurt, in order to love you must break open, in order to have peace you must face chaos."[1]

Virtually every story, example, and leadership lesson shared throughout this book includes an overt or underlying reference to one or many paradoxes or tensions. These tensions are a combination of contradictory feelings, emotions, beliefs, philosophies, behaviors, actions, and/or leadership practices that were thrown into conflict or question by losing a loved one.

Most of our book contributors managed not only to learn from their incredibly negative experiences but to somehow turn those experiences into growth opportunities that made them better people and leaders. They are the ultimate "turn lemons into lemonade" leaders.

There are too many examples of lemonade-making throughout this book to believe they are coincidences. Instead, I think there is something very consistent and important at play—intentionality. Dictionary.com defines intentionality as "an attitude of purposefulness, with a commitment to deliberate action."[2]

Our contributors experienced something terrible (the death of somebody special to them), processed and learned from losing that important person, and came out the other side a better human being and leader.

Why and how?

This phenomenon only happens through a combination of the right attitude, a persistent action learning mindset, a lot of courage and resilience, and the

DOI: 10.4324/9781003585633-13

ability to reconcile competing thoughts and emotions and the tensions they evoke. Do all these things well and you achieve intentionality.

In our last book, *The Secret Sauce for Leading Transformational Change* (Routledge, 2022), I identified in Chapter 2, "The Beauty of And," seven paradoxes that needed to be mastered to successfully lead transformational change. After all, leadership is often about reconciling competing priorities and recognizing that conflicting ideas can and often must coexist.

Lives Lost and Leadership Found builds on this notion of paradoxes, but with a twist. This book reveals that intentionality is paramount if you are going to work your way through a set of incredibly complex feelings to emerge a stronger learner and better person and leader. To extract lessons on life and leadership after losing a special somebody, you not only must find "the beauty of and" (reconcile competing priorities), but you also need to *intentionally* transition through contradictory tensions. Our book contributors repeatedly demonstrated these tendencies, which they learned on their own as well as from the special people they lost.

You must confront, acknowledge, and accept certain tough realities before you can move on to a more constructive and productive state of being. The best leaders are great at navigating these transitions. And they do so intentionally and with purpose.

If there is a simple formula to describe this phenomenon, it would be "First A, then B." The following tensions of intentionality emerged in writing our book and best illustrate this "first/then" mindset and skillset:

First...	Then...
Grief	Purpose
Fear	Courage
Fog	Clarity
Paralysis	Action
Compartmentalization	Integration
Nostalgia	Anticipation
Learning	Leading

Grief, Then Purpose

Nearly every essay in this book tells a tale of anguish and sadness associated with losing somebody special. Whether that person was young or old, healthy or ill, or was expected or unexpected to pass away, the most common baseline human reaction is to grieve over a loss. Grief is the gateway that eventually leads to finding a sense of purpose. At first, we feel terrible. Then, over time, that grief gradually gives way to the desire to turn the loss into something more meaningful. Whether to honor the person who has passed or to ensure they did not die in vain, purpose wins out over grief. Leaders find and cultivate purpose. "Grief does not change you … it reveals you," according to John Green, author of *Fault in Our Stars*.[3]

Fear, Then Courage

The leaders featured in our book often transitioned from deep fear associated with losing a loved one to an even deeper courage. But this transition is never fully completed. As Martin Luther King, Jr., Nelson Mandela, Franklin D. Roosevelt, Mark Twain, and many others to whom this quote is attributed remind us, "Courage is not the absence of fear, it is the willingness to act despite the fear."[4]

There is an inevitable tension that arises from living life without someone who has been close to us. The loss and uncertainty drive fear. And this tension often rises in direct proportion to how much of a central role our lost loved one played in our lives. But as repeatedly described by our contributing authors, fear gives way to strength and bravery. We must live our own lives, take care of those who remain around us, and make sure everyone else is "okay." That's what leaders do despite the fear. Author C.S. Lewis admitted in *A Grief Observed*,[5] "No one ever told me grief felt so like fear. I am not afraid, but the sensation is like being afraid."

Fog, Then Clarity

Many people who lose someone close to them describe a fog that descends around them almost immediately. I personally experienced this feeling when my brother and mother died. I found myself having a very difficult time focusing and concentrating on both simple and complex things. In fact, one of the reasons I waited months following their deaths to start writing this book was because I knew I needed to allow time for the fog to lift. I had to regain my ability to think and see clearly.

The ongoing tension between fog and clarity is one of the primary reasons experts advise against making big personal or professional decisions for at least a few months or more following the loss of a loved one. As composer Irving Berlin said, "The song is over, but the melody lingers on."[6] Wait for the fog to lift a bit before you drive off a cliff you did not see coming.

Paralysis, Then Action

Grief, fear, and fog inescapably breed paralysis. Under the stress of losing someone, we freeze, not knowing what to do or where to turn next. As poet Carl Sandburg reminded us, "When we lose someone we have loved deeply, we are left with a grief that can paralyze us emotionally. When they die, a part of us dies too."[7] Yet, there is a natural tension. We also have the desire and practical need to make important decisions, solve problems, and take action.

Therefore, while we may be frozen by emotional pain or fear of the unknown or lack of focus, we must act. The best leaders break through feeling paralyzed by making decisions and driving action despite whatever else is going on around them. This paralysis vs. action paradox demands the ability to focus and compartmentalize.

Compartmentalization, Then Integration

People who cope well with the competing priorities of life and death seem to have a shared superpower, the ability to compartmentalize. According to *Psych Central*, "the power of compartmentalization refers to the ability to mentally separate different aspects of one's life, allowing for focused attention on a specific task or emotion, at a given time, which can significantly reduce stress, improve productivity, and maintain emotional stability by preventing overwhelming feelings from spilling over into other areas of life."[8]

For me, it is simultaneously one of my biggest strengths and among my most prominent weaknesses. I found this same capability and curse in large supply among our book contributors.

The tension arises from the need to place the pain of loss in a separate compartment. We put it aside or behind us so we can tend to other equally important matters such as family, work, or life. Tension also surfaces when we must eventually break open the separate compartment and begin to reintegrate all the various and competing aspects of our lives. We divide things into smaller, more digestible bite-sized issues or problems so we can isolate our pain or problems and soldier on while keeping grief and fog to a minimum.

For a while, putting our feelings of loss in a separate compartment provides some relief and comfort. But being numb to the pain can only work for so long. Numbness is therefore both an asset and a liability. We eventually need to address all our competing feelings and priorities in one integrated whole. Life and leadership are about integration. As we begin to integrate our feelings once again with the daily realities and demands of life, we begin looking forward to future possibilities rather than reflecting on past pain.

Nostalgia, Then Anticipation

Respect the past while embracing the future. This entire book cherishes and highlights mostly fond memories that contributors share about the special somebodies they lost. When someone passes away, much of the initial focus is on remembering the past. We reminisce about good and bad times, special events, favorite shared activities, and what these important people taught us. Most importantly, we remember how our special somebodies made us feel.

I am reminded of the famous Maya Angelou quote, "I've learned that people will forget what you said, people will forget what you did, but people will never forget how you made them feel."[9] We are nostalgic.

Then we begin to face the tension of letting go of memories, artifacts, pictures, notes, letters, special places, favorite foods, familiar smells, books, songs, TV shows, or movies. The time comes to move forward, reawaken our sense of anticipation, and once again begin thinking about the future, not the past. Leaders intentionally transition from appreciating the past to loving what's next. A future-orientation inevitably results in learning from our experiences (including painful ones) and then turning that learning into leadership philosophies, priorities, and actions that help us—and everyone around us—move on.

Learning, Then Leading

Each essay, survey response, example, and story in this book has unique lyrics but with a common refrain. People lost a special somebody but learned important values, behaviors, philosophies, priorities, and/or leadership lessons from them. First, we learned, then we led.

It is amazing but not surprising to me that there can be so much wisdom derived from the pain of losing someone we loved, respected, and admired. While this "learning to leading" idea is the foundational premise of *Lives Lost and Leadership Found*, I don't think I fully understood the magnitude of our endeavor. Now I do.

In a strange way, we all do. To borrow from Winnie the Pooh, "How lucky (we are) to have something that makes saying goodbye so hard."[10]

Notes

1. Giselle Ibarra, "One thing I've learned, life is a paradox. In order to heal you must hurt, in order to love you …," *X*, accessed January 11, 2024. https://x.com/sincerelyart/status/1745513679368675768
2. "Intentionality," *Dictionary.com*, accessed September 19, 2024, https://www.dictionary.com/browse/intentionality
3. John Green, "Grief does not change you. It reveals you," *AZQuotes*, accessed December 2024, https://www.azquotes.com/quote/1390370
4. Nelson Mandela, *Long Walk to Freedom* (Boston: Back Bay Books, 1995).
5. C.S. Lewis, *A Grief Observed* (San Francisco: HarperSanFrancisco, 2001).
6. Irving Berlin, "The song is over, but the melody lingers on," *AZQuotes*, accessed December 2024, https://www.azquotes.com/quote/1390370
7. Carl Sandburg, "When we lose someone we have loved deeply, we are left with a grief that can paralyze …," *AZQuotes*, accessed December 2024, https://www.azquotes.com/quote/1390370
8. "Compartmentalization: Definition, Benefits, and More," *Psych Central*, accessed December 2024, https://www.psychcentral.com/health/compartmentalize
9. Maya Angelou, *I Know Why the Caged Bird Sings* (New York: Ballantine Books, 2009).
10. The Walt Disney Company, A.A. Milne, *Winnie the Pooh*, "How lucky we are to have something that makes saying goodbye so hard," *AZQuotes*, accessed December 2024, https://www.azquotes.com/quote/350806

Chapter 9

The Smoothie Effect

Have you ever had a smoothie? Wikipedia defines it as, "A beverage made by pureeing ingredients in a blender. It commonly has a liquid base, such as fruit juice or milk, yogurt, or ice cream. Other ingredients may include fruits, vegetables, crushed ice, protein powder, or nutritional supplements."[1]

No one person is credited with inventing the smoothie, but the concept is thought to have originated in the 1920s. It became more popular in the 1960s when Julius Freed invented the Orange Julius to create a less acidic juice for his own consumption. The smoothie concept continued to evolve during the 1930s through the 1980s when Steve Kuhnau began experimenting with the idea due to his own lactose intolerance, leading him to found Smoothie King, now the world's largest smoothie maker.

All this relatively recent progress was preceded by hundreds of years of tradition in Mediterranean and Eastern cultures which featured pureed fruit drinks that resemble smoothies. Based on 2023 estimates, smoothies have become a roughly $12 billion global industry with an expected compound annual growth rate (CAGR) of more than 9%, which will result in industry revenues approaching $30 billion by the year 2032.[2]

Right about now, you may be asking yourself, "What does the evolution of the smoothie have to do with losing a loved one or learning something from them about leadership?" I am glad you asked!

Connecting the Dots: The Chaos of Loss and Life

I have tried smoothies from time to time but would not consider myself a smoothie aficionado. However, some of my family members and friends are. In studying their smoothie habits and preferences, I have made several observations which may help us all better understand and appreciate the connection between smoothies and losing and learning from special somebodies.

Making a smoothie involves considerable planning and preparation, including the intentional selection of ingredients, chopping, slicing, dicing, scooping, pouring, mixing, shaking, stirring, spinning, tumbling, crunching, and making

DOI: 10.4324/9781003585633-14

a great deal of noise. It is a lot like the methodical and well-conceived way we attempt to lead our lives. We have a plan. But then life (or death) gets in the way. We expect a natural order to things, and then chaos ensues.

To me, the smoothie is a perfect analogy for this chaos of loss and life. Despite all the preparation and careful curation of ingredients, what happens next in the creation of a smoothie appears to the untrained eye to be completely random and arbitrary. Everything gets thrown in a blender and must fend for itself, being tossed every which way, turned upside down, and unceremoniously mashed, smashed, and bashed into submission. There is noise, then silence. Then more noise and more silence. Someone ultimately decides the smoothie is ready for consumption, but I am never sure on what basis. It appears to be a judgment call at best.

Smoothie-making is most definitely a process. A messy and painstaking process. But some people would argue that all that work is well worth it. After all, as the saying goes, smoothies are so good and so good for you.

Smoothies also teach us the value of creatively blending a diverse and often conflicting array of ingredients one might not otherwise choose to put together. For example, I have never considered eating chocolate, kale, whey, blueberries, and protein powder at the same time. But maybe that is just me.

Despite my own reservations, smoothies do appear to be "a thing." They are a common shared experience among millions of people worldwide, and they are a great example of reconciling competing or conflicting things. Smoothies are tasty yet healthy, a lot of work yet convenient. We can't fully appreciate them until the moment we drink them. Smoothies, like lost loved ones are…

Here and gone.

Parallels, with All Due Respect …

In no way do I intend to trivialize or make light of the pain or sense of loss associated with the passing of a loved one by equating that experience to making a smoothie. That said, if we can allow ourselves a moment of humor and good cheer in honor of the loved ones we have lost, I do want to suggest that there are some parallels between the processes of learning from a deceased special somebody and concocting a smoothie.

Both experiences combine churning, spinning, turning upside down, and handling extraordinarily complex and competing preferences, textures, tastes, and feelings. Both involve the inevitable back and forth between deafening noise and more deafening silence. And when all the tumbling, crunching, and noisemaking stop, both processes result in memories we can fondly savor.

Smoothies, like learning from losing a loved one, can make us healthier, better, and stronger. And if we can manage our way through the paradoxes of conflicting ingredients and emotions, we can be better people and leaders for having lost and learned from a special somebody.

So, what does "The Smoothie Effect" teach us as leaders about what matters most in life and leadership?

1. **Ingredients**—life and leadership are a product of what you put into them, so choose high quality ingredients and people.
2. **Blending**—we are at our best when we mix and reconcile competing experiences, ideas, feelings, tastes, priorities, and personalities.
3. **Noise**—losing a loved one, grieving, healing, learning, and leading require working through inevitable accompanying chaos and tensions. That "noise" is essential to fully appreciating the silence and focus that can be found on the other side.
4. **Intentionality**—thoughtful planning and preparation for what you are trying to accomplish (and why) makes all the difference in achieving purpose, direction, speed, execution, results, and fulfillment.

Ann Hood, novelist and short-story writer, reminds us that "grief doesn't have a plot. It isn't smooth. There is no beginning and middle and end."[3] Smoothies aren't as smooth as the name would imply either, but they sure do teach us a lot about reconciling grief, learning, leadership, and competing tensions.

Notes

1. "Smoothie," *Wikipedia*, last modified September 23, 2024, https://en.wikipedia.org/wiki/Smoothie
2. Grand View Research, "Smoothies Market Size, Share and Growth Report, 2030," last modified 2023, https://www.grandviewresearch.com/industry-analysis/smoothies-market-report
3. Ann Hood, *Comfort: A Journey Through Grief* (New York: W. W. Norton & Company, 2009).

Chapter 10

From Loss to Leadership

Yogi Berra was a Hall of Fame baseball catcher and a quote machine. He was as famous for his quotes as he was for his illustrious baseball career. One of his best is "When you come to a fork in the road, take it."[1] After you let that sink in for a minute, you may realize we are at a point in this book where we have an important choice to make.

I thought a lot about whether I wanted this final chapter to be a comprehensive summary of all the ins and outs, ups and downs, and twists and turns of the book … or not. Ultimately, the answer was no.

Learn and Do

Rather than reminding you of what I hoped *you* might learn from reading this book, I have instead decided to share with you what *I* learned about life and leadership from writing this book—and more importantly what I am going to do with those lessons. After all, I am a firm believer that writing a book is not only about what you can teach others, but also about learning something yourself.

I have learned a lot and as a result I will do the following:

1. Define and confront reality more transparently.
2. Persevere and recover more resiliently.
3. Listen and empathize more compassionately.
4. Learn and teach more passionately.
5. Advocate and role model more purposefully.

Now it's your turn. What are you going to do about life and leadership based on what you learned in this book? Write it down. Make a list. Review it often. Adjust it as needed. Share it with other people. Hold yourself accountable. Do what you say you are going to do.

But please don't stop there, go a step further. If you were intrigued or inspired by reading the essays and other content in this book, consider honoring your special somebody by writing an essay of your own. Do it for yourself, for others, and/or for your special somebody.

DOI: 10.4324/9781003585633-15

See the Appendix of this book for guidance to consider when writing your essay. Writing an essay is a great way to recognize and thank your special some-body, as well as a powerful means of capturing what you have learned from this person about life and leadership. And as you will read in the Epilogue that fol-lows this final chapter, many of our essay contributors found the essay-writing process to be an incredibly cathartic and emotional experience!

Here and Gone

Speaking of cathartic and emotional experiences, it's time to close this book by fulfilling a promise I made to you back in Chapter 1, where I committed to sharing the lyrics of the song I wrote to honor my father, mother, and brother. I hope you see a little bit of yourself and your lost loved one(s) in these words. You can also listen to a recording of me performing the song by visiting https://www.consortium4change.com/here-and-gone-ziskin.

You were here and now you're gone
  Left the world in a hurry
I'm still here but not alone
  We're feeling strong so don't worry
   Here and gone

The expressions on your faces
  Light up the edges of my mind
Imagination takes me places
  Crystal clear, yet ill-defined
   Here and gone, you were here and gone

I can hear the timbre of your voices
  And the echoes of your laughter
Joys and worries and tough choices
  Lessons from before and after
   Here and gone

You were here and now you're gone
  Left the world in a hurry
I'm still here but not alone
  We're feeling good so don't worry
   Here and gone

I miss you my father
  And the time we never had
I miss you my brother
  All the good and the bad
I miss you my mother
  But I will not be scared

You taught me the power of advocacy
    To take good care of our family
Respect all but fear none
    Never give up until the work is done
      Here and gone, you were here and gone

Give a lot more than you take
    Be the best you can be and own your mistakes
Care too much, bring the good stuff
    Cherish love and time … they fade away… and are never enough
      Here and gone

I thank you my father
    For inspiring my dreams
I thank you my brother
    For believing in our schemes
I thank you my mother
    For the gift of self esteem
      Here and gone

You were here and now you're gone
    Left the world in a hurry
I'm still here but not alone
    We're feeling loved so don't worry
    We're feeling good so don't worry
    We're feeling strong so don't worry

Here and gone
    You were here and now you're gone

(Visit https://www.consortium4change.com/here-and-gone-ziskin to listen to the song as performed by Ian Ziskin.)

Be Not Afraid …

I must admit I discovered something very revealing about myself while serving as lead author of *Lives Lost and Leadership Found: Lessons from Special Somebodies*. To paraphrase many others including Woody Allen, Marcus Aurelius, Albert Einstein, Stephen Hawking, and Mark Twain "… I do not fear death, I fear not living and leading to the fullest."

How about you?

Note

1. Yogi Berra, *The Yogi Book: I Really Didn't Say Everything I Said!* (New York: Boulevard Books, 1998).

Epilogue
Feelings About Feelings

This Epilogue was not supposed to happen. It is the result of an unplanned, last-minute decision based on unanticipated feedback from this book's contributing authors. Many of these contributors shared not only their essays with me, but also their *feelings* and unexpected reactions to their essay-writing experience.

There were many honest—and often surprised—expressions of *feelings*. Catharsis. Joy. Sorrow. Tears. Pain. Smiles. Laughter. Memories. Emotional release. *Feelings.*

While *Lives Lost and Leadership Found* is a book about life and leadership lessons, it is borne of human emotions and experiences. *Feelings.* Write something, *feel* something.

So, we decided to share some of the *feelings* with you here in hopes that it will inspire you to turn to the Appendix that follows and write your own essay about your special somebody.

We wonder how that would make you *feel.*

Elizabeth Andora ...

Working on this essay has been an incredibly meaningful experience, and I'm deeply grateful for the opportunity to write about my father. Without this prompt, I might never have taken the time to reflect in this way. Thank you!

Bill Baker ...

I wasn't sure how I would feel writing this essay, or even if I could do it. Turns out, while it was emotional, it was peaceful and at the same time comforting. It feels "right" to share it.

Gina Collins ...

Writing this essay brought back the emotions of my father's life and his passing, blending the warmth of his kindness and the safe, happy feeling of his presence with the heartbreak of his loss. Mostly, it felt like time was temporarily frozen to peacefully reflect on his remarkable accomplishments, his positivity, and the genuine care he showed for others.

Shelley D. Dionne ...

I write research papers in my work life, but for the first time I finally wrote something that wasn't for anyone else; it was just for me to honor my mom. I feel like I should have done this years ago and I highly recommend it as a means for celebrating the type of love that remains even when a loved one is gone.

Barbara Frankel ...

I experienced both sadness and joy in remembering how my father lived, how he died, and his impact on others. I felt honored to be able to "memorialize" and create a legacy for him, that he mattered and still matters to me and my family.

Stephen Frenkel ...

Contributing this essay brought a lot forward for me—nostalgia for days long past, pride in both who I've had the honor to learn from as well as who I've become, and flattered that anyone would invite me to contribute on this topic among so many admired colleagues. Thank you for this opportunity.

Carol Gausz ...

This was a heartwarming experience of discovery and reconciliation, and I felt content and grateful upon completion of my essay. I feel more connected to Dad and myself as I see more clearly the things I learned from him that I value and those that motivated me to choose alternative ways to be in this world.

Lori Heffelfinger ...

I thought this would be an easy essay to write as my mother died 13 years ago. I found myself crying as I wrote it—worried that I wasn't doing her justice and still feeling the deep pang of sadness that I lost her so soon, alongside reliving the numbness I felt planning her funeral and dispersing her assets.

Salima Hemani ...

Writing this essay about my dad's life and death was both emotional and cathartic, bringing up a mix of gratitude, pride, sorrow, and joy as I reflected on his life and the leadership lessons that he taught me. While some parts were painful to recall, this process has left me feeling deeply connected to him and grateful for how his legacy still continues to shape my life.

MaryAnne McCormick Hyland ...

I feel grateful to have the opportunity to help keep the memory of a beloved colleague alive.

Jonathan "Jake" Jacobs ...

Writing this essay was extraordinarily cathartic after holding it in for more than 60 years. I'm about to show my grown children another side of their dad.

Simon King ...

Losing my mum was devastating but being able to reflect on and write about the impact she had on the lives of so many people made me realize she will always be part of me and gave me further courage to live my life with the values she stood for.

Anna-Sophia Kristjansson ...

Writing the essay about Auntie Nancy revealed the profound, layered lessons she imparted and their lasting impact on my life. Her wisdom continues to resonate, shaping not only my journey but also my son's. I also found my essay has been healing for everyone in my family. I didn't expect that.

Mitch Lippman ...

Writing this essay was the first time I sat down and gathered/synthesized so many memories and emotions about this relationship. The process helped me find a new sense of peace with the loss and renewed joy about the time we spent together.

Katie Lopez ...

Immersing myself in the stories of my grandmother brought a sense of close-ness to her memory and also sadness, reminding me that I still miss her so much. Ed Sheeran says it best in his lyrics: "I wish that heaven had visiting hours ... the things she'll learn from me, I got them all from you."[1]

Orly Maravankin ...

Writing about my mom's life and passing stirred emotions far deeper than I expected, underscoring our profound bond and her enduring influence on me. It also deepened my appreciation for the breadth of leadership lessons she imparted, which continue to shape who I am and how I lead.

Lacey Leone McLaughlin and Jamie Snyder Smith ...

We were emotional and inspired, but most of all, grateful that it brought us together to laugh, learn, and reflect. Connecting, remembering, and spending quality time together was an unexpected and cathartic joy.

Sally Breyley Parker ...

While the initial act of writing tributes to my dad and my dog, Scout, came easily to me because of my love and respect for these two beings, the real gift was in tying their two stories together. It was the first time I saw the common threads in their lessons about life and leadership which deepened both my love for them and their impact on my life.

Cheryl Perkins ...

Writing this essay was bittersweet, as it reopened the wounds of loss but also filled me with joy and pride in honoring the incredible women my mother and sister were. It was a healing process that deepened my appreciation for their impact on my life.

Pallavi Ridout ...

I felt great joy in writing this essay honoring my father. This was something I have been wanting to do for the past few years and this essay is a wonderful beginning to a book dedicated to my father that is to be published in a year's time.

Sade Salazar ...

I feel as though I was holding a candle my grandmother lit—carrying her light forward to brighten paths unknown.

Sonya Sepahban ...

Writing about my dad, I felt an unexpected warmth and closeness to him. The experience itself has left me more convinced than ever that being curious about our loved ones can open our hearts to deeper understanding and appreciation for them, even after they are long gone.

Scott Span ...

Writing this essay came easier than I expected, including smiles and groans, and was both cathartic and frustrating. Writing did bring up happy memories and I am glad to be able to share learnings with others in hopes they can benefit. However, it was also a frustrating experience as it raised some unfinished business I'm still processing.

Shannon Wallis ...

I am truly humbled, honored, and blessed to share the story of my mother, Patricia Gray, the first example of leadership in my life. As I reflect on the many gifts of love and service she gave her family and friends, I am inspired to be a similar example for my own daughters and the leaders who trust me with their souls, teams, and organizations.

Samantha Wasserman ...

Writing this essay, I felt I was both honoring someone formally that I was not invited to honor previously (by not being allowed to come to his funeral) and that I became more deeply connected to him and to my mother. My mother says that she also feels clearer on her connection to him for having read it.

Note

1. Ed Sheeran, "Visiting Hours," *Genius*, accessed December 2024, https://genius.com/Ed-sheeran-visiting-hours-lyrics

Appendix
My Special Somebody

The Epilogue immediately preceding this Appendix features many references to the deeply cathartic, emotional, and personal experiences our contributing authors had in writing their essays. And the essays themselves in Chapters 5–7 further reveal and underscore the power of storytelling and the accompanying lessons learned about life and leadership.

There was a lot of pain, passion, pride, and purpose encapsulated in each essay—as well as the opportunity to honor a lost loved one. We now welcome and encourage you to take this journey with us by writing your own essay about your own special somebody.

You may decide to write it just for yourself or to share it with others. The choice is yours. When you are ready, here are some suggested guidelines to make the experience as painless and enjoyable as possible:

1. **Your Special Somebody**—Decide who you will write about and this person's relationship to you: father, mother, grandparent, spouse, life partner, brother, sister, child, friend, colleague, boss, mentor, etc. When referring to this person, use words you are comfortable with and that have meaning for you (even nicknames).

2. **Length and Structure**—Write in a free-flowing and creative way to get started, but plan for an essay of 1,500–2,000 words (a few hundred words more, or less, is fine) to help keep your essay focused and readable. Also, include a title for the beginning of your essay as well as sub-headings every few paragraphs to emphasize key points you are trying to make along the way. It is okay, perhaps even preferable, to write your essay in full, and then go back later to insert a title and sub-headings.

3. **Essay Attribution**—If you are planning to share your essay with others, be sure to include your name (and perhaps your title at the top). If the essay is just for you, there's no need to worry about including your name or title (presumably, you know who you are!).

4. **First Paragraph**—Include the first and last name of the person you are writing about as well as that person's relationship with you. Help the reader to get to know your special somebody.

5. **Essay Sections**—While you are free to be creative and write in any order you prefer, here is a suggested order and flow:

   – **Description of your special somebody**: personality, strengths, weaknesses, gifts, superpowers, passions, role played in your life, what made the person special to you, and why you loved or cared about this person.

   – **Job, career, hobbies, volunteer interests, etc.**: describe how your special somebody's experiences and interests affected you, your relationship, and what you learned from this person about life and leadership.

   – **Death**: characterize the circumstances around this person's death. Was it sudden, expected, due to illness, an accident, or suicide? How recently or long ago did the person pass away? What were the relevant dates and/or other facts? Include feelings and emotions you experienced that help explain how this special person's death had a profound effect on you (what was the individual experiencing and what were you experiencing at the time)?

   – **How this person handled death/dying and what it taught you**: to the extent it is relevant to your story, did your special somebody handle dying and death in a way that taught you something important about this individual, values held, leadership role in life, etc.?

   – **What you learned about life and leadership from this special person**: highlight and summarize what you learned from this individual in both life and death. Try to distinguish between what you learned from the person in the moment vs. what you may have learned upon further reflection after your special somebody passed. What still sticks with you now? These lessons might be positive (things you respect or would like to emulate) or negative (things you do not respect or would not want to emulate).

   – **Three Things I Learned About Life and Leadership**: use this heading for the final section of your essay. Below it, list the three most important things you learned from the person you lost and number them 1–3. Since this section is intended to summarize and highlight the most important life and leadership lessons you learned from your special somebody, keep each of the three items to a word, a phrase, or a sentence.

6. **Focus**—The above-referenced life and leadership lessons should reflect (where possible) philosophies, values, actions, behaviors, beliefs, priorities, and/or accomplishments this person taught you that have had and are having a significant impact on you as a leader and person. Try to focus on 4–6 things (or even fewer) that are most important to you.

7. **Emotion**—In describing the cause, circumstances, and impact of this person's death on you (and others), use as much candor, transparency, and emotion as you feel comfortable with sharing, consistent with what you feel is appropriate to honor this person.

The above guidelines are offered to support you in the essay-writing process and are very similar to the guidance provided to our contributing authors in advance of them writing their essays for this book. You are welcome to follow these guidelines where helpful and to modify or ignore them based on your needs—just as our essay contributors did!

Most importantly, write in a way that honors your special somebody … and yourself.

Acknowledgments

In the Introduction to this book, I highlighted the importance of *The Spirit of Abundance*. This philosophy of generosity, community, and willingness to share experiences epitomizes the way our book was conceived and written. I cannot thank enough the hundreds of contributors who made *Lives Lost and Leadership Found: Lessons from Special Somebodies* a remarkable journey. Our essay authors, survey respondents, and supporters span business leaders, clients, coaches, consultants, academics, students, members of our Consortium for Change (C4C) (https://www.consortium4change.com), as well as many other colleagues, collaborators, and total strangers. We came together to explore how to lose a loved one and find leadership lessons along the way. Thank you all for sharing your wisdom and emotions.

This book project required hands-on program management from start to finish, and I would like to recognize and thank Matt McGovern (https://www.700acres.com) for his outstanding leadership, attention to detail, and execution. We could not have done this book without you. I would also like to express my appreciation to Melissa Farr for her terrific work on the book cover and helping us capture the essence of what we were trying to convey. Likewise, special thanks to my executive assistant, Gina Sorrells, and program managers, Carolyn Rearick, Roz Jackson, and Heather Coleman-Otuyelu for providing excellent ongoing support with other aspects of our business, thereby allowing me to focus my attention on this book as needed. I am also extremely grateful to Lacey Leone McLaughlin, my business partner, friend, and co-founder of the Consortium for Change (C4C) for her constant belief in our work together and in me.

To the team at Routledge, Taylor & Francis Group, including senior editor Meredith Norwich, who provided expert guidance and encouragement throughout the publishing process, Bethany Nelson, Imran Mirza, and all the others who played a part in this project, THANK YOU!

Special thanks and recognition go to our book's research assistants (my former MBA students) Jack Dickson, Connor Forte, Sade Salazar, and Jackson Yaeger as well as to Ekhoe Ame-Ogie (for whom I proudly serve as a mentor).

You all helped dig deeper on important facts or survey themes that were essential to our story.

To my family including wife (Susan), sons (Tyler, Eric, and Matt), daughters-in-law (Amy and Kajsa), and granddaughters (Zoe and Leah), I cannot tell you how much I appreciate your love, inspiration, and trust. And finally, to my father (Ted), mother (Marilyn), and brother (Adam) ... and all the special somebodies featured in this book, we honor your memories and everything you have taught us about life and leadership.

Contributing Author Bios

Ekhoe Ame-Ogie is a seasoned human resources leader and executive coach with expertise in leadership development, team dynamics, and organizational culture, guiding executives to enhance their leadership skills, navigate complex challenges, and drive meaningful change. As the HR leader for Deloitte West Africa, Ekhoe is dedicated to fostering leadership excellence and believes in the power of strategic coaching and HR to build resilient, high-performing organizations.

Elizabeth Andora is a senior HR executive with experience designing and developing human capital strategies, scaling organizations, and guiding leaders. Rooted in a commitment to authenticity, meaningful connection, and courageous action, her passion is to drive transformative growth by helping leaders unlock their full potential and guide organizations to scale with purpose.

Bill Baker, Chief HR Officer of Wolters Kluwer, is a business leader focused on achieving results through the engagement of talented people. His work centers on cultivating environments where people thrive and are appreciated for their talent, innovation, and delivering for stakeholders.

Dr. John W. Boudreau, Professor Emeritus of Management and Organization and a Senior Research Scientist with the Center for Effective Organizations at the Marshall School of Business, University of Southern California, is recognized worldwide as one of the leading evidence-based visionaries on the future of work and organization. He is known for his breakthrough research on the bridge between work, superior human capital, leadership, and sustainable competitive advantage.

Alysia A. Bullock is an independent human resources consultant and accredited executive coach. Leveraging 25-plus years of HR partnership experience with global leaders in pharmaceuticals, biotech, consumer packaged goods, and other industries, she founded Incite-HR, an organization dedicated to accelerating the impact of leaders and teams through 1:1 coaching, leadership development, and HR Advisory partnership.

Gina Collins, **J.D.**, Healthcare Executive, is a senior healthcare leader with more than 20 years of payer and provider sector experience in strategic planning, negotiations, operational excellence, and compliance. She is known for her leadership in fostering collaborative cultures and building high-performing, results-driven teams.

Jack Dickson is a recent MBA graduate at Binghamton University School of Management, where he focused on Leadership and Consulting, with a background in Finance and Marketing. Passionate about making a difference, he combines his analytical skills with a strong commitment to helping others.

Shelley D. Dionne is the Dean and Professor of Management at Binghamton University's School of Management and a Research Fellow in the Bass Center for Leadership Studies where she explores multilevel issues surrounding team leadership and workforce development.

Connor Muldoon Forte is a recent MBA graduate from Binghamton University School of Management and a new professional. He enjoys traveling, hiking, movies, and spending time with family and friends.

Barbara Frankel, Founder and President of Coaching Initiatives LLC, and Adjunct Faculty Member at Quinnipiac University School of Business, is an executive coach and leadership effectiveness consultant with 20 years of experience enhancing the performance and success of executives, teams, and organizations. Prior to leading her own business, Barbara worked in human resources for JPMorgan Chase and American Express.

Stephen Frenkel, Founder and Lead Consultant, Voyager Executive Consulting LLC, is an executive coach and team performance consultant with more than 20 years of experience in leadership development, organizational optimization, conflict resolution, and change management. His mission is to help leaders and teams perform at their best, enjoy the experience, and have a positive impact at work, at home, and in their communities.

Carol Gausz, **PCC, MSOD, MPA**, is an executive coach and consultant who founded Blue Heron Associates Inc. in 2001 after 20 years leading strategy and change in several organizations. She enjoys partnering with leaders to help them unleash potential for themselves, their teams, and their organizations.

Lori Heffelfinger, **PCC, MSOD**, Executive Coach and Founder, President, and CEO of The Heffelfinger Company, is a lifelong learner and guide to leaders and teams.

Salima Hemani, **PCC, SHRM-SCP**, Founder and CEO of SZH Consulting, is an organizational development expert and executive coach known for designing transformative solutions that elevate organizational health and effectiveness in complex, competitive landscapes. With a background in senior leadership roles at top global firms, she has a track record of successfully guiding Fortune 500 companies, government agencies, and nonprofits toward sustainable change and growth.

MaryAnne McCormick Hyland, Ph.D., currently serves as the Dean of the Robert B. Willumstad School of Business at Adelphi University in New York and has been a faculty member teaching Human Resource Management in the business school since 1999. MaryAnne is a graduate of Rutgers University and Loyola University Maryland.

Jonathan "Jake" Jacobs, a Founding Partner at Rose Snyder & Jacobs, has more than 40 years of experience in business and financial consulting, specializing in compliance and services for entrepreneurial ventures, publicly owned companies, and high-net-worth families. He is the leader of the firm's Merger and Acquisition Practice.

Susan Kelliher, retired CHRO of The Chemours Company, is a senior human resources executive with extensive experience guiding large-scale transformation in global companies, including industrial manufacturing, defense, retail, and technology. Susan's career is defined by a passion for developing the best and brightest people from diverse backgrounds and creating great places to work.

Simon King, BSc Hons, Chief People Officer, Daiichi Sankyo Inc., is a senior human resources executive who has worked in key biopharma companies, dedicating his career to creating cultures and organizations where colleagues can bring their best selves to discover and develop medicines that change the standard of care. Married to Fiona, with two children—Molly and her partner Jaime, and Sam and his wife Liza—Simon volunteers for Ronald McDonald House, runs, white water kayaks, skis, and spends time with family and friends when he's not working.

Anna-Sophia Kristjansson, MSc Neuroscience, Founder and CEO of Lexicon Lens, began her career in marketing before transitioning to talent management, where she developed a passion for aligning business and people strategies to drive measurable results. Married to Orn and the proud mother to their son, John-Thor, Anna-Sophia rides horses and engages in equine-assisted leadership learning, tends to her robust four-season vegetable garden, practices ballet, cooks, and enjoys time with her family.

Mitch Lippman, Founder of The Mitch Lippman Group, Inc., is a coach, facilitator, and leadership trainer who provides ongoing executive coaching, team coaching, and leadership development coaching to clients in many industries around the globe, helping them tap into their background, story, strengths, and experience to uncover their unique leadership styles. He's particularly sought-after to coach women and LGBTQ leaders in tech, and is based in Los Angeles.

Katie Lopez, CHRO, Panavision Inc., has more than 20 years of experience in HR leadership roles in fortune 500 global companies such as Nestle, Northrop Grumman, and most recently as CHRO for Bonduelle Fresh Americas. Katie is a proud mother of two daughters, Addison and Amelia, and wife of 21 years to Alberto; and in her spare time, she volunteers in leadership roles on independent school boards.

Lacey Leone McLaughlin, President of LLM Consulting Group, is an executive coach and talent management professional with demonstrated experience in designing and delivering cutting-edge consulting services to Global/ Fortune 100, midsized, and entrepreneurial-led start-up companies. She has more than 20 years of experience helping leaders deliver business results by focusing on clearly identified personal and organizational goals.

Orly Maravankin, Ph.D., PCC, President and Founder of Edge Consulting, is an award-winning executive coach to seasoned executives and senior teams, as well as a renowned thought leader in the areas of brand strategy and innovation. Drawing on her blend of expertise in human behavior and business, she equips leaders at premier companies—from Fortune 100 firms to startups—with powerful, personalized tools to thrive and unleash their greatness.

Sally Breyley Parker is the Founder of TimeZero Enterprises, a strategy, design, and development consultancy that helps organizations achieve their potential. Her passion is social process innovations that release the authentic power of the human spirit and result in inventive strategies, innovative designs, and transformed businesses grounded in a deep sense of purpose.

Cheryl Perkins, CEO and Founder of Innovationedge LLC, is a thought leader with more than 35 years of experience in innovation. She is also a renowned business strategy expert, prominent keynote speaker, published author, and creative catalyst in brand-building initiatives.

Pallavi Ridout is an executive coach, dynamic facilitator, and motivational speaker who likes to compete in Toastmasters speaking championships and travel the world. She has coached a variety of C-Level, senior, and emerging leaders on topics such as leadership acumen, executive presence and emotional intelligence, and is an active proponent of empowering women, running a "Leading a Life of No Regrets" life-purpose transformation practice for female professionals.

Eva Sage-Gavin is a recognized Fortune 500 business leader, board director, and most recently Senior Managing Director for Accenture's Global Talent & Organization practice. Sage-Gavin's career is built on a strong foundation of Chief HR Officer and executive roles at global consumer and technology companies, including PepsiCo, The Walt Disney Company, Gap Inc., Sun Microsystems, and Xerox Corp., as well as international public affairs and nonprofit leadership.

Sade Salazar, MBA Student, Binghamton University School of Management, is the Founder of Éxito Hispano, a transformative organization committed to empowering the next generation of Hispanic leaders as they navigate the complexities of being first-generation students. A distinguished Hispanic Scholarship Fund Scholar, Sade has earned more than 25 awards for academic excellence and exemplary student leadership throughout her studies, including being selected as a 2024 NAHR Master Student as well as the inaugural recipient of the prestigious Bernard M. and Ruth R. Bass Scholarship at Binghamton University.

Sonya Sepahban is a proven global business leader, public company board director, and currently the CEO of OurOffice Inc., an innovative tech company in the HR space. A sought-after thought leader who frequently contributes to panels, podcasts, and industry research studies, she began her career as a NASA engineer, aspiring to become an astronaut, and went on to hold senior executive roles in the aerospace and defense industries, and in her most recent leadership role is focused on transforming organizations and advancing workplace equity through data-driven solutions.

Adrienne Shoch is the Founder of 5 to 1 Consulting, a leadership development firm in Asheville, North Carolina, with more than 25 years of global experience in consulting, training, and coaching across diverse industries and disciplines. Her holistic approach to development blends neuroscience, mindfulness, and communication skills with positive leadership to enhance decision-making, build trust, and deepen human connection.

Jamie Snyder Smith, SAHM, is a stay-at-home mom who works professionally in program manager and consulting roles. She has held leadership positions, managed team production operations, and performed seismic exploration for an oil field, receiving a BS in Industrial Engineering and an MBA from Tulane University.

Scott Span, MSOD, CSM, ACC, is a leadership coach, transformation specialist, and CEO of Tolero Solutions. Through his coaching work, he supports clients to identify and overcome what is holding them back, change behaviors, accelerate performance, and achieve their goals; while through his consulting work, Scott helps clients to survive and thrive through change and transition, creating people-focused cultures and a great employee experience.

Michele Stowe is an executive coach, speaker, and the Founder of SkyRocket Coaching. With her lived experience in the C-Suite of a large non-profit organization and 20 years of HR leadership, Michele now works with purpose-driven leaders to help them realize their full potential and leave a lasting impact in their communities.

Shannon Wallis, President, Cascade Leadership, is a distinguished facilitator, executive coach, author, and keynote speaker who has worked on six continents and whose work has reached more than 20,000 leaders worldwide. Prior to founding Cascade Leadership, Shannon was the global director of high-potential leadership development at Microsoft and the chief architect of an award-winning global leadership program.

Samantha Wasserman, **MA**, President of Growth Curve Consulting and Coaching, is a certified executive and team coach, leadership and succession advisor, and organizational growth and culture transformation consultant. She has specialized in the growth and transformation of companies for more than 25 years through coaching their executives and building capabilities in their teams.

Jill Wrobel is the Executive Vice President and Chief Human Resources Officer, Brunswick Corporation, a global leader in recreational marine, having previously held HR executive roles of increasing responsibility at Walgreens Boots Alliance and PwC. She has a dual degree in mathematics and finance from the University of Illinois Urbana-Champaign, is a Fellow of the Society of Actuaries, and lives in the Chicago suburbs with her husband Jeff and two children, where she enjoys cooking, yoga, podcasting, and traveling.

Jackson Yaeger holds an MBA from Binghamton University School of Management, where he concentrated his studies on Leadership and Organizational Science. He draws inspiration from a diverse range of leaders who align with his passions, including Captain America, Mark Messier, Jon Snow, and his own parents.

About the Lead Author

Ian Ziskin, President of EXec EXcel Group LLC, has more than 43 years of experience as a business leader, board advisor and member, coach, consultant, CHRO, entrepreneur, teacher, speaker, and author. His client base and corporate work span more than 25 industries and includes Fortune 1000, entrepreneurial, publicly traded, and privately held businesses.

Ian is widely recognized as a trusted advisor to CEOs, C-Level executives, operating and HR leaders, and board members. He is Co-Founder of the Consortium for Change (C4C), a community network of coaches and consultants, and was also Co-Founder of the CHREATE Project, designed to address the future of work and HR. Ian has been an Adjunct Professor at the Binghamton University School of Management MBA program, where he taught leadership and HR.

Ian's global business leadership experience includes 28 years in Chief Human Resources Officer and/or other senior leadership roles with three Fortune 100 corporations: Northrop Grumman, Qwest Communications, and TRW. He has also served on numerous Boards of Directors and Advisory Boards for organizations including National Academy of Human Resources (NAHR), SeekOut, SucceedSmart, Randstad Risesmart, Humantelligence, Allegis Partners, Axion Health, Executive Networks, SHRM Foundation, USC Center for Effective Organizations, USC Marshall School of Business, HR Policy Association, Center for Advanced Human Resource Studies (CAHRS) at Cornell University, Personnel Round Table, and Human Resources People & Strategy.

He has held appointments as an Executive in Residence at the Binghamton University School of Management, Cornell University School of Industrial and Labor Relations, and USC Center for Effective Organizations. His current pro bono work includes teaching and coaching CHROs at the National Academy of Human Resources and leading the HR HeRoes Academy for early career HR leaders, among other projects.

Ian has written or co-edited five books, *Lives Lost and Leadership Found: Lessons from Special Somebodies* (2025), *The Secret Sauce for Leading Transformational Change* (2022), *Black Holes and White Spaces: Reimagining the Future of Work and HR with the CHREATE Project* (2018), *THREE: The Human Resources Emerging Executive* (2015), and *WillBe: 13 Reasons WillBe's are Luckier than WannaBe's* (2011), and he is a contributing author to *The End of Jobs* by Jeff Wald (2020), *The Rise of HR: Wisdom from 73 Thought Leaders* edited by Dave Ulrich et al. (2015), and *The Chief HR Officer: Defining the New Role of Human Resource Leaders*, edited by Pat Wright et al. (2011). He has written dozens of articles, blogs, and book chapters on the future of work, HR, and leadership, as well as on coaching and HR's role with boards of directors, among other topics. He is also a frequent podcast guest.

Ian has a Master of Industrial and Labor Relations degree from Cornell University, where he held a research and teaching assistantship based on scholastic achievement, and a Bachelor of Science degree in Management from Binghamton University, where he graduated magna cum laude. In 1988, *Human Resource Executive* magazine named Ian one of 12 "Up and Comers in HR." In 2007, he was elected a Fellow of the National Academy of Human Resources, considered to be the highest honor in the HR profession. Most recently, Ian has been recognized as a Top 100 HR thought leader by peopleHum and Engagedly.

Index

For Product Safety Concerns and Information, please contact our EU representative: GPSR@taylorandfrancis.com Taylor & Francis Verlag GmbH, Kaufingerstraße 24, 80331 München, Germany.